THE FAVORED DAUGHTER

ONE WOMAN'S FIGHT TO LEAD
AFGHANISTAN INTO THE FUTURE

FAWZIA KOOFI

WITH NADENE GHOURI

palgrave
macmillan

To my mom, who was the kindest,
most talented teacher in the world;

to both my daughters, who are the stars of my life;

and to all women of Afghanistan

THE FAVORED DAUGHTER
Copyright © Fawzia Koofi, 2012.
All rights reserved.

First published in France as *Lettres à mes filles* by Michel Lafon.

First published in 2012 by PALGRAVE MACMILLAN® in the U.S.—a division of
St. Martin's Press LLC, 175 Fifth Avenue, New York, NY 10010.

Where this book is distributed in the UK, Europe and the rest of the world, this is
by Palgrave Macmillan, a division of Macmillan Publishers Limited, registered in
England, company number 785998, of Houndmills, Basingstoke, Hampshire RG21
6XS.

Palgrave Macmillan is the global academic imprint of the above companies and has
companies and representatives throughout the world.

Palgrave® and Macmillan® are registered trademarks in the United States, the
United Kingdom, Europe and other countries.

ISBN: 978-0-230-12067-9

Library of Congress Cataloging-in-Publication Data

Koofi, Fawzia, 1975–
    The favored daughter : one woman's fight to lead Afghanistan into the future /
Fawzia Koofi with Nadene Gourhi.
        p.   cm.
    Includes bibliographical references and index.
    ISBN 978-0-230-12067-9 (hardback)
    1. Koofi, Fawzia, 1975–   2. Women legislators—
Afghanistan—Biography.   3. Legislators—Afghanistan—
Biography.   4. Women—Afghanistan—Biography.   5. Afghanistan.
Ulasi Jirgah—Biography.   6. Women—Social conditions—
Afghanistan.   7. Children—Social conditions—Afghanistan.   8. Women's
rights—Afghanistan.   9. Human rights—Afghanistan.   I. Gourhi,
Nadene.   II. Title.
DS371.43.K66A3   2012
328.581092—dc23
[B]

                                                                2011025829

A catalogue record of the book is available from the British Library.

Design by Letra Libre

First edition: January 2012

10 9 8 7 6 5 4 3 2 1

Printed in the United States of America.

CONTENTS

PROLOGUE

September 2010

The morning I wrote the letter that begins Chapter 1, I was due to attend a political meeting in Badakhshan, the province of Northern Afghanistan that I represent as a member of the Afghan parliament. Badakhshan is the northernmost province of Afghanistan, bordering both China and Takjikistan.

It is also one of the poorest, wildest, most remote, and culturally conservative provinces in all of Afghanistan.

Badakhshan has the highest rate of maternal mortality and child mortality in the entire world, due in part to its inaccessibility and crippling poverty, but also in part to a culture that sometimes puts tradition ahead of women's health. A man will rarely seek hospital treatment for his wife unless it's clear she won't survive otherwise. With childbirth, this often means a woman may undergo three or four days of agonizing labor. By the time she reaches a hospital—often on the back of a donkey after traveling over rocky mountain tracks—it is usually too late to save both mother and child.

On the day I wrote the letter I was warned not to travel because there had been a credible threat that the Taliban planned to kill me by planting an improvised explosive device (a roadside bomb) underneath my car. The Taliban dislike women holding such powerful positions in government as I do, and they dislike my public criticisms even more.

They often try to kill me.

Recently they have tried even harder than usual to murder me, threatening my home, tracking my journeys to work so they can lay a bomb as my car passes, even firing on a convoy of police vehicles that was supposed to protect me. One recent gun attack on my car lasted for 30 minutes, killing two police-men. I stayed inside the vehicle, not knowing if I would be alive or dead when it was over.

I know the Taliban and those others who seek to silence me for speaking out against corruption and bad leadership in my country will not be happy until I am dead.

But on this day I ignored the threat. I have ignored countless similar threats, because if I didn't, I could not do my job.

But I felt the threat. I always feel it. That's the very nature of threat, and those who threaten know that.

I awoke my eldest daughter, Shaharzad, who is twelve, at 6:00 A.M. and told her that if I didn't come home from this trip in a few days, she was to read the letter to her ten-year-old younger sister, Shuhra. Shaharzad's eyes, full of questions, met mine. I placed my finger to her lips and kissed her and her sleeping sister on the forehead as I quietly left the room and closed the door.

I regularly tear myself away from my children to do my work, despite knowing I might well be murdered. But my job is to represent the poorest people of my nation. That purpose, along with raising my two beautiful daughters, is what I live for. I could not on that day, and will not ever, let my people down.

Dear Shuhra and Shaharzad,

Today I am going on political business to Faizabad and Darwaz. I hope I will come back soon and see you again, but I have to say that perhaps I will not.

There have been threats to kill me on this trip. Maybe this time these people will be successful in doing that.

As your mother it causes me such bitter pain to tell you this. But please understand I would willingly sacrifice my life if it meant a peaceful Afghanistan and a better future for the children of this country.

I live this life so that you—my precious girls—will be free to live your lives and to dream all of your dreams.

If I am killed and I don't see you again, I want you to remember a few things for me.

First, don't forget me.

Because you are young and have yet to finish all your studies and can live independently, I want you to stay with your aunt Khadija. She loves you so much and she will take care of you for me.

You have my authority to spend all the money I have in the bank. But use it wisely and use it for your studies. Focus on your education. A girl needs an education if she is to excel in this man's world.

After you graduate from eighth grade, I want you to continue your studies abroad. I want you to be familiar with universal values. The world is a big, beautiful, wonderful place and it is yours to explore.

Be brave. Don't be afraid of anything in life.

All of us human beings will die one day. Maybe today is the day I will die. But if I do, please know it was for a purpose.

Don't die without achieving something. Take pride in trying to help people, and in trying to make our country and our world a better place.

I kiss you both. I love you.
Your mother

PART ONE

ONE

STORIES OF OLD

Even the day I was born, I was supposed to die.

I have stared death in the face countless times in my 35 years, but still I'm alive.

I can't explain this, other than knowing that God has a purpose for me.

Perhaps his purpose for me is to govern and lead my country out of the abyss of corruption and violence. Or perhaps his purpose is simply for me to be a good mother to my daughters.

I was my father's nineteenth child out of a total of 23, and my mother's last child. My mother was my father's second wife. When she fell pregnant with me she was physically exhausted from the seven children she had already given birth to. She was also depressed at having lost my father's affections to his newest—and youngest—seventh wife. So she wanted me to die.

I was born out at pasture. During the summer months, my mother and a host of servants would make the annual journey to graze our cattle and sheep in the highest points of the mountains, where the grass was sweeter. This was her chance to escape the house for a few weeks. She would take charge of the entire operation, gathering enough dried fruit, nuts, rice, and oil to sustain the small party of travelers for the three months or so they would be away. The preparations leading up to the trip would be a source of great excitement, my mother packing and planning every last detail before a convoy on horses and donkeys set off across the higher grounds.

My mother loved these trips. As she rode through the villages, her joy at being temporarily free from the shackles of home and housework, and being able to breathe in the fresh mountain air, were evident to all.

There is a local saying that the more powerful and passionate a woman is, the nicer she looks while sitting upon a horse in her burqa. It was also said that no one ever looked more beautiful on horseback than my mother did. It was something about the way she held herself—her uprightness, her dignity.

But the year I was born, 1975, she was not in a celebratory mood. Thirteen months earlier she had stood at the large yellow gates of our *hooli* (house), a large, sprawling, mud-walled, single-story structure, and watched a wedding party descend the path that snaked down from the mountains through the center of our village. The groom was my mother's husband. My father had chosen to take a seventh wife, a girl who was just 14 years old.

Each time he remarried, my mother was devastated—although my father liked to joke that with each new wife my mother became yet more beautiful. Of all his wives my father had loved my mother, Bibi jan (literally translated, the name means "beautiful dear"), the most. But in my parents' mountain village culture, love and marriage very rarely meant the same thing. Marriage was for family, tradition, culture, and obedience, all of which were deemed more important than individual happiness. Love was something no one was expected to need or to feel. Love only caused trouble. People believed unquestioning duty was where happiness lay.

My mother had stood on the large stone terrace safely behind the hooli's gates as the party of more than ten men on horseback ambled its way down the hillside, my father dressed in his finest white *shalwar kameez* (a long tunic and trousers), brown waistcoat, and lambskin hat. Beside his white horse—with bright pink, green, and red wool tassels dangling from its decorated bridle—were a series of smaller horses carrying the bride and her female relatives, all wearing white burqas. They were accompanying the bride to her new home, which she would share with my mother and the other women who also called my father husband. My father—a short man with close-set eyes and a neatly trimmed beard—smiled graciously and shook hands with the villagers who came out to greet him and witness the spectacle. They called to each other, "Wakil Abdul Rahman is here! Wakil Abdul Rahman is home with his most beautiful new wife!" His public loved him and they expected no less.

Wakil (Representative) Abdul Rahman—my father—was a member of the Afghan parliament, representing the people of Badakhshan, the same people who I represent today. For as long as my family can be traced back, local politics and public service have been our tradition and our honor.

Politics runs through my blood as strongly as the rivers that snake all over Badakhshan.

Before my father and I became members of parliament, my father's father, Azamshah, was a community leader and tribal elder.

The Badakhshani districts of Darwaz and Koof, where my family and my last name originate, are so remote and mountainous that even today it can take up to three days to drive there from the provincial capital of Faizabad. And that's in good weather. In winter the small mountain passes are completely closed.

My grandfather's job was to help people with their social and practical problems, connecting them to the central government in Faizabad and working with the provincial district manager's office to provide services. He never once flew on a plane or drove a car, and the only way he could physically take issues to the government authorities in Faizabad from his home in the mountainous Darwaz district was on horseback or on donkey, a journey that often took him a week to ten days.

Of course, my grandfather wasn't the only one who traveled this way. Horseback or foot was the only way any of the villagers could connect with the bigger towns: It was how farmers could buy seed, how the sick could reach a hospital, how families separated by marriage could visit each other. Travel was only possible in the warm spring and summer months, and even then it posed great dangers.

Atanga was the greatest risk of all. Atanga is a large mountain bordering the Amu Darya river. This clear green river is all that separates Afghanistan from Takjikistan on the other side. The river was as dangerous as it was beautiful. In spring, as the snow melted and the rains came, its banks swelled to bursting, creating a series of deadly fast-flowing currents.

The Atanga crossing was a series of rough wooden stairs fastened to either side of the mountain, for people to climb up and then down the other side. The steps were tiny, rickety, and slippery. One small trip or mistake and a person would fall straight down into the river and be swept away to certain death.

Imagine returning from Faizabad holding the goods you've just purchased, be that a 15-pound bag of rice, salt, oil, or other precious cargo that had to last your family all winter. Tired after one week of walking, you have to risk your life negotiating a deadly pass that had probably been the demise of many of your friends and relatives already.

My grandfather could not bear to see his people killed this way year upon year, and he did all he could to force the government to build a proper road and a safer way to pass. But although richer than most people in Badakhshan, he was still just a local official living in a remote village. (Although a district today, back then Koof was considered a village.) In the end, traveling to Faizabad was as much as he could do. He had neither the means nor the power to travel to Kabul, where the king and central government were based.

Knowing change would not come in his lifetime, my grandfather decided his youngest son would take over his campaigning role. My father was just a little boy when my grandfather began grooming him for a future in politics. Years later, after months of solid lobbying, one of my father's biggest successes in parliament would be the realization of my grandfather's dream to get a road built over the Atanga Pass.

There is a famous story about the road and my father's audience with King Zahir Shah to discuss the project. He stood in front of the king and said, "Shah sahib, construction of this road has been planned for years, but there is no action—you and your government plan and talk but do not keep your promises." Although the parliament at that time was made up of elected representatives, the king and his courtiers still ran the country. Direct criticism of the king was rare, and only a brave or foolhardy man would attempt it. The king took off his glasses and looked long and hard at my father before stating severely, "Wakil sahib, you would do well to remember you are in my palace."

My father panicked, thinking he had gone too far. He hurriedly left the palace, fearing that he would be arrested on the way out. But a month later, the king sent his minister of public works to Badakhshan to meet my father and make plans for the construction of the road. The minister arrived, took one look at the mountain and declared the job impossible. There was no more to be said; he would return home at once. My father nodded sagely and asked him to go for a short horse ride with him first. The man agreed, and they rode together to the top of the pass. As they dismounted, my father grabbed the man's horse and raced back down, leading it behind him, leaving the minister alone on the mountain all night long to give him a taste of what it was like for villagers who got trapped on the passes.

The next morning my father returned to pick up the minister. He was furious, half bitten to death by mosquitoes, and he had lain awake all night terrified that he would be eaten by wild dogs or wolves. But now he had a clear understanding of how harsh life was for the local people. He agreed to bring engineers and dynamite so the pass could be created. My father's pass at Atanga is still there, and this feat of engineering has saved thousands of Badakhshani lives over the years.

But long before the pass was built and my father became a member of parliament, my grandfather had appointed the little Abdul Rahman an *arbab,* a leader of the village. Even at the age of 12, this effectively gave him the powers of a tribal elder. He was asked to settle the villagers' land, family, and marriage disputes. Families who wanted to arrange a good match for their daughters' weddings came to him for advice on picking suitable husbands. Before long he was negotiating road-building projects, raising funds, and meeting with the provincial officials in Faizabad. Despite being barely more than a child, he had the support of local people, so these officials were prepared to deal with him.

These early years gave my father such a solid grounding in the issues facing our community that by the time he grew into adulthood, he was ready to lead. And the timing was perfect. For this was the beginning of real democracy in Afghanistan. In the decade between 1965 and 1975, the king decided to establish a democratic parliament, and to allow people to be involved in the decision-making process by voting for their local members of parliament.

The people of Badakhshan felt they had suffered years of neglect from the central government and were thrilled at the opportunity to finally have their voices heard. When the elections came, my father was voted in as the first-ever member of parliament from Darwaz.

He was representing some of the poorest people not just in Afghanistan but in the world. A huge responsibility.

But these are also people who have their pride, who stick to their values. People who can be as wild and angry as the ever-changing mountain climate, but also as fragile and strong as the wild flowers that grow on the granite river banks.

Abdul Rahman, being one of them, knew this better than anyone, and took on his new role with nothing short of dedication.

On the day of his first address to parliament in Kabul, local people gathered at our house in the village of Koof to listen to his speech. In those days radio was the only contact with the outside world. My father had inherited the radio, a chunky wooden Russian wireless with brass controls, from my grandfather. It was the only radio in our village.

No one in Koof, except my elder brother Jamalshah, knew how to turn on the radio or even how to increase the volume. My mother was bursting with pride that her husband was a member of parliament. She threw open the gates of the hooli to allow the public in to hear the speech and called for Jamalshah to turn on the radio for her.

But he was nowhere to be seen. In panic she ran through the village calling him but couldn't find him anywhere.

The speech was about to start, and back at the hooli a crowd was gathering. Cousins, village elders, women, and children, some of whom had never heard a radio before—all wanted to hear their new representative address the parliament. She knew she couldn't let my father down but had not the faintest idea how the contraption worked.

She went close to the radio and tried all the knobs but nothing worked. As the crowd watched her in anticipation she felt a sense of rising panic and fear, and started to cry. Her husband was going to be humiliated and it would be her fault. If only she had found Jamalshah. Where was that boy? In pure frustration she brought her fist down hard on the top of the radio. Amazingly, the thump worked, and the thing spluttered and crackled to life.

She couldn't quite believe her luck. But still, no one could hear it, as the volume was too low. She hadn't the faintest idea what to do. Her friend, my father's fourth wife, suggested bringing in the loudspeaker. The women had no idea what it did or how it worked but had seen the men use it before. They carried it over and placed it next to the radio, doing what they could to connect it. It worked. The parliament proceedings were live. The entire village heard my father's speech. My mother beamed with joy.

My father soon gained a reputation as one of the hardest-working members in the king's parliament. Although Badakhshan remained desperately poor, these were good days for Afghanistan overall. The nation was secure, the economy and society were generally stable, but this wasn't something our neighboring countries could easily accept. It was the height of the cold war, and Afghanistan's strategic and geographical importance was already defining the tragic fate that would come later.

My father was outspoken, straightforward, and hard working, respected not only in Badakhshan but across the country for his generosity, honesty, faith, and fierce belief in traditional Islamic values. Yet he was unpopular with some in the king's court for refusing to kowtow to the elites or to play the political power games so many of his political peers took delight in. He was an old-fashioned politician, one who believed in the nobility of public service and helping the poor.

He spent long months in Kabul advocating for roads, hospitals, and schools. Some projects he was successful in getting funds to complete, others evaded him. The Kabul-based rulers did not see our province as a particularly important one and it was hard to get funding for major projects, something that constantly angered my father.

My mother recalled how before the annual parliamentary recess, she took the whole month to prepare for his arrival—preparing different kinds of sweetmeats and dried fruits for him, cleaning the house, sending the servants to the mountains to collect wood for all the cooking his arrival would inevitably involve. In the evenings, a long queue of donkeys loaded with wood entered the hooli gates, my mother giving directions stating how high or how big to make the piles in the wood store at the corner of the garden. In her own way she worked as hard as my father did, never accepting second best and always seeking perfection. But my father barely thanked her for it. At home he could be a terrifying tyrant. My mother's bruises were testament to that.

Each one of his wives was a political match. By marrying the favored daughter of a nearby tribe or local power holder he strategically consolidated and secured the power base of his own local empire. My mother's father was an important local elder from the next district who had previously fought with my father's village. By marrying her he essentially secured a local peace treaty.

A few of his wives he loved, two he divorced, most he ignored. Throughout his life he took a total of seven wives. My mother was without a doubt his favorite. She was petite with a pretty oval-shaped face and pale skin, big black eyes, shiny long black hair, and neatly arched eyebrows.

It was she he trusted the most, she who kept the keys to the safe and the food stores. She he entrusted to coordinate the cooking at his huge political dinners. It was she who took charge of the servants and other wives as they cooked endless supplies of scented pilau rice, gosht (lamb stew), and fresh hot naan in the hooli's kitchen.

A row of servants and brothers would stand from the kitchen entrance into the entrance of the guest house next door where my father entertained the guests, passing piping hot pots along. Women were not allowed to enter these exclusively male areas. In our culture a married woman should not be seen by a man who is not her relative, so on these occasions my brothers, who would never otherwise be expected to do any housework, had to help.

My father expected everything to be perfect for such celebrations. The rice was to be fluffy, and each grain individually separated. If it was, he smiled with satisfaction at his good fortune and his most excellent choice of wife. If he found a few grains stuck together his face would darken, and he would politely excuse himself from his guests, walk into the kitchen, and, without saying a word, grab my mother by the hair, wrench the metal ladle from her hands, and beat her across the head with it. Her hands—already scarred and misshapen from previous beatings—would fly to her head to try and protect herself. Sometimes she'd be knocked unconscious, only to get up again and, ignoring the servant's frightened stares, rub hot ash into her head to stop the bleeding, then ensure that in the next batch of rice, the grains fell apart perfectly.

She endured this because in her world the beatings meant love. "If a man does not beat his wife then he does not love her," she explained to me. "He has such expectations from me and he only beats me when I fail him."

I appreciate that this may sound strange to modern ears, but it was what she genuinely believed, and it sustained her.

Obeying my father was not only done out of a sense of duty or fear, it was done for love, because she truly and utterly adored him.

So on the day that wife number seven came home, my mother watched with sadness as the wedding procession wound its way through the village. She stood on the terrace next to a servant woman who was grinding flour in a giant stone mortar and pestle. Normally, as the lady of the house, she wouldn't take on the grinding herself, but today she grabbed the pestle and ground it into the mortar stone furiously, fighting back her tears. Self-pity, even on this day, was not a luxury she was allowed. She was responsible for cooking the new bride's feast, and she had to ensure that the young wife's first meal in this home would be of the finest delicacies and treats, befitting the status of Abdul Rahman's home. If she didn't prepare a delicious feast, he would be angry.

There was one part of the ceremony, however, that was just for her. As head wife she was to greet the party and place her fist firmly on top of the new bride's head to denote her superiority and the new bride's submission as a wife lower down the scale. She looked on as, once safely in the hooli gates, three women—the mother, bride, and her sister—were helped to dismount. They removed their burqas, and the beauty of the two younger women was displayed for all to see. Both of them had long black hair down to their waists. One stared directly at my mother, all confident green eyes and raven locks. My mother put her fist down firmly and calmly on the woman's head. The woman looked aghast, my father coughed and laughed, and the other girl turned scarlet with embarrassment. My mother had picked the wrong woman, placing her fist on the sister's head instead. Her hands flew to her mouth in consternation, but it was too late, the wedding party had moved inside to begin the feast. Her one chance to officially show this young woman just who was in charge was gone.

Now, 13 months later, my mother was giving birth in a remote mountain shack. Bereft at the loss of favor of the man she loved, she was alone and wretched. The young wife had given birth to a son three months earlier, a healthy bouncing baby boy called Ennayat with beautiful large eyes as wide as saucers. My mother hadn't wanted any more children and knew this one would be her last. For the entire pregnancy she was sick, pale, and exhausted, her body simply giving up on bearing children. Ennayat's mother, however, was glowing and even more beautiful with first pregnancy happiness, her breasts firm, her cheeks flushed.

While six months pregnant herself, my mother helped deliver Ennayat into the world. As his lungs filled with his first breath and he screamed out loud his arrival, Bibi jan held her hands to her stomach and prayed silently that she too would give birth to a boy, a chance of winning back my father's favor. Girl children in our village culture were considered nothing, worthless. Even today, women pray for sons because only a son gives them status and keeps their husbands happy.

For 30 hours my mother writhed in agony during my birth. She was semiconscious by the time I was delivered, with barely enough energy to muster her dismay at the news I was a girl.

When presented with me she turned away, refusing to hold me. I couldn't have been more different from Ennayat. He was a rosy-cheeked bundle of health. I was blue, mottled, and so tiny I was barely formed. My mother was so weak she was on the verge of death after the birth. No one cared if the new girl child lived, so while they focused on saving my mother, I was wrapped in cloth and placed outside in the baking sun.

I lay there for almost a day, screaming. No one came. They fully expected nature to take its course and for me to die. My tiny face was so badly burned by the sun that I still had the scars as a teenager.

By the time they took pity on me and brought me back inside, my mother was feeling better.

Amazed I had lived and horrified at the state of my burnt face, she gasped in horror as her initial coldness melted into maternal instinct. She took me in her arms and held me. When I finally stopped crying, she began to weep silently, promising herself that no more harm would ever come to me. She knew that for some reason God had chosen for me to live and that she should love me.

I don't know why God spared me that day.

Or why he has spared me on the several occasions since then, when I could have died, but he did.

But I know he has a purpose for me.

And I also know he truly blessed me by making me Bibi jan's favorite child from that moment on, forging an unbreakable bond between mother and daughter.

Dear Shuhra and Shaharzad,

Early in my life I learned how difficult is it to be a child in Afghanistan, especially a girl child.

The first words a newborn daughter will often hear are the commiserations given to her mother. "It's a poor girl, just a girl."

It isn't much of a welcome to the world.

Then when a girl reaches school age, she faces the problem of whether or not she will get permission to go to school. Will her family be brave or rich enough to send her to school? When a brother grows up he will represent the family and his salary will help feed the family so everyone wants to educate their sons. But in our society girls usually get married and join the husband's family, so many people see no point in educating them.

When the girl reaches the age of 12, relatives and neighbors may start to gossip about why she isn't married yet. "Has someone asked her for marriage?" "Is anyone ready to marry her?" "She may not be a good girl, which is why no one wants to marry her."

If the family doesn't care about this gossip and lets the girl reach 16, the legal age for marriage, and allows her to marry someone of her choice or at least agree to the choice her parents have made, then she will have, at least in part, a happy life.

But if the family is under financial pressure or listens to other's gossip and marries their daughter off before she's 15, then this little girl who heard "poor girl" at her birth will become a mother herself. And if she gives birth to a girl child then her little girl will hear the same words, "poor girl," at birth, and so it goes on to her daughters' daughters and their daughters.

This is how I was born. The "poor girl" of an illiterate woman.

"Just a girl" would have been my life story, and probably yours too. But the bravery of my mother changed our path. She is the hero of my dreams.

With love,
Your mother

TWO

"JUST A GIRL"

The early part of my childhood was as golden as the mountain dawn—the light that tumbled directly from the sun across the Pamir mountain range down through the valley and onto the roofs of the mud houses in our village. My memories of that time are hazy, like images from a film, bathed in the colors of orange summer sun and white winter snow, the smells of the apple and plum trees outside our house, my mother's radiant smiles, and the scent of her long, dark, plaited hair.

Koof district, where we lived when I was a child, is one of the most remote corners of both Badakhshan and Afghanistan. The Koof valley is lush and fertile, banked with trees of rich greens and yellows, colors I've never seen anywhere else. Our house looked out at a sparkling blue river, pine and elm trees growing tall along the grassy banks that rose steeply into the mountains.

The noises I recall from my early childhood are of a donkey braying, the sound of hay swishing as it is cut, the sound of the trickling river water, and the peals of children's laughter. Even today my village sounds just the same. And Koof remains the only place in the world where I can close my eyes and fall blissfully, peacefully asleep within seconds.

In front of our house was the garden, organized into market efficiency by my mother. We grew everything we needed: fruits of all kinds, peppers, olives, mulberries, peaches, apricots, apples, and huge yellow pumpkins; we even cultivated silk for weaving carpets. My father took great delight in importing trees and seeds from abroad, and our garden housed one of the only black cherry trees in all of Afghanistan. I remember the day it arrived and the sense of importance and occasion as the seedling was planted.

During the warmer months, in the late afternoon the women would come and sit among the mulberry trees for half an hour or so; this was the only time of day they could relax. Each one would bring a small dish of something to eat, and they would sit, gossiping and chatting while the children played around them.

In those days many villagers wore wooden shoes, as it was difficult for them to go to Faizabad and buy conventional shoes. The shoes were strong— there was an old man in the village who used to make wooden shoes, like carved gondola boats. He would put nails in the base so that when women went to fetch water in winter, they didn't fall over. My fondest dream was to own a pair of these shoes. They were not for children, as they were tough, and when women came to visit and left them at the door I'd put them on and go out to play in them. Once I was wearing a beautiful embroidered dress my mother's friend had made for me. I wasn't supposed to go out in it, but I didn't want to take it off, so I put on the wooden shoes and went to play with my friends near the water spring. Of course, I fell over in my big shoes and tore the dress.

But my world began with the hooli kitchen, a mud-plastered room with three large wood-fired ovens at one end, a deep bread oven called a *tanur* in the center, and a tiny high window at the other end.

Like most Afghan village women of her generation, my mother spent more than half her life in the kitchen, sleeping, cooking, and taking care of the little children. And in the kitchen she reigned supreme.

The women baked bread three times a day, sometimes 50 or 60 loaves a day, so the room was always full of smoke from fires. Then between bakes they had to prepare lunch and dinner. If my father had guests, the heat would become unbearable because wood was burning on all four ovens. On those occasions we would all feel the sense of excitement, and I would boost my popularity by bringing my friends into the kitchen to eat the leftovers. Most of the villagers were much poorer than our family, and the chance to taste unusual and fine foods was too good for them to pass up. We children were never allowed anywhere near the guest house, and if we ever thought to risk a peek inside, one quick glance from one of my father's security men guarding the doorway sent us running for cover.

But away from the eyes of the men of the house, the kitchen was a place of laughter and women's voices, a place where children were guaranteed treats from the many pots of dried fruit and sweets lining the shelves. A place where, on cold winter nights after the bread was finished, we would sit with our feet inside the dying embers of the *tanur*, a carpet over our legs to keep us warm.

At night we would unroll our mattresses and sleep there. And my mother would tell us stories. She would start with stories closer to home. She talked to us openly about her marriage and how she felt when she first met my father, about how hard it was for her leaving her childhood behind to become a wife, with all the duties that entailed. But then she would regale us with stories of faraway queens and kings, castles and warriors who gave all for honor. She told us love stories and stories about big wolves that used to make us scream. I would listen and look out the window at the moon and stars. I was certain I could see the entire sky.

I had no idea the rest of the world lay beyond the big mountain at the end of the valley, and I didn't care. My mother loved me and I loved her; we were inseparable. It was as if all the love she had lost from my father in those later years she recollected somehow and gave to me twice over. She had recovered from her initial disappointment in my being a girl, after a story was recounted to her by my aunt Gada, my father's eldest sister. Informing him of my birth upon his return to the village, the aunt declared: "Abdul Rahman, your wife has given birth to a mouse, a tiny red mouse." He laughed and demanded to see me, the first time he'd ever asked to see a newborn girl child. Looking at my scarred face and the third-degree burns caused by the sun, he threw his head back and uncharacteristically laughed out loud: "Don't worry, my sister," he told my aunt. "Her mother has good genes. And I know one day this little mouse will grow to be as beautiful as her mother."

When my mother heard this story she cried tears of joy. For her it was my father's way of sending a message that he still loved her, and that she should not feel like a failure for providing him a last daughter instead of a son. She recounted that story often. I must have heard it hundreds of times.

But by then my father was a distant man, and politics was becoming a very dangerous game in Afghanistan. The regime had recently changed from a kingdom to a presidency. Dawoud Khan removed King Zahir Shah through a peaceful coup d'état while the king was abroad in 1973 and declared himself the first president of Afghanistan. When he took power, he suspended the constitution and abolished the parliament.

My father was soon imprisoned for disobeying the president. He was vocal in his criticisms of the new regime and put pressure on Dawoud to bring back the constitution and reinvest parliament with power. The rumblings of political discontent were heard across the country. Unemployment was rising, social problems were increasing, and Afghanistan's neighbors, Pakistan and the USSR in particular, were once more beginning to play out their own political strategies on our soil.

In these days my father was mostly needed in Kabul and was rarely home. When he was away our house was relaxed and children's laughter rang through the rooms. But when he was there, the women of our household nervously floated down corridors, preparing meals for his guests and trying to keep the children silent so as not to disturb him.

My friends and I were generally happy when my father was home because we could be as naughty as we liked and steal chocolate, safe in the knowledge my mother was too busy worrying about him to stop us.

I have few real memories of my father. I remember him always walking, wearing a shalwar kameez. He wore a smart brown wool waistcoat over it, and he always had his sheepskin hat on and his hands clasped tightly behind his back. The hooli had a long flat roof, and in those days he would walk along it for hours and hours. He would start pacing back and forth in the afternoon and continue through the evening. He was just walking and walking and thinking, and always in the same position, with his hands behind his back.

I think I had a sense even then that was my father was a great man. That whatever the stresses and troubles he brought home to us, even the beatings, were partly because of the pressure he was under. The pressure of maintaining a home and extended family the size of ours, the pressure of politics, the pressure of representing some of the poorest people in Afghanistan. He barely had any time to himself. When he was home our guest house, a single-story dwelling at the back of the hooli, was always full with visitors, those seeking his advice or his wisdom to solve a family dispute, those bringing news of errant tribes or violence in the mountains, the desperate and the needy wanting his help. His door was closed to none of them, and light relief was something he had no time to enjoy. How then could he be blamed for demanding the most from his family?

I don't condone my father's behavior in beating my mother the way he did, of course, but those times were different and it was the norm. And I know at other times he was a good husband to her, as much as tradition allowed. Perhaps today I understand him more than ever because I understand his workload. I understand the pressure of politics, the feeling of never having any time alone or free from duty, the burden of responsibility. I think my mother understood that too, and it was why she endured so much.

Under the sharia law system my father espoused, a man is supposed to show justice to all of his wives equally, sharing himself without favor among them. I too believe in sharia justice. In its purest forms it is a fair system because it is a system based on Islamic values of justice and is what all Muslims should believe.

But affairs of the human heart are different, and in polygamous marriages it is bound to fail. How can a man help it if his heart prefers some wives over others?

My father's suite of rooms was called the Paris Suite, decorated with hand-painted murals by an artist brought especially from Kabul. The room had two windows looking out over an apricot garden, and in the summertime the room was washed in a cool apricot-scented breeze. No modern air conditioning could ever come close to that natural coolness which was coupled with a delicate scent.

Each night he was home, a different wife shared his bed. The only wife who didn't go there was his first wife, the Khalifa. In order to take more wives than the sharia-allowed maximum of four, my father divorced two of his original wives and made his first wife what is known as a Khalifa. Under this agreement a woman retains the title of wife and is cared for financially, but loses the intimacy that comes with marriage and never sleeps with her husband again. I remember the sadness in this woman's eyes, the power and status that should have come to her naturally as first wife totally destroyed by her forced sexless status.

Instead, my mother, the second wife, became head wife. The Khalifa never showed my mother any anger or disrespect, but I wonder if she too had felt devastated and hurt when my father first brought my mother home or when she was given the head wife status. How was it for the poor Khalifa to be usurped by a teenage girl?

I like to think my father looked forward the most to the nights he spent with my mother. She recalled how after the necessary intimacies, they would lay there until the early hours just talking, and he would tell her stories of his work, share with her the strains of his political life in Kabul, and give instructions for how she was to handle the land, the latest wheat harvest or sale of some cattle in his absence. She was so authoritative when he wasn't there that she earned the local nickname—"deputy wakil sahib," deputy representative sir.

The harder the times were for him politically, the more he relied on my mother. So long as his home was harmonious and ran like clockwork, he could deal with all the machinations and dealings that parliament could throw at him. It was she who kept the farms and business running, she who kept order in the house, who solved disputes between the wives. This was something she needed a certain amount of her own political skill to negotiate.

Certain wives, particularly the third one, Niaz bibi, resented my mother's status and tried to turn my father against her. This woman was intelligent and frustrated by her life of drudgery, so she can't be blamed for being jealous of the few freedoms and small powers my mother had over her. But her attempts to win my father's favor this way always failed, not only because my father didn't like to think badly about my mother, but because of my mother's own abilities to foresee a situation arising and take evasive action.

Her strategy was kindness. She could have beaten the younger wives, made them do the hardest work, but instead she tried to create a happy house, one where all children were loved equally and where wives could work together as sisters and friends. When one of the younger wives was caught stealing from the household food store, a large locked cellar at the back of the kitchen, my mother didn't tell my father, knowing that he would give her a vicious beating. Instead she dealt with the matter herself, secretly. This strategy slowly earned her the gratitude and loyalty of the others.

Only one wife, number six, wasn't chosen for her political usefulness but for her practical homemaking skills. She was a stunningly beautiful Mongolian woman chosen for her ability to weave the most beautiful Mongolian rugs and carpets. She taught my mother this art, and the two of them would sit for hours together in comfortable silence weaving, their hands rhythmically spinning and threading richly colored yarn while I sat and watched.

But my mother's best friend was wife number four, Khal bibi. She called my mother "Apa," which means elder sister.

Once, my mother became sick with a serious eye infection, and considering the absence of any doctors in the village, a female elder suggested that if a person were to put their tongue into the eye and licked it clean each morning, the natural antibiotic in the saliva would heal it. Such was the closeness of their friendship that Khal bibi volunteered without hesitation. Each day for eight weeks she licked my mother's swollen, pus-filled eye until, as the elderly lady had promised, it healed.

But my mother and Niaz bibi, wife number three, could just never get along. One day, as the women sat on the floor eating naan for breakfast, the two began quarrelling. I was only about 18 months old, but I somehow sensed the enmity between them. I toddled over to Niaz bibi and yanked down hard on her plaits. She gasped with shock and began laughing, taking me in her arms and cuddling me. She and my mother forgot their quarrel and both laughed out loud: "This one, Bibi jan, is a very clever girl, just like her mother," laughed my mother's enemy, showering my face in kisses.

Even at that early age I had a sense of the injustice of the position of women in our culture. I remember the quiet despair of the wives were who weren't loved or noticed by my father, and the trials of those who were.

I recall watching in horror once as my father chased my mother along the corridor and began to beat her. I flew at him, kicking out at him and trying to protect her. He flung me aside with one arm.

Once, he viciously tore out a chunk of her hair during a beating. Her brother visited a week later and, as was the custom, spent time with the men of the family, meaning my mother was unable to talk privately to him about what had happened. When he left my mother prepared his lunch for his long journey on horseback across the mountains home. She cleverly hid the locks of her torn-out hair in the wrapping. After a full morning's riding, he stopped at a clearing for lunch, unwrapped his food, and found his sister's hair. He understood the message immediately, mounted his horse, and galloped straight back to our house, challenging my father and telling my mother her family would ensure she would be granted a divorce if she wanted it. Her family support was unusual. Most women were encouraged not to complain about beatings and to endure them in silence. Often girls who fled to a family home would be returned by their father to the very husband who had hurt them. Beating a woman was normal, a part of marriage. Girls grew up knowing it had happened to their mothers and grandmothers and expecting it to happen to them. But Bibi jan was close to her parents, whom she visited every year, and her brothers loved her. Her brother sat with her in the hooli garden and told her she was free to leave with him, that he would take her home, now, if that was what she wanted. At this time in her marriage she was at the point of despair, constantly depressed. She suffered splitting headaches, her stiffened hands didn't work well due to the injuries she received from the beatings with the metal ladle, and she was tired of the constant humiliations of each new wife. She had had enough. She almost went through with the divorce.

But she knew that leaving her husband meant losing her beloved children. In Afghan culture, as is the norm in most Islamic cultures, children stay with their fathers, not their mothers, after divorce. She couldn't bear to give her children up and leave them behind, even if it meant an end to her own sufferings.

She asked to see her children and looked into their eyes and faces. She said nothing, but told me years later she could see herself reflected in her children's eyes. She couldn't leave them. So she told her brother she would stay with her husband and her children, and that he should go home. Reluctantly he got back onto his horse and left. I have no idea how my father reacted after her brother left. Did he beat my mother again for her insolence and for daring to tell her brother? Or was he tender and kind and regretful, realizing just how close he had come to losing the woman he needed? Probably a bit of both.

I remember my sisters being married off one by one. The first sister to be married had a trousseau brought specially from Saudi Arabia. Caskets of fine cloth and gold jewels befitting the importance of the marriage of a daughter of Abdul Rahman were brought to the hooli and unpacked with care as we all gasped, oohing and aahing over the treasures inside. On that day she became an important commodity, a jewel to be traded. But that was the only time in her life she was treated with such importance.

Unlike the boys, the girls' birthdays were never celebrated, and none of my sisters went to school. People saw no purpose in wasting money educating a girl because she would not be around to contribute financially to the household after she married.

I also recall the day my sister-in-law arrived. She had been married to my elder brother at the age of 12, the same age my daughter Shaharzad is today. He was 17 and they were expected to begin a full physical relationship immediately.

It is unthinkable to me that my own daughter should suffer a forced physical relationship at such a tender age as this poor girl. She was still such a child that my mother had to help her bathe and dress in the mornings. I wonder how it felt for my mother to bathe this girl and see the injuries inflicted on her by her own son. I wonder if she recoiled in horror at the injustice of it all. But this was their life and the fate of women. Perhaps all she could do was try to comfort the girl, give her the lighter chores to do, and know that just as the elder women had done, the girl would grow to accept her fate unquestioningly and without complaint. It was a conspiracy of culture that bound them all, and none were free to challenge it.

Without even being aware I was doing so, I broke boundaries and challenged these norms. Partly this was because one of my best friends was Ennayat, the son of my father's seventh wife. Despite the initial rivalries surrounding our births, he and I were instant best friends, a special brotherly and sisterly love that has lasted to this day. He was naughty and mischievous, and I even more so. Knowing that as a girl I was more limited, I was always challenging him into more naughtiness on our joint behalf. We were joined in our naughtiness by Muqim, my mother's son who had been born two years before Ennayat and I. We were the three little musketeers.

I was forever getting them both into trouble. We'd sneak into orchards and steal apples or I'd make them steal from my father's stores and distribute it to my friends.

I remember one day filling our shirts full of dried apricots from the kitchen, Ennayat encouraging me to stuff my shirt as full as I could. I tied my belt under the stash to hold it in. As we sneaked back across the garden in front of the wives who were preparing food on the terrace, the apricots began to leak one by one. I tried to walk with my back to the wall so they wouldn't see, just as a large pile of apricots plopped on the floor. I was mortified, and Ennayat was furious with me for failing in our mission. The women just laughed indulgently at us. Another of our favorite games was to steal cake and eat holes in it from the bottom up, then place it back so no one would notice, until of course they came to eat it.

A few weeks ago I asked Ennayat to recall what I was like at that age, and he replied in that dry, humorous style typical of big brothers all over the world: "You were ugly and very very annoying."

Today Ennayat, and indeed all my other brothers, are the most wonderful brothers any girl could wish for. They support my political life, campaigning for me and protecting me when they can.

But growing up, we never forgot that they were boys and I was a girl. And in our family, boys were the only ones who really mattered.

As we grew older they'd be expected to go to school and achieve something with their life. My fate was to stay at home with the other girls until I was to be married.

Boy children had power—within the household a brother's word or order was often more powerful than even the word of a mother.

Muqim would follow my mother and ask for sweets. She wouldn't give him many because such delicacies were usually reserved for the guests. He'd get angry, stomp his feet, and leave the room, but then my mother would take hold of my hand, and, without looking at my face, secretly slip me some sweets. If Muqim saw he would be furious and tell my mother that if I ate those chocolates he would prevent me from going out. As a boy he had the power and authority to do that, to control what I did or did not do, regardless of what my mother said. I hated the idea of not playing outside with my friends, so I would give him the sweets begrudgingly and run out to play.

I heard the word *dukhtarak* often and early in my life. It's a common derogatory term to call a girl child, and it roughly translates as "less than a girl."

Instinctively, I hated it. Once, when I was no more than five years old, one of my older cousins called me *dukhtarak* and ordered me to make him a cup of tea. I stood up in a room full of people, my hand on my hip, and replied: "Cousin, I shall make your tea, but you shall never call me this name again." Everyone in the room fell apart laughing.

And I heard it the only time my father ever spoke directly to me. He had organized a political rally in our garden and wanted to share some news reports with those gathered. He placed large speakers in the trees and it was the first time we'd ever heard stereo sound. We were curious, so we sneaked as close as we could get without being seen so we could listen. But I soon became bored and started to make noise. My father was trying to talk and suddenly the sounds of my squeals disturbed his ears. He stopped talking and turned directly toward us. He stared at me and I froze for what felt like minutes. Then he shouted: "*Dukhtarak!* Girls! Go away you girls!"

We ran as fast as our legs could carry us.

I was so scared of him after that I didn't ever want to see him again, terrified that if he saw me even weeks later he'd be so angry that he'd kill me.

But in my childhood fantasies, I could not have imagined that it was he who would be killed, and that my golden existence was about to come to a brutal end.

Dear Shuhra and Shaharzad,

I know this seems like a very long time ago to you, but I grew up in the 1980s.

That was a time of great political changes around the world, but a time when the people of Afghanistan suffered from the Soviets, communists, and from the countless commanders of the mujahideen.

These years were the beginning of disasters for the people of Afghanistan, and for my childhood.

When the communist Saur Revolution started,* I was exactly three years old, an age when a child needs love, security, and the warm bosom of home.

But most of my friends' parents were talking about migration to Pakistan and Iran, preparing for a life as refugees.

Children listened as their parents whispered about new equipment people had never seen before, equipment called "tanks" and "helicopters."

We overheard terms like "invasion," "war," and "mujahideen," but they were meaningless to us.

Children didn't understand, but they sensed something in the way their mothers seemed to hold them closer at night.

---

*The Saur Revolution is the name given to the Communist People's Democratic Party of Afghanistan (PDPA) takeover of political power from the government of Afghanistan on April 28, 1978. The word "Saur" refers to the Dari name of the second month of the Persian calendar, the month in which the uprising took place.

This was widely seen as the start of de-facto soviet rule in Afghanistan, with a pro-Soviet puppet government appointed after the revolution. Once in power, the PDPA implemented a Soviet communist agenda. It moved to promote state atheism and carried out ill-conceived land reform, which was resented by virtually all Afghans. It changed the national flag from the traditional Islamic green color to a near-copy of the red flag of the Soviet Union, a provocative affront to the people of this conservative Islamic country. The PDPA also imprisoned, tortured or murdered thousands of members of the traditional elite, the religious establishment, and the intelligentsia.

I am happy you have never experienced such uncertainty and fear of a time like this. No child should ever have to feel it.

With love,
Your mother

THREE

A TERRIBLE LOSS

The year was 1978, and both the mujahideen and the Russians were beginning to make their presence felt in Afghanistan for the first time.

It was the height of the cold war, and the Soviet Union was keen to show strength. The USSR was working under an expansionist agenda in those days, and Afghanistan lay between Moscow and the warm-water ports of Pakistan, where the USSR wanted to place its naval fleet. To do so it needed control of Afghanistan and was beginning to exert its strategic influence to ensure that happened. Eventually, the USSR invaded Afghanistan.

In later years Afghan fighters, known as the mujahideen, defeated those Russians invaders and became heroes among the people. But at the time the Afghan public knew them only as anti-government rebels.

The mujahideen first made their presence felt in Northern Badakhshan. The central regime in Kabul was in upheaval: The king had been forced into exile, but his successor President Khan did not last long. He and his entire family were assassinated in his palace, and communist sympathizers, Nur Muhammad Taraky and Hafizullah Amin, took control. Taraky became the first communist-backed president, but a few months later he was killed by Amin on the orders of the USSR government in Moscow.

Amin then took over the presidency with the support of Moscow. He is remembered as probably the cruelest president in the history of Afghanistan. His regime was terrifying; torture and arrests were commonplace. He tried to kill anyone who opposed the government—intellectuals, teachers, religious leaders, anyone who dared to say a word against the ruling forces would be dragged from their house at night and, if they were lucky, taken to Puli Charkhi, Kabul's largest jail, where they faced interrogation and torture. The unlucky ones were thrown into the rivers. In those days Afghanistan's rivers witnessed thousands of lives being taken, all without reason or trial.

During this time my father continued his work, trying to stay focused on helping Badakhshan even through those days of terror. He remained outspoken, despite the risk of torture or more imprisonment. But perhaps the regime knew he was more useful to them alive than dead. The mujahideen rebels were beginning to make their presence known, and the government was nervous. The rebels had a stronghold in Badakhshan. Eventually the government ordered my father back to his province with instructions to settle the mujahideen or else. They made clear the penalty for failure would be death.

A man of peace, my father was certain he could reason with the mujahideen; after all, they were his fellow Afghans. He understood the political uncertainties of the time and the calls for more social justice. These were men from his own province, Badakhshanis just like him, and he was sure that once he had spoken to them he could calm their fears, listen to their complaints, and offer to help them in exchange for their cooperation with the government. But the Afghanistan my father thought he knew—the values of country first, Islamic tradition, and natural justice that he believed in so strongly— had already begun to change.

He arrived in Badakhshan on his mission with a heavy heart. He had no love for the Amin regime and in truth didn't know what was best for the people of Afghanistan. He gathered his provincial elders together in what is known as a *jirga,* a meeting of tribal leaders and elders, and explained to them what he had seen in Kabul: a government who didn't want young people to be educated for fear they would turn into dissidents; a government who killed with impunity; a land where teachers and intellectuals lived in fear; an Afghanistan where government opponents were simply crushed. After the heady years of King Zahir Shah's reign, when Afghanistan was regarded as one of the world's fastest-developing countries, after all that promise of democracy, it was crushing to see the reality of communist rule.

Some of the Afghans who had gone to the mountains to fight with the mujahideen truly believed they were there to fight for the future of Afghanistan. My father was still a government servant but he understood the mujahideen and respected them in many ways. He simply didn't know which way to turn, and asked the elders what they should do.

The *jirga* debated for hours. Some wanted to join the rebels; others wanted government rule for better or worse. But in the end local needs won the day when one man stood up and spoke in a clear voice. "Sir," he said. "We are already very poor, we can't bear to have a fight. We should talk to them and bring them down from mountains, why should we fight?"

Finally the group agreed to go and talk to them. My father gathered hundreds of local elders from all over the province. They rode on horseback for over a day to reach the rebels' camp. The Pamir mountain range is as high and as treacherous as it is beautiful. Fertile lush valleys soon give way to rocks of different colors—blues, greens, and orange ochres that change with the light—then on to towering snow-covered peaks and plateaus. Even today there are few roads in Badakhshan, but then there was nothing apart from the donkey and horse tracks, some so narrow and steep that the only way to pass was to hold onto your donkey or horse's tail, close your eyes, and pray the sure-footed beast didn't slip. To fall was certain death—plunged down the mountainside into one of the icy rivers below, swept away by the rapids.

After a day and a half of solid riding, they reached the highest point of the Pamir, where it gives way to a wonderful natural plain—almost as high as the heavens. In winter men from all over the province gather here to play Buzkashi, the origins of the game now known in the west as polo. It's a skilled game, a test of rider and horse, where men must race their horses to pick up and place the carcass of a dead cow into the goal area, marked with a circle, at the end of the pitch. In ancient times, the carcass was a dead prisoner. Games are fast and exciting, sometimes involving hundreds of riders and lasting for several days. It's a game as wild, dangerous, and clever as the men who play it. It is the true sport and essence of the Afghan warrior.

But as my father rode, thoughts of the pleasures of a Buzkashi game were furthest from his mind. He remained calm and composed, still wearing his hat, leading his white horse at the head of the group. Then three men suddenly appeared in the middle of the road and pointed rifles at them.

One of them shouted, "Wakil Abdul Rahman, so it is you. I have waited a long time for this chance to kill you."

My father shouted back in a cool voice: "Please listen to me. The government of Afghanistan is strong. You cannot defeat it. I come here to ask you to work with it, to stand together and to cooperate with us. I will listen to your needs and I will take them to parliament."

The man simply laughed and fired a shot. Other shots rang from out from behind the mountains. Pandemonium ensued. The village men—who were mostly unarmed—ran for their lives. My father's horse had been hit, and as it reared up in pain he lost his stirrup footing and was half dragged along as his mount galloped. The wounded animal headed for a small river that ran along the edge of the Buzkashi pitch. Some of the younger men tried to follow him but he shouted at them to flee and to save themselves. "I'm an elder," he yelled as he was dragged along. "They will talk to me but they will kill you. Just go."

The mujahideen gave chase and found my father.

They held him hostage for two days. I don't know if they gave him an opportunity to talk, if they listened to his reasoning and considered his offers, or if they beat and humiliated him. All we know is that two days later they executed him, shot him straight through the head.

News of his death reached the village quickly. Despite the remoteness of the region news has always traveled fast, a sophisticated system of a person passing on urgent messages at each hamlet along the way. And of course some of the men who had accompanied my father had already arrived home and reported the shooting of his horse. In Islam a body must be buried within 24 hours facing Mecca. The idea of my father's body being left alone on the mountainside without proper burial was one my family couldn't bear. He had to be brought back. But the mujahideen sent word to warn us that they would kill anyone who attempted to retrieve the body. No man wanted to be shot and killed themselves just to bring home a dead body.

So it fell to a woman to show bravery. My aunt Gada—my father's elder sister—stood up, gathered her long skirts, and put on her burqa, announcing to the shocked male gathering that she, Gada, would go retrieve the body of Wakil Abdul Rahman. As she strode out of the room and straight up the path to the mountains, her husband and my father's cousin had little choice but to follow her.

After walking for 13 hours they found him, his body dumped halfway between the village and the rebel camp.

I was three and a half years old, and I remember clearly the sadness of the day he was shot, listening to both men and women weep, alarmed by the fear and confusion in the village.

I lay awake all night listening, until at around 2:00 A.M. I heard my aunt's voice ringing out loud and clear as she approached the village. She was carrying my father's wooden staff and tapping it on the ground.

"Wakil Abdul Rahman is here. Get out of your beds. Come to greet him. He is here. We have brought him. Wakil Abdul Rahman is here."

I leapt out of bed thinking, "He's alive, my father's alive." Everything was going to be ok. The father was here. He would know what to do. He would restore order and stop everyone crying.

I ran into the street barefoot. I stopped dead in my tracks at the sight of my mother weeping and grabbing at her clothes in horror. I darted past her and saw my father's dead body. The top part of his skull, where the bullets had entered, was missing.

I began to cry. I didn't yet fully understand the enormity of what had happened but I knew that our life would never be the same.

The body was brought into the hooli and laid out in the Paris Suite before burial. My mother alone went to see the body and prepare it for the funeral. Only she of the wives said her final goodbyes to him. In the room where her children were conceived, the room where husband and wife had, in all too rare moments, lain and talked and created their own private world together, she endured this task, as she had endured everything else in her harsh life: with dignity and duty. She didn't scream or wail out loud; she washed and prepared the body in accordance with God. In his death, just as in his life, she did not fail my father.

In the morning thousands of local people poured into Koof to say a final goodbye to him. Their sadness and fear for their own futures created an atmosphere so heavy that it felt like the very sky was falling down on our heads.

Gray-haired old men with beards, white turbans, and green coats sat in the garden crying like babies. My father was buried on a peak behind the hooli, facing Mecca and the valley of Koof he so loved.

For the villagers, losing the man who had championed their causes and supported their needs was a turning point. It marked the beginning of the political upheaval that was about to become full-blown war in Afghanistan.

For my family, losing my father meant losing everything: our lives, our wealth, our figurehead, our reason for being.

Dear Shuhra and Shaharzad,

When I was a little child I didn't know the words "war," "rocket,"
"wounded," "killing," "rape."

Words which sadly all Afghan children are familiar with today.

Until the age of four I knew only happy words.

I long for those nights of summer when we would all sleep on
the big flat roof of my uncle's house. His house was just next door to
the hooli but it had the roof with the best view of the valley so all the
family liked to gather there.

Until late at night my mother, my uncle's wives, and my small
mother—my father's fourth wife and my mother's best friend—would
sit and tell old stories.

We children sat under the blue sky, or under the bright yellow
moon to listen to these sweet stories. We never closed the door at
nights and had no security men with guns like we do today, because
there were no worries about thieves or any other dangers.

In these happy times and with everyone being nice to me, I
couldn't even begin to imagine how I had begun my life, that my
mother was not happy when I was born and put me in the sun
thinking I'd die.

I never felt that my birth had degraded my mother the way it did.
I felt only that I was loved.

But this happy life didn't last for long. I had to grow up fast.

My father's murder was just the first of many more tragedies and
deaths to hit our family.

And being forced to leave those beautiful gardens of Koof, with
cold spring water and big trees, the experience of being refugees and
homeless in our own country ended my childhood.

The only thing which didn't change was the constant smile of my
mother, your grandmother.

With love,
Your mother

FOUR

RUNNING

Although she grieved for the man she loved, my father's death was in many ways the making of my mother.

In those first few months, her natural leadership abilities and skills came to the fore. It was she who took control of the family, organizing resources, deciding the fate of children. Her years of practice as my father's right hand, of political organizing and efficient home management, of keeping the peace within our extended family, allowed her to lead our family out of this dark period. Her priorities were keeping the children together and safe. She received many offers of marriage, but for the same reasons she had once refused to divorce my father—the fear of losing her children—she refused all suitors.

Not all of the wives fared so well.

Ennayat's mother—still young and somewhat flighty—married a handsome young man who had worked for my father as a shepherd guarding the family cattle. He had gone to Iran to find work and recently returned, bringing with him exciting consumer goods, including a tape recorder, not found in our little village. He wooed her with his tales of the sophisticated life in Iran and with that tape recorder.

But as is normal in our culture, a stepfather has no obligation to take the children from a previous marriage, and he refused to care for them. Aside from Ennayat, she had borne my father three other children: Ennayat's brother Hedayat, sister Nazi, and a six-month-old son, Safiullah. She insisted on taking the children with her to her new home, but the new husband refused to feed or clothe them. When my mother visited a few weeks later, she found Ennayat and his two older siblings crying in the yard. They were not allowed in the warmth of the house and were hungry and dirty. She took them home with her immediately. But the young woman refused to give up her baby. My mother, who was sympathetic to her, left without baby Safiullah. It was something my mother regretted forever, because a few days later he got a fever and was left to die without food or comfort. We heard that he cried alone for hours, his little face covered with flies, while this man would not allow his mother to even pick him up. He died a lonely, horrible death. Ennayat has never gotten over it and named his own first-born son Safiullah in his memory.

Khal bibi, who had been so dear to my mother, was luckier. She married a local leader, a kindly man who had no previous children. In a gesture almost unheard of in our culture, he raised her two sons like his own, even leaving his property to them when he died.

Niaz bibi, the wife who didn't get on with my mother, married a teacher and remained in Koof. Despite her and my mother's disagreements, years later, when I was campaigning for parliament, this man helped me enormously, arranging transport for me and accompanying me on the campaign trail. The extended family structure is hard for people in the western world to understand, but in my view it is a wonderful thing. Those ties transcend generations, petty arguments, and geography. Family is family.

Zulmaishah, the Khalifa's child and my father's eldest son, inherited the hooli. He was later killed, and Nadir, the child of my fifth mother—one of the wives my father divorced—inherited it and still lives in it to this day.

But in those first days and weeks after my father was killed we didn't have much time to grieve, because the world beyond the mountains was getting closer, and the rapidly disintegrating political situation was about to come crashing down on us.

A few days after his death, the commanders who had killed my father came looking for us. We ran up to the fields where our cattle were and hid behind a large rock ledge. We watched as they looted the house, stealing all they could carry—the radio, the furniture, the pots and pans, they took it all.

Then, a few weeks later, we were all sleeping on the roof of my uncle's house when they came back in the middle of the night. They awoke us by hitting us all with their rifles. They were yelling and screaming, demanding to know where the sons of Abdul Rahman were. My brother Muqim was just six years old, but if they had found him they would have killed him. Somehow my mother managed to pass him to a neighbor on the next roof, who hid him underneath her skirts. In some parts of Afghanistan shalwar kameez are the norm for women, but village women in Badakhshan wear loose pantaloons covered by long, full skirts. Those skirts saved my brother's life that night. The mujahideen took my sister and my sister-in-law, my elder brother's wife. Both girls had just turned 16. They started to beat them. My uncle tried to stop them but he was beaten back. They took the girls off the roof and down toward the hooli. My uncles and male cousins were screaming at them, telling them this was against Islam, that this was *haram,* forbidden, and that no Muslim should touch a woman who is not his blood relative or his wife.

We were forced to watch from the roof as they beat the girls all night long, pistol whipping them and hitting them with rifle butts. They kept demanding to know where the weapons were hidden, but no one claimed to know. My mother was white as a sheet and grim-faced, but she said nothing. We all watched as they put the bayonet of the gun to my sister's chest and pressed it until she began to bleed. We had a guard dog called Chamber who was chained near the gate of the hooli. So desperate was he to protect his family that he tugged until his chains broke free; he ran toward the men, barking and snarling, ready to bite, but they simply turned and shot him dead. They beat the two girls until dawn, when the call to prayer was heard over the mountain. They left, presumably to go pray.

Two days later they came again and threatened to kill us all. This time they forced Nadir, who was a teenager, to show them where the guns were. My mother had known all along and had even watched as her daughter and daughter-in-law were beaten without betraying the whereabouts of the weapons. My mother knew that with the guns gone, our last method of protection was gone. They had taken everything we had; the next time, they would kill us.

The men of the village were so horrified by what had happened to the girls that night that they sent a message to the mujahideen, saying that if they came back to our village they would meet resistance. They would take up shovels, pick axes, and staffs, whatever they had, and use it to protect their women. The mujahideen agreed not to terrify the village, but they wanted the family of Abdul Rahman dead. Their commander gave permission for his men to execute us. This was the second time I stared death in the face.

They came early the following morning. By now the Khalifa and her children had moved to another village, so my mother was the only wife left in the hooli. Fortunately most of the children were out playing and were able to hide in neighbor's houses. My mother grabbed me and the two of us ran into the cattle house. Our neighbors frantically started to pile up pieces of dung in front of us to give us cover. I remember the smell and the choking bitter taste of the dung. It felt like I was being buried alive. I clung tightly to my mother's hand, too afraid to cough for fear they would find us. We were there for hours, silent, terrified. The only sense of security was my mother's fingers wrapped around mine. We could hear them searching for us, and at one point they came right up to our hiding place. If they had prodded the dung pile it would have tumbled down, revealing our positions, but for reasons only God knows, they didn't.

After they finally left, we came out of our hiding place to find the world had turned to terror: our hooli had been completely ransacked. My mother grabbed me, my two brothers, and my elder sister. She didn't waste time gathering our clothes, and we ran. We ran down past the garden, through the hay fields, and onto the river banks. We were leaving all we had behind and we didn't dare even to glance back. For my mother, it was as though her life was collapsing with each step she took. All the beatings, all the pain, all the years of drudgery and work, it was all to build a home and a life. A life that ended as we ran for our very survival along the river bank.

As expected, the men returned to search again, and they looked down into the valley and saw us running away. They started to give chase. They were stronger, faster. I was getting tired and was beginning to stumble and slow the others down. My sister started to scream at my mother to throw me into the river to save the others: "If you don't throw her they'll catch us and we'll all die. Just throw her."

She almost did. My mother picked me up and lifted me into the air as if to throw me, but she looked into my eyes and recalled her promise at my birth that no more harm would ever come my way. From somewhere deep inside her she gathered reserves of strength and instead of throwing me to my death put me on her back, where I clung on as she ran with me. We were the last of the group and I could hear the footsteps of the men getting closer. I thought that at any second they'd be upon us and would tear me from my mother's back and kill me. If I close my eyes today I still feel the clammy, cold, awful fear of that moment.

Then, suddenly, we saw a Russian.

WE'D REACHED THE OTHER SIDE OF THE VALLEY, which was government-controlled land. Our would-be assassins turned and ran back. We collapsed with exhaustion and relief. My mother started to weep.

That Russian was the first of many I would see in the following years. They were foreign invaders in Afghan land, and although they would bring education and development in some areas, they would commit many atrocities on innocent Afghans. This one, though, was kind to me. He was tall and blond, in army uniform, and he called me over. Hesitantly, I walked toward him. He handed me a bag of sugar, which I ran back to my mother with. It was the first, but not the last, time my mother would be forced to accept charity.

First the five of us stayed close to the river, in the home of a teacher named Rahmullah. He was just about one of the kindest people I ever met, with warm eyes that crinkled when he smiled and a neat gray beard. The family was poor and couldn't really afford the extra mouths to feed, but he had been one of my father's political supporters and he was honored to have the Wakil's family in his simple two-room home.

His garden backed directly onto the river, and I remember playing happily, splashing about with his daughters. It was a relationship that would endure. Years later he came to me for support because his daughter needed to escape a forced marriage. The family had arranged the match when she was a child, but the man in question had grown up to be notoriously violent and the girl wanted to refuse him. His family insisted the match go ahead, but Rahmullah supported his daughter's right to say no. I negotiated between the two families, eventually getting the other side to agree to break the engagement. The girl was then free to follow her dream and train as a teacher like her father. In gratitude, Rahmullah gave me all the help he could in my political campaigns. Today, if I visit the area I love nothing more than to take a simple lunch of rice and chicken by the river with this lovely family.

After staying with them for two weeks my mother was restless, confused about what to do and where to go. We heard contradictory news about our house, including that the mujahideen had burned it down and killed my sister and sister-in-law, who were still living there. Happily, the news was not accurate and the girls had survived.

My two elder brothers, Jamalshah and Mirshakay, had already moved to Faizabad before the attacks began. The elder one was a chief of police and the younger one a student. When news of what had happened to us finally reached them, they chartered a flight to Koof to pick us all up.

When the helicopter landed my mother was sobbing with relief. It was the first time I'd ever flown, and I remember running toward the helicopter ahead of the two boys and my big sister. Inside the helicopter there were two big wooden chairs; I put myself in the corner of one of the chairs, and my mother and sister sat in the other. Ennayat and Muqim had no chair, and I remember looking at them and smiling smugly because I had a chair and they did not.

In Faizabad my brother had rented us a house. He couldn't afford much on his policeman's salary, and it was a basic two-room mud shack. Local people gave my mother the basics: plates, pots, etc. The fancy imported china she was used to serving food on in the hooli was a thing of the past. She joked we were living in a dollhouse, it was so tiny, but she did her best to turn it into a home for us, putting hangings and tapestries on the walls to brighten it up.

By now I was seven. I still looked like a typical village girl, dirty hair and face, wearing baggy kameez trousers, a long scarf that trailed in the mud, and a pair of red wellington boots. I was so out of place in the big town.

From the dollhouse, I watched as the young girls went to school. These girls looked so smart and bright, and I yearned to be like them. But no girl child in my family had ever been educated; my father didn't see the need. But he was no longer here. So I asked my mother if I could go. She looked at me for a long, long time—it felt like hours—beamed a big smile, and said yes. "Yes Fawzia jan, you can go to school."

Everyone else was against it, particularly my older brothers. But my mother held fast and insisted. I was to go with Muqim to school the next day to ask permission to join. We went into the headmaster's office. I remember the office being smart and clean with padded chairs, and I felt so tiny and so very dirty. My nose was full of snot and my face was covered with dirty marks, and feeling suddenly embarrassed, I used my scarf to wipe my nose loudly.

The headmaster frowned and peered at me. How was it a dirty little village girl like me was here in Faizabad asking to be educated? "Who are your people?" he asked me. When I answered I was the daughter of Wakil Abdul Rahman he raised his eyebrows in surprise. This was how far down the social scale our family had fallen since his death. But the kindly man admitted me to school and told me to start the next day. I remember running home to tell my mother, my scarf trailing in the mud and tripping me. My little heart was so full of excitement that I forgot everything else—my father's death, the loss of our home, our life of poverty.

I, Fawzia Koofi, was going to school!

I was so determined to make the most of every moment of school it didn't take me long to catch up with the other girls, and soon I was regularly achieving second and first place in class. Nothing has ever brought me such joy as studying for an exam and receiving a top grade.

Our education was fairly basic: general studies half the day at Kockcha high school, and study of the Holy Quran the other half of the day from the mullah iman at the local mosque. My mother—herself totally illiterate—was very interested in the Quranic studies.

At night I slept alongside my brother Muqim in our mother's bed. Our routine was always the same. She would ask us what we had studied, and we had to tell her what we remembered and recite the Quran to her, and she would make verbal corrections of our readings. It was her way of being involved in our education, and she loved it.

By the time I got to Pamir high school, the first high school in Faizabad, I was a confident child. I cut my hair short in order to look like the other girls. My brothers were furious, but again my mother calmed them down and, I believe, secretly enjoyed my newfound confidence and development.

Sometimes we'd have access to television and I would hear about Margaret Thatcher in the UK or Indira Gandhi, the prime minister of India, who remains a heroine of mine to this day.

I would watch them with my mouth open and think to myself, How is it possible that a woman stands in front of all those people? How can a simple woman lead them? And where does she find the power to speak to the all those people?

Other times, my friends and I would climb on the roof of my school to play. Slowly my horizons were broadening. When I was a toddler, I used to stand in the kitchen of the hooli looking up at the sky and thinking my whole existence was there. Now I stared from the roof at the streets surrounding the school. I believed then that the whole sky stood on the mountains around Faizabad, and all the world, my world, was in that city and its surrounding areas.

I was extremely happy there until the age of 11, when my brother Jamalshah got a promotion within the police force and was posted to Kabul. We were to go with him. I think the day we moved was one of the most exciting days of my life. Not only was I thrilled to be moving to the exciting capital city, a place I had only seen on TV, but I was transferring to a big high school there. I was fit to burst.

Kabul was exactly as I had dreamed it would be—noisy, exciting, and loud. I marveled at the yellow taxi cabs with black stripes down the sides, the blue Millie buses with female drivers in smart uniforms (the Millie was Kabul's electric bus system, one of the few electric bus system in the world at the time), the glitzy shops with all the latest fashions, and the smell of delicious barbequed meat floating from the hundreds of restaurants. The city embraced me, and I loved it back with all my heart.

For the next three years we stayed in Kabul, and they were some of the happiest years of my childhood. My mother loved the city, too. She found shopping in the big bazaars tremendously exciting and stimulating. It wasn't much, but these were levels of independence she could never have dreamed of when she was married to my father. The same was true for me. I experimented with fashion and talked about poetry and literature with my friends. We'd walk home from school along tree-lined boulevards, carrying our books with pride. These new school friends seemed so sophisticated and glamorous to me. Their families had houses with swimming pools; their mothers were chic with bobbed hairstyles, and their fathers indulgent and kind, trailing behind them the faint scent of aftershave and scotch whisky. Some of these girls even wore makeup and nail varnish. I was banned by my brothers from trying it, and I recall one day when I'd secretly put some on at a friends house. I also borrowed some of her clothes, long socks and a short skirt. My friend and I were casually sauntering around, pleased with how cool we thought we looked, when Jamalshah drove past in his car. He saw me and slowed down, staring out the open window. I didn't have time to hide, so I turned and faced the wall. My thinking was if he couldn't see me I couldn't see him. But of course he did. And he was waiting for me when I got home. He made like he was going to beat me so I ran away to hide. As I ran I heard him bellow with laughter, calling my mother to tell her the tale. She laughed too, and shamefaced I quietly snuck back in for dinner.

Those days in Kabul were free and light and fun.

But once again the wider world was about to collide with my little world.

Dear Shuhra and Shaharzad,

When I was young I felt like my life changed all the time. Each time we found a safe place to live or a moment of calm, the war forced change back upon us.

I hated change in those days. All I wanted was to stay in one place, in one home, and go to school. I had big dreams but I also wanted a contented life. I want the same for you, too. I want you to fly free and find your dreams, but I also want you to have a happy home, a husband who loves you, and one day experience the joy of having children of your own.

Even in your short lives you've had to experience more changes than I would have wished for you. Tolerating a bad situation is often easier than having change forced upon us. But sometimes I worry that I have asked you to tolerate too much. My long absences, your fears that I will be killed and that you will be left motherless.

But sometimes tolerating something is the wrong approach. Being able to adapt and start anew is an ability that all great leaders have shared. Change isn't always our enemy and you need to learn to accept it as a necessary part of life. If we make a friend of change and welcome it in, then it may choose to treat us less painfully the next time it comes to call.

With love,
Your mother

FIVE

A VILLAGE GIRL AGAIN

I t was the beginning of the 1990s. Apartheid in South Africa had ended. In Europe the Berlin Wall was coming down, the great Soviet empire was dismantling, and the cold war was reaching its final years.

The mujahideen fighters were seasoned veterans by now. They fought a successful war of attrition against the Russian invaders. And in 1989 they succeeded in sending the Soviet army retreating back to Moscow. Crowds cheered and clapped as the Red Army was forced to make a humiliating defeat. The fighters' morale had never been higher and many people saw them as heroes. The most popular of them all was Ahmed Shah Massoud, the man known as the Lion of Panjshir. He was seen as the most brilliant and clever of all the mujahideen warlords and the man who was the real strategist behind the Russian defeat. His image is still found on posters all over Afghanistan today.

But now, with the Red Army gone, the fighters were eager to seize full power over the government. They sent their armies sweeping toward Kabul. The mujahideen resented what they saw as a puppet government that, even though the Russian military presence had gone, still had very close links to Moscow. The government was led by President Mohammad Najibullah. For three years the Afghan army under his control fought to keep the mujahideen at bay, but eventually they were overwhelmed and his government collapsed.

People hoped this would bring stability and a new, purely Afghan-led government. But almost immediately after they defeated the government, the mujahideen began to fight among themselves. With the common enemy defeated, simmering ethnic tensions rose to the surface and they could not agree on how to share power. These battles between different commanders would eventually turn into the Afghan civil war, a bloody, brutal war that lasted more than a decade.

I was 16 years old when I heard the news on the radio that President Najibullah had been arrested by police while trying to flee Afghanistan. We were all shocked by what was happening and very worried for our country.

We had been living in Kabul, where I went to school. But the week it happened we were in our home province of Badakhshan. We were back in the city of Faizabad, visiting relatives on an extended holiday.

The day after the report of the president's arrest we could hear shooting coming from the mountains above Faizabad.

The Afghan army had set up positions on one side of the mountains that ringed the city, while on the other the mujahideen had also dug in. The two sides were exchanging fire with rifles and machine guns and occasionally artillery. It seemed to me that the mujahideen were firing a lot more than the army, who didn't seem to have as many guns or as much ammunition as their enemy.

The army soldiers just seemed to be defending their positions and weren't offering much resistance. Many Afghan soldiers had already deserted in large numbers. Many were unwilling to fight their countrymen, but the soldiers also knew exactly what the mujahideen were capable of doing. During earlier battles, Russian soldiers had been tortured and killed. The torture became more gruesomely creative as time went on. Sometimes they burned people alive. Other times they would ask a prisoner his age and then nail that number of nails into his skull. Still other times they would cut a prisoner's head off and pour boiling oil into the corpse. When the hot oil encountered the nerve endings, the decapitated body moved around for a few seconds as if it were dancing. This form of torture was aptly called the "dead man's dance."

The Afghan army knew that it was the new enemy and couldn't expect any more mercy than the Russians had. Many soldiers simply slipped off their uniforms and returned to normal civilian life.

After two days of fighting, the mujahideen were declared the new government. Peace talks for the surrender and handover of power had already started at a conference in Geneva two years earlier, in 1989. So when the government in Kabul collapsed, few were surprised. Suddenly Faizabad was full of mujahideen fighters who had come down from their mountain positions.

I remember watching them, thinking how interesting and grizzled their faces looked.

These were men who had been living in mountain camps, subsisting on scarce rations and fighting almost daily battles for several years. In my mind, soldiers wore smart uniforms, so it was very strange to see these casually dressed men in jeans and sneakers. I wondered how some of them could ever readjust to civilian and civilized life. And I was not alone in that thought. The government offices were suddenly full of these men, and they terrified the locals; many schools shut their doors because parents refused to send their daughters, fearing they might be raped by these ex-fighters who now stalked the city streets.

But overall, most people in Afghanistan were happy that the Russians were gone and still hoped that the mujahideen would settle their disputes and form a decent government.

For me, however, these political changes marked a very depressing period in my life. I was 16 years old, and suddenly, if I wanted to travel around the city, I had to wear a burqa for the first time in my life. The mujahideen were not religiously fundamental and they did not impose the wearing of the burqa. The need to wear it was more a matter of safety. With so many male soldiers around it just wasn't a good idea for a young girl to show her beauty on the streets.

It was very common for women like my mother, my aunts, and my elder sisters to wear a burqa. But younger women like myself didn't identify with the traditions of wearing them. In the old days a burqa was a sign of nobility, but it also had practical uses. It was designed to protect a woman from the harsh elements, the burning sun, dusty sand, and fierce winds. I know that many people in the West today see the burqa as a sign of female oppression and religious fundamentalism. But I don't see it that way.

I want the right to wear what I think is best, but within the confines of Islam. Covering the hair with a head scarf and wearing a long loose tunic that covers one's arms, chest and bottom is enough to satisfy the Islamic rule of being modest before God. Anyone who says a woman must cover her entire face to be truly Islamic is wrong. A burqa is definitely not an Islamic requirement but is usually worn because of cultural or societal reasons.

I am also aware that in some Western countries, wearing a face-covering burqa has become a political issue, with certain politicians and leaders wanting to ban it by law. While I believe that all governments have a right to de-termine the laws and culture of their own countries, I also believe in freedom of choice, and I think Western governments should let Muslim women wear what they want.

As a young girl, however, I did not want to wear a burqa. One day my mother, sister, and I got dressed up in our nicest clothes for a party at my aunt's house. I was very pleased and felt beautiful. I was even wearing a little bit of makeup. Before the arrival of the mujahideen I would have just put a head scarf on before stepping outside. But my mother had gone to our neigh-bor's house and borrowed a burqa, which she insisted I wear.

I was furious. I had never worn a burqa in my life, and here I was in my nicest clothes with my hair and makeup done, ready for a party, and she was insisting I cover myself in a heavy blue sack.

I refused and we flew into a terrible argument. I argued, "Suddenly the mujahideen come to town and the whole world changes," while my mother pleaded, cajoled, and threatened that it was for my own protection. She ar-gued that the soldiers could not be trusted if they saw me uncovered and that I should hide myself to avoid unwanted trouble. I was crying, which only made me angrier because it ruined my makeup. I started doing that teenage thing where I decided that if I had to wear a burqa then I simply wouldn't go to my aunt's at all. Eventually my mother talked me around. I did want to go to the party, and having spent so long getting ready it would be a shame not to go. And so I begrudgingly pulled the burqa over my head and reluctantly took my first steps into the streets of Faizabad and this strange new world.

Peering through the tiny blue mesh eye slot, I felt as though everything was closing in on me.

The mountains seemed to be perched on my shoulders as if the world had somehow grown both much larger and much smaller at the same time. My breathing was loud and hot inside the hood and I felt claustrophobic, like I was being buried alive—smothered beneath the heavy nylon cloth.

In that moment I felt something less than human. My confidence evapo-rated. I became tiny and insignificant and helpless as if the simple act of don-ning the burqa had shut all the doors in my life I had worked so hard to open. My school, the pretty clothes, the makeup, the party—all meant nothing now.

I'd grown up seeing my mother wear the burqa, but I felt as though it was merely something of her generation and that it was a cultural tradition that was slowly dying out. I had never felt any need nor had been asked by my family to conform to it. I saw myself as part of a new generation of Afghan women, and the burqa's traditions didn't represent my ambitions, for myself or my country. Unlike my mother, I had an education, one that I was eager to expand upon. I had opportunities and freedoms. One of them was the freedom to choose whether or not to wear a burqa—and I chose not to.

It wasn't that I had, or have, a particular problem with burqas. They are traditional and can offer women some degree of protection in our society. Women all over the world must occasionally deal with unwanted attention from men and for some women, wearing a burqa can be a way of avoiding that. But what I object to is that someone can impose a decision about what to wear. How would women in the West react to a government-enforced policy that made them wear miniskirts from the onset of puberty? Islamic and cultural ideals of modesty are strong in Afghan society, but they are not so strong that a woman must, by virtue of her gender, be hidden beneath a blue sack. Covering the hair with a head-scarf is enough to satisfy the Islamic rule of being modest before God.

When we got to my aunt's house, I was relieved to get the burqa off. The experience had left me feeling shocked and scared about what my life and my country was turning into. I couldn't enjoy the party and instead kept to myself, reliving the horrible experience of the walk, suffocating beneath the tiny walls of my portable cell. All the while I plotted how to best get home—how I would dash back, hoping to avoid anybody I knew. I wasn't ready to admit to myself, let alone anybody else, that a burqa had become part of my life.

The following day Kabul airport was closed by the mujahideen. The flights between Faizabad and Kabul stopped running. Our sense of isolation from the capital became very real. I was very worried about what was happening there. I was particularly concerned that my school, if it hadn't already been destroyed in the fighting, might be closed and I would never be able to return to my studies.

We listened closely to the radio for any scrap of news. It was hard to know what to believe. The warlords were smart enough to seize the radio and television stations, and even in Faizabad rumors abounded about what was happening in the capital. The radio announcer told us the schools were open and girls were to attend. But the reality was parents were reluctant to send their daughters to class because they didn't think it was safe.

We could see the changes on the television. At that time, Afghanistan had some highly respected women presenting the evening news. They were smart and glamorous and executed their jobs with utter professionalism. As a girl they were important role models for me. I loved following their changing hairstyles as much as I loved listening to them report the international news. They were living proof Afghan women could be attractive, educated, and successful. But suddenly, the beautiful, intelligent female news presenters with their perfect hair and makeup that I had so admired disappeared from the screens. In their place dowdy women in scarves stumbled their way through the news. This change made me very worried.

I went to my mother in tears one day, upset and scared and frustrated by the situation. She just listened to me as I poured my heart out, and when I had finished, she announced that we would find a temporary admission at a school in Faizabad.

I missed Kabul and the heady glamour of my friends' houses. But I was pleased to be back at school, even though the school in Faizabad, which had once so felt so large and overwhelming to me, now seemed tiny and parochial.

And I was stuck with the burqa. I began to get used to the feeling of being enclosed, but I couldn't get used to the heat. There was no bus service in Faizabad, and so I would walk to school in the sun while the sweat ran down my body. I found I sweated so badly that my skin developed black spots from the perspiration and lack of air.

Despite my discomfort I found myself making lots of friends. I was enjoying being back in the classroom and the opportunities that came with it. My teachers invited me to take part in some gardening classes after school, where we could learn about plants, propagation, and soil care. This was Badakhshan, where even today the understanding of biology and farming science is very basic, so it seemed like an interesting way to spend time with my new friends.

Unfortunately, my mother wouldn't let me continue my gardening classes. Even with my burqa she was scared her teenage daughter might attract the roaming eye of a mujahideen fighter. Every minute I was outside the house was another minute that might lead to an unwelcome marriage proposal; and a mujahideen marriage proposal is not one you turn down without serious consequences. To do so would almost certainly invite the mujahideen to take what they wanted by force. As far as my mother was concerned, going to school was an essential risk; learning about plants was a luxury her beautiful daughter could live without.

The arrival of the mujahideen had changed so much about my world outside the house. But it changed my home life in unexpected ways, too.

I had been back at school for a month when my half-brother Nadir appeared at our door one day. He was the eldest son of the wife my father had divorced. I hadn't seen him for 15 years, when he disappeared as a boy to fight the Russians. The man who stood in our living room was now a mujahideen commander. He and his men were responsible for the supply routes into Koof, to ensure the fighters there had enough arms and ammunition. It was a very important role and not a position the generals handed out lightly. My mother was glad to see her stepson, of course, but she wasn't shy about venting her displeasure at his job. If this had angered my brother he would have been, at least as far as the mujahideen were concerned, within his rights to beat her or maybe even kill her for such insolence. But he didn't. Such was my mother's way and the respect she commanded within our family that he apologized to her. He was a man now, he said, and he knew right from wrong. His priority now lay with doing what was best for the family.

He wanted to take me to his village, where he could protect me from the other mujahideen. His rank within the fighters would be enough to guarantee my security there. But he was clear that while I remained with my mother in Faizabad, not even his influence was sufficient to prevent local gunmen from forcibly marrying me should it occur to them.

This was my mother's greatest fear, and so it was decided I should go with Nadir to the village where he lived in the Yaftal district.

The only way there was on horseback. And later that day he arrived at the door with two white horses wearing tasseled bridles. I hadn't ridden a horse since I was a little girl. And as ever, my burqa conspired to make my life difficult. Trying to even sit on a horse while wearing a burqa is a challenge, let alone riding an animal through busy traffic. It startled at every blaring horn and strange noise. In the end my brother had to take the reins and lead the horse through the city, while I did my best just to stay on. Every time it kicked or bucked he would rein it in, controlling it just as I thought I was about to fall onto the road. I had never felt more backward than I did that day. Here I was, dressed in a burqa, while being led on a horse. I felt like I had regressed to my mother's or grandmother's generation. At that moment it looked like neither my country nor my life was ever going to progress into something better.

We rode out of Faizabad and on to my brother's house. It was several days' riding and the roads were very poor, barely even dirt tracks. I had taken control of the horse, so I was pleased with myself. The burqa still made it difficult for me to ride, especially when trying to steer the horse around corners. With my restricted vision I was very disoriented. And if the horse stumbled in a hole it was very hard to retain my balance.

As night fell we came to a village where we could rest. Although we had only been traveling a day, already I could see the differences in the people. The village women were very welcoming and were eager to talk to the new arrivals. As we spoke I noticed how filthy their hands were, black with dirt from long, hard days working in the fields and irregular bathing. Their clothes were those of simple rural peasants, which I suppose shouldn't have surprised me, but I just couldn't shake the feeling that somehow I had gone back in time. First the burqa, then the horse, and now the dirty village women who lived their lives in much the same way as their grandmothers and their grandmothers before them—it was like watching my country's future unravel before my eyes.

When I woke I found I was very stiff and sore. Horse riding can create aches in places you never thought possible. But I was still pleased with myself to be riding unassisted through such tough country after such a long time out of the saddle. You need to be skilled to ride in this part of Afghanistan. Sometimes your life depends on it.

I had been living with Nadir and his family for two weeks when we went to visit an uncle and some of my other distant family in a nearby village. I was sitting with a woman who knew my mother when she asked me if I was in Kabul when my brother Muqim had been killed. I was completely shocked because I hadn't heard anything about this. Everybody in the room could see the look of horror on my face and they realized I didn't know. My uncle was first to react. His instinct was to deflect the subject, and he tried to suggest the woman was asking about another of my half-brothers who had been killed by the mujahideen 15 years previously.

That brother had been among a group of village men who helped fight off the mujahideen when they attacked the town of Kohan. He spent all night firing out of a small bathroom window in his house, armed with just a pistol. In order to reach the high window, his poor wife had to crouch on all fours and he stood on her back. Both he and his wife survived that battle, but he was a marked man after that. He fled to Takjikistan for a while but eventually tried to sneak back into Afghanistan. That was when they caught him. In another sign of the strength of the extended family, my mother spent the night going from local commander to local commander, begging for his release. He wasn't her blood son, but like all the other wives' children, she loved him as her own. But she failed and he was executed with a bullet to the head the following morning at dawn.

But I knew all about this story. And I was only a little girl when it had happened. So why would she ask me if I was there? Despite what the family said to the contrary, I was sick with worry that they were really talking about my brother Muqim. He lived in Kabul and I feared it was he who had been killed. I was in shock. I felt like I was having a heart attack. I didn't want to eat anything. I felt sick. I just wanted to sprout wings and fly to Kabul to check if he was alright.

On the way back to his house, Nadir continued to protect me, saying that the lady had made a mistake. I knew in my heart he was wrong, but I chose to believe the lie rather than accept the terrible truth.

Perhaps it was the uncertainty of whether Muqim really was dead or not, but I found life in the village very difficult after that. I was really beginning to miss my family, especially my mother. I was having trouble adjusting to life in the country, too, and I found myself longing to be back among the bustle and energy of a city, preferably Kabul. Everything was just so unfamiliar. I even found the basic village food of boiled meat and naan inedible. I began losing weight. Most of all I was missing my classes.

There was no television or radio, so once the evening meal had been eaten and tidied away, the family simply went to bed—normally by seven o'clock each night. It was far too early for me. To occupy myself on those quiet evenings, as I lay in bed I would go over different math problems, formulas for chemistry and physics. It kept my mind occupied and helped me feel at least some connection with the lessons I missed so much. And as I remembered the numbers and symbols, part of me hoped I could soon return to Kabul and find it like it was when I left more than a year ago.

Not long after, I asked Nadir to let me return to Faizabad. I missed my mother so much and really needed to be near her. I started discussing this with my family, but it was decided that instead of returning to Faizabad, my mother, sister, brother-in-law, and I would all move back to Kabul together. Mirshakay, my mother's second son, was by now a police general in the capital, and he had decreed Kabul to be safe enough.

I took a flight to the city of Kunduz, where I met up with the others. I was so happy to be back with my family, and especially my mother. I did not tell her what I had been told about Muqim's death, because I still couldn't bring myself to believe it was true. When I felt the nagging sickening waves of unease wash over me, I simply shut it out of my mind. My mother was very pleased to have me back, too, and although neither of us knew what to expect in Kabul, we were all very excited to be returning.

From Kunduz we had to take a 186-mile bus journey. That July was very hot, even by the usual summer temperatures of Afghanistan. The sun scorched the mountains, and the rocks became so hot around midday that you could not touch them for fear of burning your hand. The wind whipped up the dust so that it swirled around in little tornados, getting everywhere—in houses, inside cars and machinery, constantly in your eyes.

I was becoming used to my burqa, but of course I still resented it. The dust did not respect women's modesty, and it would find its way inside the blue cloth and stick to my sweating skin, making me itch and wriggle even more than usual. At least on the horse ride to my brother's house I was in the open air, but when I was crammed into a stifling bus with my family and dozens of other people trying to get to Kabul, the temperature inside my burqa was unbearable.

The road from Kunduz to Kabul is one of the most dangerous in Afghanistan. It has improved over the years, but even now it can be a nerve-wracking journey. The road's narrow, rutted surface winds around the jagged mountains in spirals that on one side pierce the turquoise sky, while on the other plunge hundreds of feet down to the jagged rocks of the gorge below. Many unfortunate people have met their deaths down there. There aren't any safety barriers, and when trucks and larger vehicles like our bus met while going in opposite directions, they would squeeze past each other a few inches at a time while the wheels teetered along the crumbling lip of the cliff.

I have always been nervous in cars. I sat in my bouncing, swaying seat listening to the roar of the bus's engine as the driver worked his way furiously up and down the gears, occasionally tooting his horn to remonstrate passing motorists. Fortunately I had my physics calculations and formulas to distract me, and I would happily drift off in a trail of numbers. Anything to keep my mind from the rivers of sweat that ran down my back and matted my hair inside the hood of my burqa.

As the heat of the day began to wear off, the mountains turned lilac. The landscape softened, and now and then we passed a shepherd squatting near his flock of goats and sheep as they grazed the sweetest grass around the river-beds and shadier spots. Donkeys snuffled among the wild poppies, and every few miles the burned and abandoned remains of a Soviet tank or truck lit-tered the side of the road.

When we approached the outskirts of Kabul, tired, still damp with sweat, and irritated by the layer of dust that tickled our noses and made our skin itch, our bus slowed to a crawl in a long line of traffic that stretched out in front of us. Hundreds of cars blocked the road, packed bumper to bumper. We waited, uncertain of what was happening. Without air flowing through the windows it became unbearably hot once again. Many of the children were crying, pleading with their mothers to give them water. A man with an AK-47 rifle approached the bus, sticking his bushy black beard and brown *paqul* hat (a wool round shaped hat, usually grey or light brown in color) through the door. His shalwar kameez was sweat-stained and dirty. The passengers strained their ears to hear the conversation. The delay, the gunman told the driver, was because a mujahideen commander, Abul Sabur Farid Kohistani, was being appointed prime minister of the new government, and the roads in the capital had been closed as a security precaution to let his convoy through. I took it as a bad sign. Not even the Russians had needed to bring an entire city to a halt to move dignitaries around. Kabul was in the hands of the muja-hideen; they were veteran fighters, not politicians or civil servants. How could they run the country efficiently?

When the roads were eventually opened again we made our way through the city. There were signs of recent fighting—destroyed buildings and burned-out vehicles, and mujahideen stood at checkpoints, guns at the ready. We went to my brother Mirshakay's apartment in an area called Makrorian, a series of Russian-built apartment blocks. He lived on the fifth floor, and the apartment was very busy. He'd had been given a very senior job at the Ministry of the Interior, where he was helping run the police force. He was a very important man, and when we entered the apartment the living room was full of guests, men mostly, waiting to speak to him. Some were there on official business—

police policy and organization. Others were there to plead the case of friends or relatives who were in jail; while others, many from Badakhshan, were making a social visit. It was a chaotic scene. He came to meet us on the third floor and I burst into in tears. The city was so different from the last time I was here, and I was afraid of what it meant for my family and my country. But I was most concerned that my brother Muqim wasn't there to greet us, too. It played to my worst fears. I knew in my heart he was dead, but his absence confirmed it to me. Still, nobody seemed prepared to acknowledge the fact.

When I asked where he was, I was told he had gone to Pakistan and planned to go to Europe. When? I asked. About 40 days ago, I was told. But I knew I was being lied to. Then I saw his photograph on a shelf in the living room. The frame had been decorated with silk flowers. It was an ominous sign, and the first outward confirmation of my worst fears.

"Why did you decorate the photo frame with flowers?" I asked my sister-in-law. She squirmed uncomfortably. "Because, you know, since Muqim went to Pakistan I just miss him so much," she replied. My heart sank and I knew she was lying. In Afghanistan we decorate a photograph with flowers as a sign of mourning, as a tribute. My family was trying to protect me. But I didn't need protecting—I needed the truth.

Later that evening I was casually exploring the apartment, picking up the books and photographs that lined my brother's living room. I found a diary and opened it out of bored curiosity rather than genuine suspicion. Inside was a poem. It was the terrible truth laid out in verse.

Written by a man called Amin, who had been my brother's best friend, it was a poem of lament, describing how Muqim had been killed. I had read only the first three lines before a scream exploded from my lips. It was more a wail of anguish than rage. Here was elegant proof of Muqim's murder. A murder no one in my family seemed prepared to openly acknowledge. My mother and brother rushed into the living room to see what was the matter. I was crying uncontrollably and barely able to talk. Instead I just stood there, holding the journal in my hand, waving it at my mother. She took it from me with trembling hands. My brother looked horrified, but he didn't stop my mother from staring down at the poem. Unable to read the words, she looked up at me blankly. "It's about your son," I whispered. "He's dead." The time for lies, no matter how well intended, was over. My mother's scream was heartbreaking. Its piercing crescendo echoed off the concrete walls, drilling down into our brains. The irrefutable evidence of my brother's death had struck me like a hammer blow. For my mother it was almost crushing. My family gathered in the room, the secret of Muqim's fate now in the open.

That evening our grief bonded us—myself, my mother, my sister, my brother and his two wives, my three aunts. We were all left weeping and asking why? Why a young man who was so good and strong had been taken so unfairly away from us. Another of our family's brightest shining stars was gone.

Dear Shuhra and Shaharzad,

Family.

It's a simple word but it is possibly one of the most important words a child will ever learn. Family is the home that a child is born into, the place where they should be kept safe, warm, and protected. Whether it is hail or rain or even rockets and bullets that pierce the night air, a family should be there to protect a child. Safe in the house, a child should sleep soundly in its mother's arms with a father standing by.

Sadly, many children, you included, don't have two parents. But you are still lucky because at least you have me—a mother who loves you and tries to make up for the loss of a father in your lives. Some children don't even have that. So many poor Afghan children lost everyone in the war and have no one left to care for them.

Siblings are also such an important part of family. I had so many brothers and sisters I almost lost count. Our extended family had rivalries and jealousies, especially among my father's wives. But never were the children made to feel unloved. Each mother loved all the children equally and it was a wonderful thing to know I was loved by so many mothers. When my father, your grandfather, died, my mother took responsibility for trying to keep all the children together so that we stayed a proper family.

My siblings and I fought and argued and sometimes we'd get in fights and kick and punch and tear at each other's hair, but we never stopped loving each other. And we never stopped looking out for each other. I battled against my brothers very hard to remain at school and be independent, and even though they didn't like it, they loved me and they let me do it. Of course now they are so very proud of their little sister the politician. They are also proud of themselves that they were open-minded enough to help me achieve my dreams, because in doing so we've helped to keep our family name and our political honor.

I wish I had given you a brother, a decent fine young man who would have loved his two sisters so much. I am sure you would have squabbled and fought with him, too. But I know you'd have loved him. I would have named him after the brother I lost. Muqim.

With love,
Your mother

SIX

WHEN JUSTICE DIES

A short story for Shuhra and Shaharzad:

The wind and the rain lashed down from the Hindu Kush mountains on to Kabul that Friday night. The dusty roads quickly turned to mud, thick and slippery underfoot. Open sewers filled with brown water and burst their filthy banks, forming ever-growing, stinking ponds. The streets were deserted, except for a barely discernable movement in the shadows. A man breathed heavily in the dark, the rain catching in his beard and forming rivulets that cascaded into the ankle-deep puddle he was standing in. His shalwar kameez clung to his skin as he shivered in the wind that whipped at the sodden clothing. He loosened his grip on the AK-47 assault rifle. The Russian-made gun was heavy and he was mindful of how slippery it had become in the rain, but it was his nerves that made him grip it tighter than he needed to. He made his way slowly, deliberately, through the black quagmire, placing each foot carefully, testing the ground before trusting it with his full weight.

He turned to face the six-foot-high compound wall and delicately lifted his gun onto the top. Even on a night like this the clatter of a badly controlled weapon could carry a long way. Steadying his balance, he paused, hands held up at shoulder height, before springing, cat-like, grasping the top of the wall cleanly with both hands. He dug his toes into the bricks, searching for grip on the wet surface. The muscles in his arms and back strained as he fought to

control his weight. Throwing his right elbow onto the top of the wall,
he pressed his face into the rough cold cement, swinging his left leg in
an arc to catch the high edge. Heaving the rest of his torso onto the
top of the wall, he panted silently, scanning the dark compound for
any sign of guards. Seeing none, he dropped to the ground, his feet
splashing noisily as they made contact. He pushed the safety lever on
his AK-47 down with his thumb, clicking it into the firing position.
Crouching low, he used the shadows of the fruit trees to move toward
the main house. Inside, everything was dark. The rain obscured his
vision and he fumbled at the brass door handle. It turned with a
scrape of the bolt. He held his breath now, easing the door open a
crack, slowly widening it as his eyes adjusted to the dark room. It was
quiet inside. The sound of the rain was muffled against the heavy roof
tiles, but he was aware that he was dripping loudly on the tiled floor.
He walked in his crouch, moving across the living room, gun poised.
The tap-tap, tap-tap of his sandals on the floors sounded amplified
against the close brick walls of the hall. He found the bedroom door
and paused. He readied the gun, holding it pistol-style in his right
hand, and with his left, tested the knob. It gave, and opened a crack.
And then, in cold blood, this man murdered my brother.

THE ASSASSIN HAD EMPTIED his gun at Muqim as he lay sleeping in bed. A Kalashnikov's magazine holds 30 bullets. The gunman held the trigger down until the gun was empty. Then he fled.

My sister-in-law woke to the gunfire. She and my brother Mirshakay were asleep upstairs on the other side of the house. My brother tried to calm his wife, assuring her the firing was probably just someone shooting in the air in celebration of the victory over the Russians or a wedding party. That was when a neighbor started shouting from outside the yard that Muqim had been shot.

He was only 23 when he died. Tall, handsome, and clever, he was one of my favorite brothers. We had grown up playing and fighting and loving and falling out. A kind word from him would make me smile for hours; a harsh word would bring tears to my eyes in an instant.

He, Ennayat (the son of my father's last wife), and I had been playmates our entire lives. Muqim had narrowly survived being murdered as a little boy in the dangerous days following my father's death. He had lived only because a quick-thinking neighbor hid him from the would-be assassins under her skirts. This time there was no one to hide him.

He had been a law student with a black belt in karate, which was very exotic for that time, even in Kabul.

It was such a devastating blow when I learned of his murder. I felt like it was a part of me that had been killed. After my father's death all my brothers had taken on a much greater role in my life. Muqim relished his new patriarchal powers and would order me about, telling me to wash my socks or brush my clothes. I was the adoring little sister and I didn't mind his bossiness. I just wanted his approval and attention.

Normally he encouraged my education, and he would tell me "Fawzia, I want you to become a doctor." That would always make me feel very special, knowing that he believed in me so much. But sometimes if he was upset and frustrated, he would forbid me from going to school the next day, wagging his finger at me sternly and stating: "You are not allowed to go to school. Tomorrow you stay at home. You are a girl. For girls home is enough."

So even though we loved each other dearly, he could still be very traditional in his outlook, although it seemed to be his way of dealing with stress. He was a bit like my father in that way. Usually the day after he'd banned me from going to school he would come home with a gift—perhaps a new schoolbag or pencil case. Then he would ask me to go back to school and remind me of how smart he thought I was and what great things I was going to do. He was different from my other brothers—if one of them said I couldn't go to school, they really meant it. But with Muqim I knew it was just talk and it would pass.

From the clothes he wore to the food he ate, Muqim was always very specific about what he wanted in life. So when he told me he was in love with a girl he met at university, I knew he was serious. He was in his first year of law school and she was starting her medical training. When he told me she was very beautiful, I didn't doubt that, either. He used to point to my prettiest doll and say, "She is beautiful like that doll. Except she has blue eyes."

He had loved her for four years, but in that time he had never been able to tell her how he felt. He used to spend hours hanging around the front of her house, hoping for the merest glimpse of her. Muqim had sent her letters to tell her of his love, but she sent them back unopened. She was a very traditional girl, and a traditional girl doesn't open letters from unsanctioned suitors. But he was hoping to change his status and get the approval of her family. He was looking forward to my mother's return to Kabul because she was going to visit the girl's family and propose the match. If my father had been alive he would have done it, but instead it fell to my mother in her role as matriarch. But he was killed before he could make the proper approaches. Some people have asked me if the girl's family had arranged his murder. I do not believe this was the case.

Coming to terms with the death of a loved one is always hard. The sense of loss is enormous, and the hole their absence leaves in your life feels like it will never be filled. The ache of knowing you will never see that person again throbs like a bad tooth. Except there's no painkiller you can take to relieve the pain.

The fighting between the mujahideen forces and the government meant the police were unable to mount much of an investigation. Even my elder brother's status as a senior police commander could do little to bring Muqim's killer to justice. The only evidence the killer left was a sandal abandoned by the wall as he fled. But it was the type of sandal worn by men all over Afghanistan and this was long before the days of DNA testing and forensic evidence. Afghanistan was in a state of war, and people die during war. The fact that Muqim's death was murder meant little under the circumstances. Hundreds of people were being murdered every day, women were being raped, and homes were being looted and destroyed. Food and water were scarce. Justice was in even shorter supply.

Mirshakay blamed himself for Muqim's death. Not only had he failed him as a policeman, by not capturing his killers, but he felt personally responsible for his murder. As a police general he had a team of bodyguards. They would travel with him everywhere, and at night their job was to guard the house as he and his family slept inside. But because it was Friday, a day of prayer, observance, and family, and also such a horrible wet night, my brother had felt sorry for his bodyguards and dismissed them early, telling them to go home and be with their families. Muqim got home about 10 P.M., having been to the gym. He was soaked to the skin in the rain and was complaining about an eye infection. My sister-in-law fetched her kohl from her makeup bag. In my home province of Badakhshan women often use a type of kohl eyeliner made from herbs found in the mountains, and one of the benefits of the herbs is that they are very good for treating eye infections. So she put some on his eye, and then he went to bed. That was the last time anyone saw Muqim alive. If the bodyguards had been on duty, there's no way the gunman could have entered the house, and he'd still be alive. Mirshakay's rage ate at him, and he felt it was his fault his brother had been killed.

One of the great questions we ask ourselves in life is "Why?" Why does anything happen? As a Muslim I have my beliefs. I believe them to be true, and they are a large part of me. I believe God alone decides our fate. He chooses when we live and when we die. But even that certainty doesn't make the painful events and losses of my life easier to bear.

With Muqim's death we simply didn't have any answers.

Why would somebody kill such a kind, intelligent, gentle young man as my brother? He was a brilliant young student trying to make a life for himself. He wanted a career and a wife and a family. He wasn't a threat to anybody. But his life was taken away in an instant. In Islam a dying person is supposed to recite the name of Allah three times before passing away. Poor Muqim didn't have time to do that.

And not having time to say a proper goodbye was something I was also becoming used to.

Dear Shuhra and Shaharzad,

As you grow older you will learn about loyalty. Loyalty to your faith, to family, to friends, to your neighbors, and to your country. In times of war our loyalty can be sorely tested.

You must be loyal to the true and good nature of your Islamic faith, helping and loving those around you even when you might feel you cannot.

It is important to be loyal to your family, both those alive and dead. Our bonds of family do not cease at the grave, but we must also be careful not to remember the dead at the expense of the living.

You must be loyal to your friends, because it is the action of a true friend. And if they are true friends then they will also be loyal to you, and ready to act when you need their help.

You must be loyal to your fellow Afghans. There are many of us and we are not all the same. But you must be able to see past those ethnic and cultural differences and remember the thing that unites us together—Afghanistan.

And you must be loyal to your country. Without loyalty to our country we have nothing as a nation. We must work hard and wisely to improve our country for your children and their children.

Loyalty can be a hard lesson to learn sometimes, but there are few lessons more valuable.

With love,
Your mother

SEVEN

THE WAR WITHIN

I was glad to be back in Kabul and was eager to resume my old life, or what little of it remained under what was now becoming full-blown civil war.

We were still living in my brother's apartment in Makrorian. (The word *makrorian* roughly translates as "living space.") The apartments had been built by the Russians using the latest technological advances, such as a communal hot water system serving over ten apartment blocks, each housing up to 50 apartments. Despite being shelled countless times, many of the Makrorian blocks have survived even today, and the hot water system even still works. Today it is still a sought-after neighborhood.

During this time, Kabul was divided into different sectors. The central parts, Khair Khana, Makrorian, and around the King's Palace, were controlled by the mujahideen government, which was then headed by President Burhanuddin Rabbani, a former general from Badakhshan and a man my family knew well—hence my brother's senior position at the Interior Ministry. The famous "lion of the Panjshir," Ahmed Shah Massoud, was his minister of defense.

The west of Kabul was controlled by a man named Mazary, the leader of an ethnic group called the Hazaras. (Said to be the direct descendants of Genghis Khan, the Hazaras are identifiable by their classic Mongol looks, round faces and large almond-shaped eyes. They are unusual in being Shia Muslims; the majority of Muslim ethnic groups in the country are Sunni.) An area on the outskirts of Kabul, Paghman, was controlled by a man named Sayyaf and his people. Yet another area was controlled by the fearsome Abdul

Rashid Dostum, the leader of the ethnic Uzbeks. Just outside the city walls, towards the south, was Gulbuddin Hekmatyar, the leader of a group called Hizbi Islami; a second Hizbi Islami leader, Abdul Sabur Farid Kohistani, was the prime minister.

Essentially, despite having a shared government and having been allies when fighting the Russians (during which time they were given the name "Northern Alliance," as most of them originated from the north of Afghanistan), these commanders were now fighting each other for power. As the civil war grew more brutal, short-term allegiances shifted and changed with the weather.

The fiercest opponent of the mujahideen government was Hekmatyar, who was unhappy with his role in the government and wanted more power and seniority. Every day, his men fired scores of rockets into Kabul from their base in the higher ground at the edge of the city. The rockets exploded in marketplaces, schools, hospitals, and gardens, and scores of people were killed or injured. Sometimes the situation changed overnight. A group that had previously supported the government might suddenly turn against it and start fighting. A few days later, with hundreds of civilians dead, the group might use the national TV station to announce it had all been a misunderstanding and it was now supporting the shared government again. The public had no idea what would happen from one day to the next. Probably our leaders didn't either.

Despite the turmoil happening around me, I insisted on resuming my English lessons. They were too important to me to give up, even though that meant regular journeys through the streets, which was now the battleground for the mujahideen commanders to play out their deadly power struggle.

It should have been a simple, short taxi ride to class, except the journey to my lessons took me through some of the areas of the fiercest fighting. Some neighborhoods and streets had to be avoided entirely, while others had to be crossed whatever the risk. I would take a convoluted route that changed depending on which side held the upper hand. Gathering intelligence from people on the street was as essential to successfully navigating the route as was the driver's ever-present search for the scarce supplies of petrol. Packs of gunmen would roam the streets and the danger of snipers was constant—their choice of target indiscriminate. A crack from a rifle accompanied by the dull thump of the bullet would often send some poor soul toppling to the ground, their desperate search for food, water, or medicine brought to a premature end. Machine gunners set up in the damaged homes around key intersections, their positions carefully chosen to both conceal themselves and give the maximum field of fire—all the better to catch your enemy in the open. They were often little more than the tops of heads among the gloom of their cover, but it was understood that from among the rubble they were peering over their steel gun sights for any sign of movement. Vehicles often drew the deadliest attention, but they were still the fastest and safest way to travel. On more than one occasion my car was targeted by rocket artillery. Some roads were pre-targeted by the artillery commanders. When their spotters signaled an approaching car, all they needed to do was open fire and chances were the car, or truck, or possibly even a tank would be blown off the road. I remember once the rockets came rushing down toward me. But over our heads, the boughs of trees struck upward like fingers waiting to catch the projectiles. The rockets hit the branches and exploded, filling the street with shrapnel and shards of splintered wood as we sped along the road and out of range. If it were not for the trees, the rockets would have ripped the flimsy car apart, and both me and the driver with it.

Few taxi drivers would risk going out in the fighting for the meager price of a fare. Those who were brave enough to do so were motivated by the threat of starvation. No fares meant no food, for them or their families, and that would spell a death even more certain than the bullets that hummed through the air. Often it was impossible to find a taxi to take me to class.

So on those days I would have to walk, darting from cover to cover, avoiding the areas where I knew the gunmen were and praying I didn't unknowingly stumble into others. And after class I would have to walk back, too, sneaking along alone in the dark. Sometimes it took me as long as two hours. It was very dangerous for anybody to be on the streets at night, but especially a young girl by herself. Aside from bullets, I ran the risk of being raped. When night fell the shooting became more unpredictable. Nervous in the dark, the gunmen's fingers would curl a little tighter around their triggers, and even a loud footstep or the tumble of rubble could attract a burst of bullets.

Often my mother would be waiting nervously outside our apartment, keeping watch for me. She would be standing at the bottom of our apartment building dressed in her burqa, peering out into the night and scanning the shadows. The occasional clatter of gunfire echoing across the sky would send her heart jumping into her mouth. Her imagination must have tormented her as she waited for her daughter to reappear from her journey through the war zone. Her relief at my return was obvious, but she never showed it by hugging me. Instead, she would be quick to scold me, saying: "Even if this course makes you president, I don't care. I don't want you to be president. I want you to be alive."

My brothers and sisters didn't like me taking such great risks either, but they would never tell me directly. Instead they would nag my mother and ask her to stop me from going.

But my mother would probably have thrown herself headfirst into machine gun fire if it meant I could still go to school. She was illiterate but fiercely intelligent. By watching me become educated she was somehow educating herself, too. She took genuine delight in talking to me about my classes and her commitment to me never wavered. She just ignored my siblings' pleas and nagging, placating them with her winning smile. But I am sure she felt a wave of fear every time I disappeared into the night. A fear that must have been made more acute by the recent loss of her son, my brother Muqim. His death affected the whole family, but none more so than my mother. Every morning she would visit his grave and put fresh flowers on it. But this simple loving act of a bereaved mother soon gave way to more erratic and, for the family, more worrying behavior.

By now the city was turning into a killing zone. In the neighborhoods where the fighting was worst, we heard reports of hundreds of civilians being killed each night. We could hear the crackle of gunfire ripple across the city. On still nights it would echo off the hills and mountains that surround Kabul, making the whole city feel haunted by the terrible events it witnessed.

Rocket fire was very common. The rockets would land without warning, sometimes destroying a family home, leaving its residents buried beneath the earth walls; other times destroying a shop, a school, or a group of women buying vegetables for the evening meal at a market stand. All you would hear was the whizz as they flew through the air, then the whizz stopping suddenly as seconds later they fell and detonated. You never knew where or on whom they would land.

One night I was cooking the family meal of rice and meat when I realized my mother wasn't home. It was 7 o'clock in the evening and normally she would be in the kitchen or organizing other aspects of household life. I had a nasty feeling I knew where she had gone, and if I was right, I knew I had to go in search of her. I was still in my mourning period for Muqim, so I put my black head scarf on and slipped out the door. A guard near our apartment building told me he had seen which direction she left in, and I knew my worst suspicions were right. She was on her way to visit my brother's grave.

There weren't any taxis about and buses weren't running at all, so I set off on foot toward the center of the city. At first the streets were eerily quiet. The Kabul I knew was bustling in the evening with cars and motorbikes and people walking to visit friends. Now it was deserted, cleared by the rattle of gunfire that lay between me and my brother's grave.

I kept walking nervously, aware that somewhere ahead was my mother. I began to see bodies in the street, freshly shot or torn to pieces by explosions, the corpses not yet beginning to bloat. I was so terrified. But I realized I wasn't afraid of dying as much as I was scared of the knowledge that these dead bodies were someone's family. And that tomorrow, it could be my family lying here.

When I got to an area called Dehmazang I came across a taxi. The driver had removed the back seat and he was piling it with bodies. He was covered in blood; his white shirt now streaked crimson, with darker flecks congealing around the pockets and buttons. His car looked like a slaughterhouse as the victims of the fighting, men and women with twisted limbs and shattered heads and torsos, oozed their blood into the footwell, where it formed thick pools that dribbled through the rusted holes in the floor and onto the dusty road beneath. The driver, clearly in shock, was lathered in sweat as he tried to stuff another corpse into his car. In Islam, a swift burial is very important, and I'm not sure it even occurred to him that his life was in danger. He simply worked at his grim task like he was loading sacks of rice. I just stood and stared at the strange sight for a moment. He and I were the only people on the street that warm summer night. The only sound was the crackle of gunfire and the grunts of a middle-aged taxi driver risking his life to ensure a group of people he'd never met got a fitting burial.

When he was satisfied he could fit no more bodies in his car he started the engine with a cloud of blue exhaust smoke and drove toward the hospital, the back doors still open, the passengers' dead limbs dancing as the suspension sagged over every bump and pothole. The sight of the dead and dying made me think of my family and I had to battle with my mind, as it kept imposing their faces onto these nameless victims. I wasn't far from the graveyard now, and I knew I had to keep going and find my mother.

It was getting dark and I was walking past Kabul University when a group of uniformed men shouted at me. They wanted to know were I was going.

I didn't answer them and instead just lowered my head and walked faster. One of the men raised his gun and asked me again, "Where are you going?"

I stopped.

I turned, looking into the gun.

I lied.

"I'm looking for my brother. Somebody said they had seen his body just around the corner. I need to go and check," I said.

He thought about it for a moment before lowering his gun: "OK, go."

I hurried off, heart pounding. For a moment I had thought they were going to do something worse than shoot me.

The cemetery was a dusty spread of earth covering several football fields. Years of war and fighting had preempted life's inevitable consequence and the newest graves were cramped together—oblong piles of small rocks with a roughly hewn gravestone pushed into the ground for support. On the higher ground, where the more prestigious plots lay, graves were often fenced with iron palings, now silently rusting in this lonely place. Tattered green flags, a sign of mourning, flew over them.

My mother was hunched over the grave. I could see her gently organizing the bright bunches of yellow silk roses. She didn't hear my footsteps as I approached, completely immersed in her thoughts. She was shaking as she cried and caressing a photograph of my brother. He looked so young and handsome. She turned and looked at me. I stood there in tears of relief at having found her and sadness at the scene. I felt overwhelmed and I knelt beside her. For a long time the two of us were holding each other and crying. For a while we just sat there, talking about my brother and how much we missed him. I asked her why she risked her life coming out here at night—did she not see all the dead people and the men with guns, and did she not realize how worried I was? She just gave me a sad, tearstained look as if to say, "You know why," before turning back to the photograph.

We sat there so long I didn't realize how dark it was getting. There were few working street lights because of the battle. I started to get very scared. We were still crouched over the grave, collecting our thoughts. We were now in a great deal of danger. We couldn't risk going back the same way we came. It was too far and too dangerous to even attempt. So we resolved to wait another hour until it was completely dark, and then sneak out of the graveyard. We made for a shortcut we knew well—it led to a house that my father had lived in when he was a member of Parliament. The house was on the edge of the city, in an area called Bagh-e-bala. Some relatives had been living there to keep the house safe for us. We wouldn't be able to get home that night, but at least we would be out of danger if we could get there.

We crept through the tiny alleyways that separated the houses. Any noise or panicked movement could draw attention in the form of bullets. My mother and I inched our way forward, up the hill and toward safety.

The house was built in traditional Kabuli style, made from large gray-brown bricks and very square, with small windows to keep the heat out in summer and the warmth in during the freezing winters. A sloping roof of curved tiles ran parallel to the hill. At the back was a courtyard with fruit trees and flowers. As we hammered on the door I wondered if the trees were still there. My relatives answered the door. They were visibly scared. They thought we were mujahideen coming to rob or kill them. When they realized it was us they dragged us inside and shut the door. I was so relieved to be safe, but I felt very sad to be back in this house so unexpectedly. This was actually the house my brother was living in when he was murdered. My mother knew this too, and she started crying again. We were both so physically and emotionally exhausted it was all we could do. My relatives brought us tea and some food, but neither of us could take anything aside from a little tea. Blankets were fetched and we went to bed, on my mother's insistence, in my brother's room.

Neither of us slept that night. I lay wrapped in a blanket thinking about my brother and the terrible things I had seen that day. How it felt to watch my country implode. How a taxi driver loading bodies into his car was the most decent, civilized thing I had seen all day. How a woman will walk through rocket fire to mourn a beloved son, and why men with guns who fought to free Afghanistan from the Soviets were now destroying this country to satisfy their own personal lust for power. My mother wept all night, her knees pulled to her chest, lamenting her loss. That night seemed to drag on forever. In some ways I wish it had. By dawn there was enough light in the room to see the bullet holes from the rounds that had sprayed from the gunman's Kalashnikov and killed Muqim.

That terrible sight only seemed to strengthen my mother's resolve. Her determination and pragmatism were returning. That morning she made hot green tea for me, and then staunchly announced we would be moving out of the apartment at Makrorian and moving here, closer to the cemetery. My mother's logic was impeccable as always—if you must walk in a war zone, better to make it a short walk.

My father's house had spectacular views over the city. The neighborhood was home to many affluent Kabulis. Instead of being able to enjoy the cityscape that tumbled out toward the mountains, we were now forced to witness the fighting that was raging beneath us as if the city were a horror movie. Machine guns chattered, and rockets hissed and roared as they exploded into buildings. From our high lookout we could see the two sides exchanging fire, tracers from the explosives lighting up the darkness. I watched the fighters as they organized themselves and directed fresh attacks on enemy positions. Some of the homes there had been built using colored plaster. I was watching the battle one day when an artillery rocket landed directly on top of a pretty pink house. The blast made the earth tremble and sent chunks of masonry flying more than a hundred yards into the air. Where the house stood just a few seconds previously was now a cloud of pink dust, almost a mist, settling over the surrounding houses. I saw the same thing happen to a blue house, too—there was nothing left of the house when it exploded like a ghastly firework, fading out with a trail of blue fog rolling through the streets. The tragic inhabitants inside were blown to smithereens along with their house.

For me, one of the saddest moments was when the polytechnic school got hit in the fighting. It had been built by the Russians and was a very good institution. During their time in Afghanistan the Russians had built a lot of institutions. We wanted the Russians gone because they were invaders in our land, but at the same time we had been thankful for some of the infrastructure and building they brought with them. A lot of young high school graduates continued their studies there, learning computer science, architecture, and engineering. Even Ahmed Shah Massoud had studied there. For a long time as a little girl I aspired to attend one day, too. That dream ended the day the library was destroyed. It was late in the day and the fighting was beginning to die down. I don't know if whoever fired the rocket intended to hit the polytechnic. Neither side were using it as a base, so perhaps it was an accident. Or maybe they just wanted to destroy it and what it represented. Either way, the result was the same. When the rocket exploded in the side of the poly-technic library I gave a little gasp of shock. Then, in the way one watches a horror movie, not wanting to see the end but unable to turn away from the inevitable, I watched, growing more and more sickened, as the smoke gave way to flames, licking at the gaping wound. Inside were thousands of books that had helped educate many young Afghans. Now those books were fueling an increasingly large fire. There was no fire brigade, of course. Nobody rushed to save all this knowledge that could help improve our country and educate our people. Nobody except me really even seemed to notice. I watched it burn until it was time to go to bed. I went to bed numb with the idea that so many words, so much literature and learning, had perished. But I also felt guilty for caring about books when people were burning in flames, too.

My mother quickly settled into her routine in that house.

Every morning she would wake, eat a simple breakfast of traditional Af-ghan naan bread and green tea, and make the dangerous journey to change the flowers on my brother's grave. She would take the shortcut down the hill, weaving through the alleys and rocky tracks that made up the hillside before creeping across the open ground to the cemetery. She would return a little later, puffy around the eyes from crying. It upset her but it also seemed to strengthen her, despite the risks. The routine seemed to galvanize her, and her return to the house was usually marked by a flurry of domestic activity. My relatives had been living there and guarding the property, but they hadn't turned it into a home. My mother set about this job, organizing, cleaning, and decorating. Furniture was cleaned and aired, rugs beaten, pots and pans cleaned and buffed until they gleamed black or copper. The yard was emptied of rubbish and swept.

But she never again went into my brother's room. That was left as we found it, broken and bullet marked. My mother and I never discussed clean-ing that room. It was just understood that for however long we were living here, the bedroom was to stay untouched, at least until such time my mother decided otherwise. The door was closed, and that was that. My brother was to be remembered in death, as he was in life, bright and wonderful like the silk flowers that stood on his grave—not in the violent evidence of his last living moments.

My elder brother Mirshakay would try to visit us every day. To put it mildly, he wasn't very happy about my mother's decision to stay at the house.

But he understood her reasons and for the moment was prepared to let us remain there. Sometimes he would bring my sisters, too, and on those nights we would sit down and have a meal like we might have had in more peaceful times. We would gossip and laugh, but despite the banter, there was no escaping the underlying fear we all shared for our future.

It seemed to be a turning point for the city's middle class. Until now most had been prepared to sit out the fighting and see what happened. Leaving prematurely would mean leaving your house open to looting. But with the civil war showing no signs of ending, many intellectuals and professionals fled to Pakistan. They would load the essentials for an uncertain life—mostly clothes, documents, and jewelry—into their cars, try to secure their homes, and then slip out of the city during a lull in the fighting. Most Afghans live with their extended family, so usually it was the father and his wife or wives, plus the children, driving to Pakistan. Elderly or more distant relatives were left behind to guard the house and scratch out an existence as best they could.

Nobody judged them for their decision to leave. Many who stayed behind would have gone, too, if they had the chance. And when the fighting intensified, it appeared their choice had been correct. One morning a friend of Mirshakay's appeared at the door. He was visibly frightened, having driven though some of the areas of intense fighting. He insisted we come with him immediately. My brother had sent him to take my mother and me back to the apartment at Makrorian. My mother refused to leave, and she and the man argued for a while as he pleaded with her to follow my brother's wishes. But my mother was adamant she would not leave her son's grave unattended, and there was nothing this bedraggled messenger could say or do to make her change her mind. My mother was an immovable force, and she was determined that we would remain in the house, whatever the risks.

Or so she said at the time. But the news we got just a few hours later instantly changed her mind. My mother had been out trying to buy food when she heard the story. The night before, a few doors away, a group of mujahideen had smashed their way into a house and raped all the women and girls inside. My mother showed little concern for her own safety, but the virginity and sanctity of her daughter was paramount. In Afghan culture rape is despised, but it is an all-too-common crime in times of war and peace. While the rapist can be put to death, the woman must endure a much longer punishment, where she becomes a social pariah, even in her own family. The victims of rape are often cast out like a kind of broken harlot, as if they did something to provoke the attack or inflame the loins of the man, who was driven mad by lust and unable to control himself. No Afghan man would marry a woman who had been raped. Any suitor would want to be certain his bride was pure, no matter how violent or unjust the circumstances of her deflowering.

My mother went from being determined to stay to being determined to leave. She didn't give me the full details of the attack but ordered me to collect my things and she set about doing the same. I was really scared, but I also knew better than to debate the subject with her. We were leaving. Now.

My brother's messenger had already left in his car, so the only way back to the apartment was on foot. The memories of my journey through the city the first time still haunted me, and the thought of doing it again made me feel like I was going to be sick. We'd have to run down boulevards of sniper fire, go through checkpoints, and risk seeing dead bodies left from the shelling of the night before.

My mother left our relatives with instructions to keep guarding and maintaining the house, and we nervously stepped onto the street. We started running. We both knew we had a long way to go and I think we just wanted to get it over with. We ran from house to house, careful not to linger in the open, scanning doorways and darkened windows for any signs of movement, listening for gunfire that might signal the presence of a machine gun or sniper up ahead.

We hadn't gone far when a woman came running toward us. She was screaming hysterically about her daughter. She just stood there screaming, "My daughter, my daughter."

I could hear from her accent that she was Hazara—one of Afghanistan's minority Shia Muslim population.

I was too scared to open my mouth, but my mother asked her what had happened. The woman's head was shaking with uncontrollable emotion, the blue hood on her burqa wobbling every time she convulsed with grief. Her tears formed little beads on the mesh, embroidered and glistening in the sunlight.

The woman's house had been destroyed days earlier in the fighting. She and her daughter had no alternative but to flee. They took shelter in a Shia mosque, where around 150 other women, their husbands dead or caught up in the fighting, were taking shelter.

She told us how the mosque was hit by rocket fire and caught alight, and I remembered then that I had seen the building blazing in the distance as I stared in silence through the window of my father's house.

The mosque had burned very quickly. Those who survived the explosion rushed for the exit, but in the smoke and dust and screaming dozens of others must have been trampled, or overcome by the smoke and the flames. The woman told us how she and her daughter were near the explosion when it hit, knocking them off their feet in a blast of concrete and roof tiles. When they came to, the building was already burning. Women and children were screaming and crying, running in panic. The only light came from the flames, which grew higher every second. Some women dragged their children to safety by stepping on the children of other women, while the screams of so many mothers trying to locate their youngsters separated in the dark was deafening, adding to the panic.

Her daughter spotted a hole in the wall caused by the explosion, and the pair of them crawled through it and wriggled to safety.

Earlier that morning, exhausted, dehydrated, and starving, she approached a mujahideen checkpoint, begging to be given safe passage. She told us how the mujahideen commander had agreed to allow her through so they could escape. The woman was cautious and had told her daughter to stay hidden while she approached the checkpoint. But now that they were going to go free, she called her daughter to come forward. The girl came out of her hiding place.

This was the moment the men were waiting for. They grabbed the girl. The commander dragged her into a steel shipping container that served as his field office. Then he held her down on the table and raped her in front of her mother. The daughter screamed for her mother's help as the men violated her, while others held the woman back, forcing her to watch. Some mujahideen soldiers were raping women with impunity at that time—it was every woman's greatest fear. But there were some instances where Hazara women were especially targeted. Their brand of Shia Islam is predominant in neighboring Iran, which was seen as an unwelcome source of foreign influence, giving the attacks a political overtone. It was a situation not helped by Islam's Sunni-Shia schism. Sunni Islam is the dominant form of the religion for the world's 1.5 billion Muslims. The key difference relates to a historic debate about the true successor of the Prophet Mohammed. Sunni believe the first four caliphs, or spiritual leaders, are the true successors, while Shia believe the Prophet's cousin and son-in-law Ali ibn Abi Talib is the rightful successor. It's a division almost as old as Islam itself, and over the course of history has proved as bitter and bloody as any seen in world religion. During the civil war Hazaras were massacred by many different sides, and later they were also targeted by the Taliban, who saw them as infidels. Today many Hazaras still feel they are regarded as being of lower status by other ethnic groups and are denied top jobs in government or the civil service.

When the girl's ordeal had ended, the commander simply took out his gun and shot her, as if disposing of something distasteful. Then he let the poor mother go.

After she told us her story there was little my mother could say to this poor wretched woman. She just clutched the woman's hand, and taking mine in her other hand, she started running. The three of us ran hand in hand through the battle-scarred streets, over the bodies, around the burned-out cars and through shattered buildings.

We just ran and ran, terrified of what we might run into but more fearful of what we were trying to leave behind. Around a corner we saw the most wonderful sight we could have hoped for—a taxi.

My mother urged the Hazara woman to come and stay with us at the apartment, but the woman announced she was going to try to find some relatives who lived further out of the city. They argued some more over it, but the lady was very determined. Eventually the taxi driver told us to hurry up. We got in and drove home to the apartment in Makrorian. My brother didn't know whether to shout or laugh with joy when he saw us. He was furious at my mother's refusal to come sooner and in his messenger's car. When he heard that we'd walked alone and the story of the poor Hazara lady, he threw my mother a filthy look at even coming close to risking that happening to me. But he let it go. We were home now.

But something had changed for my mother. In the weeks and months that followed she grew weaker and weaker. She began to have difficulty breathing. She had suffered allergies all her life and these started to get worse. She tried to convince us she was well and not to worry, but we could see her fading before our eyes. Yet still she fussed over me, cooking for me when I was studying, insisting I go to class, and waiting for me when I got home.

As summer turned into winter that year I felt as though the rest of the world was starting to lose interest in Afghanistan. The West seemed pleased the Soviets had been defeated and gone home, and that was all they needed to know about Afghanistan. For Pakistan and Iran, neighboring countries with a huge interest in what happens across the border, the different mujahideen commanders had become proxies, used to fight out their own battles on neutral soil. But even as the mujahideen fought for power, settled old scores, and struck deals with neighboring governments, a new power was growing elsewhere in Afghanistan. A movement was growing in the madrassas—religious schools—in the south of the country. A movement by the name of Taliban.

And the movement would one day not only shake Afghanistan, but shake the world.

Dear Shuhra and Shaharzad,

Life is a miracle given to us by God. At times life can feel like both a blessing and a curse. Sometimes life gets almost too much to cope with, but we do cope; we cope because humans have a great capacity to endure.

But we human beings aren't great. Only God is great. Humans are like tiny little insects in the wider universe. Our problems, which sometimes seem so big and insurmountable to us, are really not.

Even if we live a long time our time on earth is still very short.

What matters is how we spend our time here. And the legacy we leave behind to those left on earth. Your grandmother left a far bigger legacy to all of us than she ever knew.

With love,
Your mother

EIGHT

LOSING HER

The first time I saw the man I would marry was as my mother was dying.

In the past three months she had gotten progressively worse, and now she was barely able to breathe and too weak to move. She'd been admitted to a hospital, but everyone could see she didn't have long to go.

I had heard from rumors that a man called Hamid from a village near ours in Badakhshan wanted to send a marriage proposal to me.

One night I was sitting by my mother's bed when several Badakhshani men came to pay their last respects to her. Hamid was among them.

I was embarrassed because it's not culturally allowed to meet a man who wants to marry you until an engagement has been agreed upon. And I was still only 17. I wasn't sure I even wanted to get married.

There was a group of ten men and although I'd never seen him before, I knew instantly which one Hamid was. He was young, with a lean body and a face that was both handsome and intellectual. Not bookish as such, but with an expression of curiosity and empathy. He was someone you warmed to instantly.

I was secretly pleased my suitor was physically attractive. But I tried very hard not to look at him directly; that would have looked very bad on my part. But in the close confines of the hospital I couldn't avoid glancing at him.

My mother was sitting in a wheelchair, and she was so weak she could barely speak. But she still tried to play the gracious hostess as came so naturally to her, fussing over her guests and asking if they were comfortable. The sight of her broke my heart. At one point she asked me to remove the blankets covering her knees and to wheel her into the sunlight. Hamid leapt up and leaned over to help remove the blanket. He was so gentle with her. He rearranged a pillow behind her head with such tenderness and care, that I was taken aback. In a flash I realized this was a rare Afghan man and a man who might treat me with tenderness, too.

My mother must have had the same thought, because when the men left, she took my hand in hers and looked into my eyes. "Fawzia jan. I want you to be happy in your marriage. I like this man. I think he is enough for us. When I recover we will both go to live with him." Her eyes searched mine for a reaction, and when I smiled and nodded she beamed. Her spirit and strength still shone strong through her watery, pale eyes. I turned away, biting back tears. I wanted so much for my mother to come and live with me and this kind man, and for me to be able to look after her as she had looked after me. But she grew frailer by the minute.

I was sleeping at the hospital; I refused to leave my mother's side. But I heard that the following night Hamid sent a proposal. As is the traditional way to ask for a lady's hand, male members of his family came to our house to speak with my brother. But my brother was also at the hospital that night. A proposal can only be passed in person, so it wasn't to be.

The following morning the hospital doctor, a warm lady with gray hair and green eyes, asked to speak to me in private. She wanted to impart the news she had already told my brother the night before. "Fawzia," she said gently, "All trees blossom and all trees wither. It's the nature of life. It is time to take your mother home."

I knew what she meant. My mother was dying, there was no hope. I screamed and pleaded, and begged for her to stay in the hospital. They could try new medicine, there was hope. The doctor hugged me and shook her head silently. It was over.

We took her home and tried to make her feel as comfortable as possible. My mother she refused to rest or sit still and insisted on attempting to carry out chores as usual. My brother jokingly told her if she didn't rest he'd have to physically restrain her. For a while I lay on the bed with her. I stroked her hair and told her stories about my life at the university, just like I had always done. She told me how proud she was of me, her disbelief that the daughter of an illiterate woman like herself had become educated. And she jokingly reminded me that I may still one day be president. Normally I'd love it when she talked like this, buoyed by her dreams and belief in me. But this day I couldn't see anything but a gaping black hole, an emptiness of the inevitability that was about to come. I fell asleep. At about 2 A.M. I heard her calling for me. I found her outside the bathroom, where she'd collapsed. She hadn't wanted to wake anyone and had attempted to go to the bathroom herself. I half picked her up, half carried her back to bed. She felt like a tiny bird in my arms. The sight of her like that is a memory seared in pain across my brain. To see a woman like that, a woman of such strength, such dignity, a woman who had endured so much in her life, beatings, death, tragedy, the loss of her husband, to see her too weak to even take herself to the bathroom was just awful.

I took her to her bedroom and placed her on the mattress on the floor. As she lay back to sleep, her breath started to rattle a little.

Unlike in the days of her marriage when she was expected to either share her husband's bed or sleep on the kitchen floor, she now had a bed of her own. But she was too weak to climb in and out of it, so she slept on the mattress. I also think she secretly preferred the floor, having grown so accustomed to it over the years.

Usually when she slept there, she liked to have one of her grandchildren, my brother's children, with her. That night, she had my six-month-old niece, Katayoun, sleeping next to her. I smiled when I saw the baby's little fingers curled around my mother's hair. I had also done that as a child. I waited until I was sure she was asleep, then I crawled into her proper bed and went to sleep. That night, I had a very unusual dream in which I saw nothing but fear and blackness. I was trying to run away from it.

I woke up with a start. I looked over at my mother on the mattress and realized that her blanket was not moving. There was no sign of breathing. I lifted up the blanket and could see she was almost gone, her breathing so weak it was imperceptible. My screams woke up the rest of the family. My brother had been about to start his morning prayers. He ran into the room clutching his Quran so he could read her some verses as a last goodbye. I screamed at him to stop. I didn't want to believe my mother was taking her last breaths.

I shouted at my family to bring a doctor. Someone ran next door to a neighboring house where we knew a doctor lived. They were back within minutes, but the doctor simply repeated what everyone knew. She was passing out of this life, and there was nothing we could do. I heard his words, but I couldn't take them in. "I'm sorry," he kept saying. "I'm sorry. She's almost gone." I felt like throwing myself out of the fifth-floor window. The lights had gone out. The stars had fallen out of the sky, and I wanted to follow them. I did not see how I could live without her.

For 40 days after her death I slipped in and out of consciousness. The shock and trauma had sent my body into almost total shutdown.

I was not in a fit mental state for at least six months after that. I didn't want to talk to anybody, I didn't want to go anywhere, no one could get through to me. I am not even sure I wanted to live. My family was incredibly supportive. No one forced me to try to move faster; they let me take my grief at my own pace. They were grieving, too, but they all knew my mother and I had a special bond.

It was the first time in a long time that I hadn't shared a bed with her. I couldn't sleep unless she was laying next to me, my fingers curled in her hair. I lay awake at night and tried to imagine her there. I cried and cried for her. I wailed for my mother like I was a newborn baby.

After six months of watching me grieve like this, my family feared I'd never improve. They had a family conference and decided the only thing that might help was my return to education. My mother had died in the autumn months and now it was spring again. Term time was beginning and my brother suggested I go back to study English and also take a computer class. By now, even those brothers opposed to my education knew it was the only thing I might choose to live for.

At the time my mother had fallen sick I was due to take my high school graduation exams. I'd been too upset to take them, but the teachers arranged for me to take them now. If I didn't, I'd fail automatically. So I had to go. And of course it helped. Slowly I entered the world again.

It was coming up to my eighteenth birthday. I admitted myself to the university exam preparation classes. I had decided I wanted to study medicine at the university and become a doctor. Hamid knew that I was in this class. Sometimes, even though he wasn't supposed to, he would drive his car and park it at the end of the street. He thought that I couldn't see him. But I recognized the car and the man inside. I never approached him or waved. To do so would have been culturally indecent of me.

After a couple of weeks of this he grew braver and would walk over to greet me as I left class. It was very formal and we never discussed anything personal or our feelings for one another. He'd ask how my family was, I would reply politely, and that was that. In Afghan culture there can be no courtship or dating. We were not even allowed to speak on the telephone. We both respected that and obeyed the rules. But these little moments with him were enough for me; even if he only spoke three words to me I would live off the memory all week and replay it over and over in my head. Hamid's smile made me forget some of the pain I was in and eased my grief for my mother. I would remember her words: "This man is enough for us."

By now the fighting was beginning to calm down. The different mujahideen factions had begun to broker agreements with each other. Kabul was still a divided city, with different factions in control of different areas. But they had started negotiations with each other and began drafting a new government constitution. As the civil war drew to a close, Burhanuddin Rabbani was nominated to be president. Most people saw this as a good sign, that the war was behind us. Soldiers no longer patrolled the streets and it was safe not to wear a burqa. Although I always covered my head with a scarf, of course, I was now also proudly able to wear jeans and fashionable long tunics. The sense of relief on the streets was palpable. Cinemas that had been closed because of fighting sprang back to life, showing the latest Indian films, and children went back to play in parks that had formerly been home to snipers. The bustling streets around the center of Kabul once more smelled of kabobs as street vendors and their customers felt safe to be out after dark. The spirit of Kabul crackled and sizzled back into life.

My life was also beginning to take a regular pattern again. But I was still deeply traumatized. One of my favorite possessions was a beautiful doll. She sat in her own cart and carried a stuffed dog. I was too old to be playing with such things, really, but I needed security and comfort, and the doll seemed to give me that. I spent hours brushing her hair and putting nice clothes on her. I obsessively arranged a vase of flowers next to her cart.

Hamid wasn't the only person trying to propose to me at this time. Various mujahideen commanders also came to see my brothers to ask for my hand. Fortunately my brother would never have forced me to marry against my will. I had to agree to it. And I would not. The more I compared these men with Hamid the more I knew it was him I wanted to marry. I didn't want a soldier; I wanted the intellectual with kindness in his eyes.

Hamid ran a small finance company, a kind of money exchange. And he also taught finance part time at the university. The idea of being married to a teacher was a far more romantic notion than being married to someone who carried a gun.

His family came several times to talk to my brother and send the proposal, but each time my brother said no. My brother's biggest fear was that Hamid's family was not as rich as ours, and that there would be a big difference in how we could live and in our social life. Hamid relied on his academic salary to make ends meet. My brothers also wanted me to continue the family tradition of expanding our political networks by marrying someone from a politically useful family. Hamid's family were not that.

My brother Mirshakay discussed it with me honestly. He told me he knew I liked this man but that he was trying to protect me by saying no. "Fawzia jan, how will you cope if he loses his job? You've grown up in a family where no one had to rely on a monthly salary to live. Imagine the stress each month of having to pay for rent and food and not knowing where the money is coming from."

But my brother's concerns didn't worry me. I had always wanted to work, too. And I had this romantic notion of the life I could have with Hamid. My education had given me career prospects. We would both work, and we would both contribute to the household. We would be a team, real partners. I wanted a life where I could make the decisions along with my husband.

But this wasn't something I could explain to my brother.

Culturally, I couldn't tell him I liked Hamid, and I could never tell him that we spoke to each other outside the university. That would never have been allowed. But my silence when my brother spoke negatively about Hamid and the obvious look of pain on my face probably told him all he needed to know.

I tried to get the support of my sisters, thinking they could help win my brother over, but they were opposed to the marriage, too. They all wanted what was best for me, and in their eyes a life of wealth and status was best. They told me stories of wedding parties they'd attended where there had been thousands of guests and the bride had been given showers of gold; they tried to enthuse me about the kind of wedding I might have if I married one of my richer suitors. But it meant nothing to me. What use was gold? In that life I would have felt like a bird trapped in a gilded cage. I wanted the gift of freedom.

Also, because I came from a family where multimarriage was the norm, I knew I didn't want it for myself. My father had eight wives and my brother had two wives, so I had seen too much of the pain and jealousy the women suffered. Many of the suitors who came for me were already married, and I'd have been wife number two or three. I didn't want to destroy another woman's life in the same way I had seen my father's later wives destroy my mother. And I'd never have coped with that situation or the lack of independence that came with it. I think after even a week of a life like that I'd have killed myself.

The next winter came and I turned 19. By now I had a diploma in English and I had started volunteering as an English teacher, teaching women of all ages. It was an amazing experience for me, watching the light go on in my pupils' eyes when they understood something. I loved it.

I didn't ask for a salary, but one day the head of the course gave me about 2,000 Afghanis—the equivalent of 40 dollars. They were my first-ever earnings. I was so proud I almost cried. I didn't spend the money. I kept it in my purse and just kept looking at it. I wanted to keep it there forever.

As the snow started to fall I was finally feeling happy. I passed my university entrance exam and got a place at medical school to train to be a doctor. I was teaching and I had some independence. The raw, angry hole in my heart that was my mother's absence was still there, but the pain had dulled to a manageable level.

The fighting was becoming more and more sporadic those days. Rabbani's government had finally achieved a degree of calm. In the summer of 1995, a peace agreement was brokered. Hekmatyar agreed to lay down his arms in return for the position of prime minister within the Rabbani government. The motive behind the peace agreement was the growing influence of the Taliban in the south. No one knew much about the Taliban, other than that they were religious students who had studied at the *madrassas* in the border regions between Afghanistan and Pakistan. Stories abounded about how these young men wore white clothes and called themselves the "angels of rescue." Villagers living in the south, like people throughout Afghanistan, had grown tired of the civil war, the lack of rule of law and the weak central government. As the fighting raged in Kabul, people living in quieter provinces had felt ignored and neglected. Their overwhelming poverty had not disappeared but had only worsened in the chaos, and they were desperate for a proper government that could help them. These men who called themselves angels arrived in villages on the back of pickups and set about restoring order and security at the community level. They were like self-styled vigilantes, but for people who had been too scared to open their shops for fear of looting or to send their children to school, these vigilantes started to make individual neighborhoods safe. That was enough to foster confidence in them.

Ironically, the latest mujahideen peace treaty allowed the Rabbani government to function effectively for the first time. The civil war was over, and the mujahideen government was finally sharing power peacefully and doing a decent job of running the country. But it was all too little, too late to placate a desperate population. Calm had descended, but calm in Afghanistan is as fleeting and fragile as the life of a butterfly. The Afghan people were already looking for new heroes to believe in. The Taliban were on the ascent.

PART TWO

PART TWO

My dear mother,

I still wait and hope that you will come back. Even now my breath catches in my throat when I remember that you are not in this world. I'm a politician now. But sometimes I'm just a silly girl and I make mistakes. When I do make a mistake, I imagine you'll be there, gently chiding me and correcting me. If I arrive home later than usual, I still expect you to be waiting in the yard for me with your burqa.

I still wish I could sleep curled next to you, like I used to sleep with you until the last days of your life.

I want to lay next to you and listen again as you tell me stories of your life. Stories of your good times, bad times, sufferings, patience, and hopefulness.

Mother, your stories taught me how to live.

Those stories taught me that as a woman I should learn to suffer and be patient. I remember as a child when I was not happy during the day—when one of my brothers would tell me not to go to school, or my mind couldn't concentrate properly in class, or I would see that my classmate's father would come to pick up my friend from school with his nice car to take her home, or when my girlfriend Nooria would talk about her father and I would feel very sad and an unknown sorrow would take over my heart.

At those times I thought that I was the weakest and the poorest girl in the world, but then I remembered your stories in the night— how you married when you were 16 years old, how so often you would witness a new woman marrying my father, and how despite your pain you stayed with my father and his other wives so that your children could have a good future—these stories gave me strength.

It was important to you that my father should be the best man in the world, that is why you would always tried to make the best food for his guests, and why you always kept the yard tidy. That is why you would always be nice to the other women of the family so they didn't become jealous and create problems for him.

I think of how you would use all your natural intelligence to try to solve the problems of the poor people when my father was not around, and how after my father was martyred it was important for you that all his children—both girls and boys—should go to school and should live with you in the same house so you could be aware of their problems and be there for them.

It was important to you that my brothers should grow to be men of good character and become people who could do something for their country. You suffered and starved yourself so my brothers could study and go to university.

When I remember all this I still feel amazed that through all these problems and heavy responsibilities you laughed. You laughed all the time.

I wish I was able to face my problems laughing like you.

Mother, my entire world was in these stories.

The interesting thing was the older I became the more interested I was in these nighttime stories—they would make me feel calm and safe in bed. Maybe I was trying to escape from my surroundings.

You were my refuge from it all. The best moments in my life were after you'd finished the stories, and you would turn your attention to me.

The way you promised me I'd become something important.

How my father had also apparently told you after I was born that I would grow to become like you. Beautiful, clever, wise, and warm.

They were small words, but those words became my inspiration to struggle.

When I asked what I would become you'd smile and reply: "Maybe, Fawzia jan, you will be a teacher or a doctor. You will have your own clinic and will treat the poor patients who come from the provinces for free. You will be a kind good doctor."

Then I would laugh and say: "No Mother, maybe I will be a president."

I said this because once I heard you tell a neighbor: "My daughter tries so hard. I am sure she will become president."

I learned so many life lessons from those stories.

And I have never felt so calm and safe with anybody else as I did with you.

Mother, I learned from you what self-sacrifice really means.

I learned from you that literacy alone is not enough to bring up good children, but intelligence, patience, planning, and self-sacrifice for others is what really counts. This is the example of Afghan women, women like you who would walk miles with an empty stomach to make sure your children get to school.

I learned from you that any human, even a "poor girl," can change everything if they have a positive and strong attitude.

Mother, you were among the bravest of the bravest Afghan women.

I am glad you were not here to witness the horrors that came next in our lives—the Taliban years.

Your daughter,
Fawzia

NINE

ONE ORDINARY THURSDAY

I will never forget the day the Taliban came to Kabul. It was a Thursday in September. I hadn't gone to university that day and had been at home studying. My sister Shahjan needed to buy bread and I needed a new pair of shoes, so in the afternoon we walked to the bazaar.

I was wearing one of my favorite brightly colored headscarves and tunic. My sister told me a joke and I giggled. The shopkeeper smiled at us and said: "You ladies will not be able to come here dressed like this tomorrow. The Taliban will be here tomorrow and this will be your last day of pleasure in the market, so be sure to enjoy yourselves."

He was laughing when he said it; his green eyes were smiling and the lines around them crinkled. I thought he was joking but his joy over the repression of women made me angry. I snapped and told him this was a wish he'd be taking to the grave; it would never come true.

I only vaguely knew who the Taliban were. I knew they were religious students who had formed a political movement, but didn't know what they stood for. During the years we were fighting the Russians, the Afghan mujahideen had been joined by thousands of Arab, Pakistani, and Chechen fighters. They had been funded to help the battle against the Soviets by other countries, such as the United States, Pakistan, and Saudi Arabia. Each of those countries had their own vested interests and political reasons in helping us. While their help in our battle was initially welcomed, these fighters brought with them a fundamentalist version of Islam that was new to Afghanistan, Wahhabism.

Wahhabism originated in Saudi Arabia and is a particularly conservative branch of Sunni Islam. Madrassas (religious schools) in the border regions between Pakistan and Afghanistan promoted this type of Islam to young Afghan men, many of them vulnerable refugees barely out of childhood.

But there was a lot of misinformation in those days. Some people in Kabul even thought the Taliban were the communists coming back in a new guise. But whoever they really were, I could not and would not believe they, or anyone, had beaten the mujahideen. The mujahideen had defeated the entire might of the Red Army, so how could a few students possibly defeat the men who had done that? The idea that they would be in the shop where I was now standing was just ridiculous.

At this stage I personally didn't see much difference between the Taliban and mujahideen. As a child I had been very much afraid of the mujahideen. Now as a university student I was learning about the Taliban. In my view they were all just men with guns. Men who wanted to fight instead of talk. I was tired of all of them.

But that night we got the shocking news on BBC radio. We listened to it all night long, incredulous at what we were being told. The BBC reported that Ahmed Shah Massoud's men had withdrawn from Kabul and gone back to their stronghold in Panjshir valley. I still couldn't accept that it meant defeat. Tactical withdrawal was not an unusual military tactic for Massoud. I truly thought he'd be back to fight before breakfast to restore peace and support the Rabbani government. Most people in Kabul thought the same.

Suddenly, the front door opened and my brother Mirshakay, the senior police chief, came in looking terrified. He spoke rapidly, saying he didn't have much time. He had asked his wife to pack his bag. He, like many senior government officials, was leaving to join Massoud in Panjshir.

I had so many unanswered questions about the future. I started to argue with him. His wife began crying. He hissed at us and told us to be quiet in case anyone heard.

Mirshakay had two wives, and it was decided that one would stay in Kabul in the apartment with me, while the other would be taken by her family that same night to Pakistan, where my brother owned a house in the city of Lahore.

It all happened so quickly we could barely believe it was real. As my brother went back out the door, my sister threw a pot of water after him. This is part of our culture: if the water follows the target, it is said he will come back soon.

With Mirshakay gone, we women huddled around the radio. The latest reports stated that President Rabbani and his ministers had also fled. They had gone by plane to Panjshir and from there to Rabbani's home province of Badakhshan.

Then they reported that former president Najibullah, the man who had been regarded as Moscow's puppet and a communist sympathizer, had taken refuge with his family in the United Nations compound. Ahmed Shah Massoud had offered to take him back to the Panjshir valley with him, but Najibullah didn't trust the mujahideen anymore than he did the Taliban and feared a trap. That was to be his fatal mistake, because within hours of Massoud retreating Najibullah would be dead.

At 8 o'clock that night jets were flying overhead. My family was teasing me, joking that even in war I kept my nose in a book. Then my brother Mirshakay came home and informed us that he had to flee Kabul immediately. I was furious with him and told him he should be here defending Kabul and the government, not running away from these people. I couldn't believe the government was giving up so easily to a bunch of religious students. I wasn't particularly fond of the Rabbani government, but it was a government at least. And here were officials like my brother leaving their posts and running.

Throughout the night we barely slept. We just listened to the radio as the country unraveled around us once more. At 6 o'clock in the morning I looked out of the window and saw people wearing little white prayer hats. Everyone was wearing them all of a sudden. I quickly closed the curtain and returned to my studies. As I swished the fabric of the curtain I wanted to shut out this new world, this latest incarnation of Kabul that I didn't understand.

Then the rumors started.

It was a Friday, prayer day. Reports started surfacing that they were beating people to make them go to the mosque. We certainly realized at this stage that they weren't communists, but then, who were they?

Never in the history of Afghanistan had we experienced anything like this. It was clear they were a strange force and were not controlled by Afghans. They couldn't be, not behaving like that.

Next they killed former president Najibullah, forcibly taking him from the United Nations building, where he had gone with his family to seek sanctuary. Had he escaped with Massoud perhaps he would have lived, but his decision to stay under UN protection cost him his life. The Taliban stormed the UN compound, dragging him out and executing him. They hung both his body and that of his younger brother from a busy roundabout for everyone to see. For three days, as the bodies slowly turned yellow and bloated, they hung there as a warning. People drove past in scared silence. No one dared to take the bodies down.

Then they looted the museum, destroying thousands of artifacts reflecting the history of our land—ancient Buddhist statuettes, Kundan ornaments, eating vessels from the time of Alexander the Great, artifacts dating from the times of the earliest Islamic kings. In the name of God these vandals destroyed our history. The world took notice when they blew up the Buddhas of Bamiyan. These ancient stone statues were regarded as one of the wonders of the world. They had been built in 6th century AD, during the reign of the Kushans, great patrons of art, before Islam was brought to Afghanistan. The giant Buddhas were not only a piece of important Afghan cultural history and a sign of our enlightened past, they also represented the livelihood for the Hazara people who live in Bamiyan. The Buddhas had long attracted visitors from all over the world as well as elsewhere in Afghanistan. As a result, a healthy tourist industry had developed in Bamiyan, an otherwise poor province, which was essential income for the people who relied on the tourism.

In shocking TV footage that was broadcast around the world, the Taliban blasted the statues with rocket-propelled grenades and heavy artillery until these great monuments fell into little pieces.

Then they started destroying our minds. They burned the schools and university buildings. They burned books and banned literature.

That weekend I was supposed to have an exam that I'd been studying hard for. I had only recently started my medical degree and I was loving it. But I was told not to bother going as my medical school had closed. Women were no longer allowed to be doctors, let alone study medicine at the university.

In an instant so much of Kabuli life, the things people took for granted, were gone. Even in the war the small, pleasurable things—such as meetings friends for a cup of tea in the bazaar or listening to music on the radio—and the big things, such as a wedding party—had still been possible. But under the Taliban they disappeared overnight. The wedding ban was particularly hard for people because weddings are such a big and important event. In our culture, as in most other cultures around the world, a wedding day is a rite of passage and one that involves the whole family.

Afghan weddings are traditionally very large, anywhere from 500 to 5,000 people. Owning a wedding hall or hotel can be a lucrative business. The best ones can command high prices, and it's not unusual for families to spend 20,000 or 30,000 dollars, paying the whole bill in advance.

But on their first weekend in power the Taliban banned all weddings in public places. Hundreds of couples had to frantically cancel their day. Those couples not only lost their day, the day little girls all over the world dream about, but their families, already struggling because of the bad economy caused by war, lost their money.

The Taliban ordered people to have private ceremonies at home with no guests, no music, and no fun. It's interesting to think about some of the couples who married that weekend. Their wedding anniversaries are a kind of memorial day for Taliban rule. It wasn't the wedding day they expected, but it's something they will certainly remember until the end of their lives.

Of course many people tried to defy the ban. Proud fathers refused to allow these creatures to destroy such an important family day and attempted to go ahead as planned. Some hotel owners ignored the new rule and carried on trading as usual. But the Taliban, in black turbans, were driving around town in pickup trucks. They carried guns and whips with them, and when they heard music coming from a wedding party, they raided the location. They burst in shouting and yelling, smashing speakers, ripping tape from video cameras, and tearing photographic film. And they beat people. They beat the grooms in front of their brides and grandfathers in front of their frightened guests. They beat them senseless. I kept hearing these stories, but I still could not believe it was true. I think I was in denial.

The next day my sister went to the market to get some vegetables. This sister wore a burqa routinely so that wasn't such a problem for her. But she came back from the market in a flood of tears. She said she'd seen them beating all women who weren't in burqas and were only wearing head scarves. I listened in shock. She was describing them beating women who dressed like me.

She sobbed as she told me how she watched a man and wife laden with shopping bags push their bicycle along the street. The woman wasn't even in modern jeans or a skirt. She wore a culturally traditional shalwar kameez and had covered her hair with a large scarf. The couple was chatting when the Taliban came from behind and attacked the woman. Three of them set upon her, beating her with wire cable and thumping her around the head so viciously that they knocked her to the ground. When they started to beat the man he denied that she was his wife. To save himself he denounced his own wife.

It was horrifying, the idea that an Afghan man could denounce his wife so easily. In traditional Afghan culture men will fight to the death to protect their wives and families, but the Taliban brought with them such fear, such evil, that they twisted some of the men of our nation. Some men who had previously been good men and kind husbands became swayed into believing this warped ideology, either because of their own fear or because they were taken in by the excitement of a mob psychology.

For the next week I didn't go anywhere. TV had been banned. The state radio station had been taken over for Taliban propaganda purposes. Woman presenters, even the old ugly ones with no makeup, had been banned. A popular young male news presenter who used the wrong word in a report about the death of a Taliban commander was beaten on the soles of his feet and left in a container for three days with no food or water. He had mistakenly used the word "joyous" instead of "tragic" to describe the death. It's an understandable slip when you consider men with whips were standing behind him as he broadcast live. Who wouldn't be nervous?

I couldn't even listen to the propaganda they called news. I wanted real news. I wanted to feel connected to the outside world. Not having contact made me feel like I was in prison. But the local grapevine news, delivered from neighbor to neighbor, was unavoidable, and each story was more horrible than before.

The fighting outside Kabul continued. The Shomali Plains, the area between Massoud's stronghold of Panjshir and the city, became the new front line. Most people were still expecting Massoud's troops to come back. We couldn't believe this Taliban reality was going to be permanent.

The only place where I could meet other girls and talk was on the communal balcony of the apartment block when I was cleaning the house. Watching from the balcony, I could see other young girls in the other apartments. Young, beautiful girls were being deprived of their basic rights, of breathing the fresh air and feeling the sun. As soon as these girls heard the sound of Taliban voices they fled, running as fast as they could back inside.

I needed to connect with my mother. I was missing her so badly but was thankful she didn't have to witness this latest abomination on her country. I wanted to visit her grave but I still couldn't bring myself to put on a burqa. I didn't even own one. So I borrowed a black Arab-style hijab from my sister. It was like a large cape that also covered the whole face, so I thought I'd be safe wearing that. The streets were deserted, and fear made the air so thick you could almost cut it with a blade.

Few men dared to come outside and even fewer women; those who did were dressed in blue shuttlecock burqas, the new uniform of Afghan women. (A shuttlecock burqa is an old-fashioned, tent-like burqa, with a crocheted screen that covers the eyes. The Taliban brought this style back, and it replaced the "younger" burqas, which have a veil on the eyes, and fit closer to the woman's figure.)

They scurried along silently, doing their shopping as quickly as possible so they could get home to safety. No one talked to anyone. Shopkeepers handed over bags wordlessly, and women took them without looking up. Occasionally a Taliban pickup truck would drive by, the men inside sneering menacingly, looking for new victims to beat, as loudspeakers on top of the trucks blasted out religious teachings. I thought that by now I knew fear in all its forms and shapes, but this one was a new form again—cold, clammy, and tinged with an icy fury. My fury. After that I didn't leave the house again for almost two months.

We hadn't heard from my brother Mirshakay since the Taliban had first taken control. Like him, many other former mujahideen and government workers had fled, taking their families with them. The Shomali plains and the Panjshir valley—the province northeast of Kabul—were still under the control of Ahmed Shah Massoud. But his men weren't the only ones fleeing. Others—former communists, university professors, doctors—were also fleeing. Grabbing what they could—a few clothes, jewelry, food supplies—they loaded up their cars and left town. People left behind everything they had worked for. People who had only weeks earlier congratulated themselves on their houses surviving the civil war intact were now locking the gates of those houses behind them and walking out without a second glance.

But not all of them made it to safety. We heard stories of cars being attacked and looted. The few possessions the passengers had were taken from them, gold necklaces ripped from women's necks, earrings torn from their lobes. Some of the looters were Taliban, others were criminals taking advantage of the chaos.

As they edged out of town and closer to the front line—the other side of which would mean relative safety—many people were killed, their cars hit by rockets or stray gunfire.

I prayed and prayed for Massoud to come back. Each night I went to sleep begging him, willing him, to push back the front line into the city center. I wanted to wake up and find the Taliban and their ideas gone.

Eventually we got a letter from my brother to say he had been hiding in the house of his driver in Parwan province, just to the north of Kabul. It's a beautiful place with a river and lush valleys full of trees. In the summer people go picnic there. Traditional Afghan picnics are a lovely affair—boiled eggs, juice, and plump mulberries picked freshly from the trees.

My brother wanted his wife and children to go to him. I decided to travel with them. Even now, despite the dangers, I still could not bring myself to put on a burqa, so I wore the black hijab instead, making sure my face was fully covered. I also wore a pair of glasses to disguise myself further. Even with my face covered I feared someone would recognize me as the sister of a police officer. Although Parwan is just next door to Kabul and the direct route is only an hour's drive, it was too close to the mujahideen and Taliban front line to drive directly. We didn't want to risk being hit by a rocket so we drove south first which was the opposite direction of where we needed to go. From Sarobi to Tagab and then to Nijrab in Kapisa province—almost a day's travel on a bumpy road. We had to loop back, then around, then backward again, then forward, then backward. Other people fleeing had created new tracks over fields, puzzling circuitous tracks, some leading to nowhere, others to another loop. It was an awful journey. For the 12 hours we drove I was terrified we'd hit a land mine, be looted, or come under gunfire. We didn't dare risk stopping for a break or for water.

Once again, I felt like I was driving away from my dreams. Every time I tried to start life it was thwarted. This was no life, constantly moving, constantly escaping, living on nerves, and ever-dwindling reserves of hope.

I was also driving away from Hamid. I hadn't been able to contact him to tell him I was leaving. And I hadn't seen him since the last time I was at the university, when he'd walked over to say hello to me. I recalled watching the back of his head as he retreated to the car, loving the way the wind caught his silky hair as it ruffled into little curls. I had spoken hardly more than a few sentences to him but I truly felt that I was beginning to love him. But I knew that by leaving with my family I had no idea when I might see him again.

And now that the war was officially over, the world also began to move on. The cold war had ended and the mighty Soviet empire was collapsing. No longer was the Afghan fight against the Russians of relevance to the West. No more was it broadcast nightly on international television news. Our civil war was over and as far as the world understood it, the Taliban was our government now. We were yesterday's story. And other tragedies took the front pages.

But our tragedy was not over. And the world forgot us for those next few years, our bleakest years of need.

Dear Shuhra and Shaharzad,

*If we Afghans had been living in darkness in those years of war,
then the days that were about to follow would truly plunge us into
the blackest depths of hell. A living hell created by men who called
themselves men of God, men of Islam. But these men represented
nothing of the Islamic religion that I and millions of other Afghans
follow in our daily life. Ours is a peaceful, tolerant, and loving faith
that accords all human beings rights and equal value.*

*I want you to understand that as a woman true Islam accords
you political and social rights. It offers you dignity, the freedom to
be educated, to pursue your dreams, and to live your life. It also asks
that you behave decently, modestly, and with kindness to all others.
I believe it is a true guide to living correctly for as long as you are in
this earthly world and I am proud to call myself a Muslim. I have
brought you up to be good and strong Muslim women in the future.*

*These men called themselves the Taliban. Their form of Islam was
so alien to us it could have come from another planet.*

*Many of their ideas about Islam came from different cultures,
mostly from the Arab lands.*

*These men rode in trucks and carried guns, but they promised
the Afghan people they would keep the streets safe, restore order, and
promote strong justice and local harmony. At the start many people
believed in them, but that hope quickly turned to fear and loathing,
especially for the women and girls of Afghanistan.*

*You were lucky not to be a young woman in those days. Very
lucky indeed.*

With love,
Your mother

TEN

RETREAT TO
THE NORTH

In Parwan we stayed with my brother's driver. The man and his family were not rich, but they let us stay in an annex adjoining their house. They refused to allow us to cook, preparing all our food for us. My brother, his family, and myself were all treated like honored guests, not unwelcome burdens.

Things continued to get worse in Kabul and my sister and her husband (who was a policeman and at risk from the Taliban) came to join us. It was decided they would move on again to Puli Khumri in the north, and we would all join soon after. Although Parwan was still safe for now, it was not far enough from Kabul to remain so much longer.

And importantly for me, no one in the north forced you to wear a burqa. For me that was reason enough to go.

My sister and her husband had been in Puli Khumri, almost 200 miles away, almost one week when the Taliban started gaining ground outside of Parwan, edging closer. I was fast asleep when Mirshakay shook me awake and screamed that we needed to get into the car. The Northern Alliance had closed the Salang pass, the second-highest road pass in the world. In a feat of incredible engineering the Russians had blasted a three-mile-long tunnel right through the center of the mountain. It was a one-lane pass, only accessible in the drier months. It is also the gateway to Northern Afghanistan. The remaining Northern Alliance was worried thousands of people would now try to flee, and in doing so bring more insecurity and possibly the Taliban with them.

So in a brutal but strategic military move they ordered the pass, the escape route from south to north, closed—a move that trapped everyone on either one side or the other. And that meant we would be unable to join the others in Puli Khumri.

My brother had managed to get an approval letter from one of the mujahideen commanders that would allow us two cars to go through the pass. One for us and one for our security escort. One of the women in our party didn't have either a hijab or a burqa, so I gave her my hijab. All I had left to wear was a bright red scarf. We were trying to escape Taliban control, and by now we could hear the bombs, the fighting was coming so close. If they reached us and caught us I would be badly beaten.

The escort car was also red, a Hilux pickup. I laughed at the irony of it and wondered how much more visible we could possibly make ourselves. We drove out of the house into the main street, and people were everywhere trying to escape. A large bus drove toward us. It was full of terrified-looking people; they were crammed inside, three or four hanging out of each window, some lying on the roof. They looked like bees swarming a hive.

As we left the village for the main road we joined a convoy of cars. Thousands of people were trying to escape the encroaching Taliban. The cars were full of clothes, kitchen equipment, blankets, and animals. Everything the passengers owned. People were hanging off the sides of cars, holding on anywhere they could. An injured man hanging from one of the taxis saw our car—I think he was a fighter. He was Uzbek from appearance, with a round face and almond-shaped eyes. He looked like a mujahideen fighter. Blood was running down his leg and obviously he couldn't hold onto the side of the taxi for much longer. He made his way over to our car, holding a gun. He waved it and told our driver to stop, but the driver carried on. Then he aimed at the tire and shot. As the tire burst the car swerved and almost hit the man. I was sitting in the front of the car and I was terrified he would come and drag me out of the vehicle, but our driver held his nerve and managed to keep going. The man moved on to the cars behind, shooting desperately. I dared not look back to see if he had killed a poor family.

People had no idea where they were heading. They just wanted to get out. It was the beginning of winter, and as we rode rose up into the mountains toward the Salang pass the air temperature began to bite, the altitude made it harder to breathe, and the chill bit toes and fingers, even inside the car.

The pass was already closed and those families without letters of permission had no choice but to stay on the freezing mountain or drive back home and straight into the Taliban front line. Even with the letter it took hours and hours. The commanders didn't want their fighters on the other side of the pass to know they had lost battleground and that refugees were fleeing, so only a few cars were allowed through to make it look as normal as possible.

In the car queue my sister-in-law saw her cousin, a young girl who had recently married. She and her husband had their six-week-old baby in the car. They looked terrified and they had no letter of permission. In the freezing cold the baby would surely die. So we agreed to leave our security car behind and allow their car to take its place. Everything we owned was in the security vehicle. Our bags, money, jewelry, everything. We were promised it would be allowed through later.

On the other side of the Salang pass, the road to Puli Khumri doesn't go over the mountain but around it, precariously clinging to the edges. Normally I am terrified of such heights and flimsy roads, but on this day I was just relieved the Taliban hadn't caught us.

My sister-in-law had managed to arrange a place for us to stay. It only had a few rooms, and there were some 60 people already there. They were my brother's men, former policemen, and they now had nowhere else to go. That's why we now have so many illegal armed groups in Afghanistan. When the system collapsed those men didn't have any options, so they just went with whoever had been their officer or leader and formed a militia. My brother didn't want us to be surrounded by so many men, though, so he asked them to return home to their families.

At midnight we were told the security vehicle containing all our things had been allowed to pass and was here. I grabbed the bags as they were carried inside. I think I knew already that our jewelry was gone. The people who were supposed to be guaranteeing our safety had taken the lot. They were men belonging to another local commander who had done my brother a favor by sending us the escort, so there was little we could do. My sister went through hers, sobbing. She was almost manically searching through all the pockets. I thought she was hysterical, still hoping her jewelry was there. But then she pulled out a handkerchief and blew her nose loudly. That handkerchief was pretty much all she had left. But at least we were safe again. For now.

Once again the traumas of my birthplace had forced my life to spiral out of my control. My dreams of being a doctor were shattered. By now the Taliban had banned all women from school and university. So even if Kabul were safe enough for us to return to, which it clearly wasn't, there was zero hope of a return to my studies. Instead my days were spent in Puli Khumri cooking, cleaning, drinking chai in the garden. It was the life of boring drudgery my mother and sisters endured, and the one I had battled so hard to escape. I was very depressed. Days rolled into dusk, into sleepless nights and reluctant mornings when I squeezed my eyes shut to block out the sun and the gaily mocking light of another new day.

After a few weeks the Taliban reopened universities for men, but by then many male students, teachers, and professors—the country's intellectuals—had already fled the country. Taliban rule had transformed Kabul from a war-torn city into a dead city. I honestly couldn't say which one was worse.

People were arrested and beaten for the slightest misdemeanor. The Taliban went door to door asking people to hand over their weapons. They refused to believe that not everyone in Kabul kept guns and wouldn't take no for an answer. If someone refused to hand the gun over or genuinely didn't have one, they were arrested and put in prison. Some families had to go out and buy weapons just to give to them to the Taliban in order to release the person who'd been arrested.

One of the worst places someone could be taken was the Ministry of Vice and Virtue. Just the mere mention of this name could strike petrifying fear into the hearts of the bravest people. This pretty, white stuccoed villa had a garden full of lush grapes and scented roses. It was situated in Share Naw (what is known as the new town area of Kabul).

Here people who had been accused of crimes against religion or what were called "morality crimes" were brought to be judged. Men without long enough beards and women caught without burqas were brought here to be beaten on the soles of their feet with wire cables, while outside Taliban guards sipped tea and told jokes among the roses. Terrified Kabuli women who had been accused of lacking morality were brought to be judged for their "crimes" by bearded mullahs from the conservative countryside villages of southern Afghanistan. Until now, Kabul and those villages had been culturally and socially worlds apart. Women who had proudly worn the latest fashions and carried books to the university just a few months ago were now being judged by unwashed men who couldn't read or write.

The Olympic sports stadium, a large, round-domed building that had once rung to the sounds of applause and cricket or football glories, became home to a new kind of sport—public executions. Adulterers and thieves were stoned to death or had their hands chopped off in front of cheering crowds. In grisly scenes reminiscent of a Roman coliseum, the prisoners were driven into the center of the stadium in a pickup truck, then dragged out and walked around for the crowd's entertainment before being shot in the head or buried up to waist, then having rocks thrown at their head until they died. No matter to those judging them or the brutes casting the first stone that the thief may have stolen a loaf of bread only to feed his hungry child or that the adulteress had in fact been raped.

All this was supposedly in the name of God. But I do not believe these were the actions of God. They were the actions of men. And I am sure God would have turned away to weep.

Thousands of the Taliban's supporters flocked into Kabul. Ultra-conservative families from the south moved in, buying houses at knock-down prices from those seeking to get out and escape. Wazir Akbar Khan, which had been one of the smartest and most sought-after addresses in Kabul, with modern, architect-designed houses, beautiful gardens, and swimming pools, became known as the "street of the guests." Favored Arab and Pakistani fighters who had connections to the Taliban leadership were given houses. If the house was empty they just moved in and took over, and if it had inhabitants those living there were forcibly moved out at gunpoint.

Even today some families have still not regained control of properties they lost at this time. When the Taliban were defeated in 2001, many of those who had been refugees in Europe or America came back to try to take ownership again. But with no documents, post-war chaos, and corruption rife in government, it is a difficult process. Many people ask for my help in tracing property ownership. Few of them succeeded. And sadly, in the past couple of years a building boom has seen the often illegal destruction of hundreds of these elegant villas, with their fruit trees and grape arbors. They are replaced with what have become labeled as "poppy palaces," ugly Pakistani-style buildings with over-the-top decorations of mirrors, smoked glass, and lurid, fancy, patterned tiles. An architecture that owes nothing to Afghan culture and everything to post-conflict new money, all too often gleaned from corruption or the proceeds of the heroin trade.

Those houses that have survived both the war and the developers have stood the test of time and look just as stylish today as they did when they were built. Today different types of guests have taken over Wazir Akbar Khan. Now they are occupied by foreign aid workers and international journalists from global networks like BBC, CNN, and France 24. In response to the insecurity inhabitants feel living and working in a capital city with frequent suicide bombings, large sections have been barricaded off. In an area known as "the green zone" the streets are blocked with concrete bollards and checkpoints in an attempt to keep suicide bombers out. Those without identification or the correct passes are barred from entering or driving through, something that creates traffic chaos and is a constant source of frustration and anger among many Kabulis toward these latest guests.

The British Embassy has recently taken over an entire street of houses for their compound, blocking entrances at both ends. What was once a bustling, rich neighborhood with children playing ball games on the streets is now sadly a fortress, barred to most Afghans except those who need to travel there for work.

IN THOSE LONG DAYS that we waited in Puli Khumri, I spent every moment hoping for a return to Kabul. The front line and the areas controlled by the Taliban and the mujahideen-led government kept shifting. But what was clear was that it was the Taliban who were slowly gaining more and more ground.

I had no idea if Hamid was still living in Kabul or if he and his family had also fled. I thought of him constantly, but I also knew there was still a lot of objection from my brothers to our marriage.

One day I was sitting in the yard, enjoying the feel of the sun on my face, watching snow fall on the mountains beyond. I was yearning for the city and wondering to myself what the weather was like in Kabul when I saw Hamid's sister, her husband, and one of his uncles at our gate. I was amazed to see them. I let out a little squeal of joy.

It turns out Hamid had gone to our house, found the curtains drawn and no one there. He asked around and found out where we had gone. Then he realized that this could work in our advantage. If I was in mujahideen-controlled land that meant I was around armed militias and commanders who might rape me. Hamid figured my brother had enough on his plate keeping his own two wives safe without worrying about my honor. This might make him more open to the idea of our marriage.

So here was his sister at our door with the proposal. She and her husband, along with their three- and four-year-old kids, had come from Kabul to ask. The journey was dangerous for them. Not only was there fighting, but they had gotten stuck underneath an avalanche. It narrowly missed their car and blocked the road, meaning they had spent the night freezing. They could have been killed and I felt slightly angry at Hamid for putting them through that, but at the same time I was secretly thrilled by his newfound determination to make our wedding happen.

And Hamid was right. My brother no longer had the power he had had in Kabul. He was exhausted and stressed. But he still wasn't quite ready to give in.

In our culture if you want to say no to someone's proposal politely you don't actually say no; you just give them a list of requests that they have no way of meeting. My brother knew they had risked their lives to bring this request and he couldn't be so rude as to turn them away with no hope. But he still wasn't prepared to let this union happen. So after we had all finished dinner he quietly told them the engagement could only go ahead if they paid for a house (which would be in my name), gave large amounts of gold and jewelry, and 20,000 dollars in cash.

That was a lot of money, especially in war time and especially for this family, who although not dirt poor, were certainly not rich either. I was not allowed to be part of the negotiations, of course. Hamid's sister and I were in a room next door, but we strained our ears to the wall, trying to keep abreast of the proceedings. I gasped with horror when I heard my brother say it. But amazingly, Hamid's family agreed.

Hamid's uncle sounded a little shocked and not entirely happy, but he did a good job of recovering himself. He must have been fuming inside, but he shook hands with my brother, even going so far as to thank him profusely.

Hamid's sister gathered her children and hugged me goodbye with a warm smile before throwing her burqa back over her head. The men put on their turbans before getting back in the car. The Taliban had made the wearing of turbans and beards law for all men.

A few days later my brother drove to Kabul to meet Hamid's family again and discuss arrangements. That's a normal procedure. Even though my brother did not expect Hamid's family to meet his request, he still had to go along with the process and it was his turn to visit them and explore how their plans were coming along. But on the way he got caught in more fighting between the Taliban and the mujahideen. The Salang pass was once more closed and he was trapped on the other side. We had no news about him for 40 days. The tension was unbearable. We had no idea what we'd do if he'd been killed. His wife looked at me reproachfully, as if it were my fault he'd had to risk his life by going back to Kabul.

Eventually news came that he'd been in Badakhshan. The Taliban were gaining more and more ground, and his commanders feared they were about to take more of the central and northern provinces. So he'd been sent back to Badakhshan to help organize a new mujahideen stronghold.

Mirshakay was returned to us safely, and the green shoots of spring were already pushing through the snow when Hamid's uncle came again. This time Hamid was with him. Mirshakay was surprised, and possibly a little horrified, when they produced the 20,000 dollars in hard cash and documents showing proof of a house purchase. But he still wasn't prepared to give Hamid my hand in marriage. Even now he couldn't bring himself to say a final and direct yes.

Although the family was far from rich, they did own land in Badakhshan. So they had been able to sell some of that to get the money. It wasn't like they had nothing, but of course my brother, who owned four houses in Kabul and a house in Lahore in Pakistan, didn't see it that way.

Once again the negotiations were strictly a male affair and we women sat in a different room. That was a strange feeling for me, sitting quietly and straining my ears to hear as my future was being argued upon like a business transaction. It reminded me of my childhood in some ways, trying to sneak up to my father's guest rooms and listen to the discussions inside. As I listened I felt a strange mixture of pride, curiosity, and powerlessness.

When I heard they had the money, I let out an involuntary squeak. My life had been pretty much dust in Puli Khumri. No university, and I was unable to walk or go anywhere. I had no idea how marriage was going to be, but I figured it had to be less boring than where I was now.

But then the enormity of the situation suddenly hit me. Engagements in Afghanistan are binding and only in exceptional circumstances can they be broken. An engagement itself is as strong as the marriage contract. I started to think about all the warnings my brother had given me. His voice kept repeating my in head, "Fawzia jan, do not marry this poor man. You can have any man you want. You will not be able to survive on his monthly salary. Marry a rich man, a powerful man."

The warnings rang round and round in my head and I must admit I started to have second thoughts. But it's hard to imagine your life as a newlywed when your country is in ruins. I had no idea what was going to happen, how long the Taliban would be here, whether the fighting would ever end, where we would live, whether I would be able to study again or ever be able to work. All the plans newlyweds make together were denied us in those days. Staying alive and safe took precedence over dreams.

My elder sister saw that I'd turned a bit white. She looked at me sternly and said: "Fawzia, you must decide. Now. Right now. If you don't want this to go ahead this is your last chance to say so. Do you understand that?"

In a last attempt to tempt me away from marrying Hamid, Mirshakay had a few days earlier promised me I could go to Pakistan and stay with his second wife, who was living in his house in Lahore. I could stay with her and go to a Pakistani university. It was a great idea. The chance to study medicine again in a country not blighted by war was a good one.

But although I barely knew Hamid, what little I had seen of him convinced me we could make it work. I knew he was an unusual Afghan man, one that would treat me like an equal and genuinely support my desire to work. He wasn't rich and the future was uncertain in so many ways, but he still felt like the right choice for me. Because he was *my* choice.

As is so often the case in my family history, it took a woman for there to be decisive action. My sister told me to make a decision. I nodded a silent yes. Then she knocked and entered the men's room and asked to speak to my brother. Outside the room she bravely and sternly told him to stop challenging these poor people. They had the money as promised. It was time for him to make decision. Yes or no.

He pursed his lips and rolled his eyes dramatically, let out a large sigh, and then agreed with her, although still reluctantly. My sister prepared a bowl of sweets and put some flowers and a handkerchief with a small red flower on it inside the bowl. I still have that handkerchief. The items in the bowl were a sign of our acceptance. The bowl was ceremoniously sent into the room where Hamid was sitting. I wish I could have seen the joy on his face when he saw it and realized his dreams were coming true at last. The sharing of sweets is the traditional Afghan way of formalizing an engagement. The sweets are shared and the groom's family puts money in the bowl to pay for the wedding.

Hamid took a sweet, unwrapped it carefully, and ate it, then put another 5,000 dollars inside the bowl. He'd been prepared for this cost, too. At this stage the bride's family often also puts money into the bowl to share the cost of the wedding, but my brother was still a little disgruntled with himself for giving in. So he added nothing. Even now he was pointedly refusing to make it easy for them.

The next day they came back again for lunch. I was in the kitchen from early morning. As I washed rice and peeled cucumbers I smiled as I realized how much love I was pouring into the cooking. The simple pleasure of preparing food for those they love is something all women feel at some time. It must be something so ancient within us, so much a part of our biology and nature. I was reminded of my mother cooking for my father and how she always wanted things to be just perfect for him. Here I was, doing the same. As I chopped the vegetables I made sure to cut them just so, into lovely little straight pieces that would be a delight for him to eat.

I was still not allowed to see my husband-to-be. The only glimpse I got of him was as he and his family left. I hid behind a curtain at the window and sneaked a glance. I think he knew I was going to be watching him, because he stopped and paused, pretending to scratch his head. I think he thought about sneaking a glance back at me, too, but he obviously decided it was too risky in case my brother saw.

As Hamid walked to his car I felt a surge of excitement. It had been almost six years since Hamid's first proposal. He'd never given up on his quest to marry me. I was 21 years old and I was going to be a bride.

Dear Shuhra and Shaharzad,

So many times myself and other members of our family survived because of the kindnesses of other people. People who risked their own lives to help us, offer us shelter, or hide us from danger.

And we weren't alone. All over our country ordinary men and women opened their doors to people who needed them.

Neighbors turned a blind eye as little girls scurried under the cover of darkness to secret girls' schools in underground basements. These schools were run by brave, wonderful Afghan women, who despite the dangers to themselves, knew they couldn't let the Taliban destroy the education of a generation of girls.

We had so many widows in those days. There were thousands upon thousands of women who had lost husbands and fathers and who were now the main breadwinners in their family and responsible for ensuring children were fed.

But the Taliban denied all women the right to work. So these women, who had already lost so much, were forced to beg and rely on the kindness of strangers. Many didn't survive and many of the widows' children died of disease or starvation. But many other widows and their babies did survive, because those people on the streets who saw them begging did not walk by. Even though they didn't have much for themselves they still gave what little they could. This is what it means to be a true Muslim. To give alms to the poor is one of the main tenets of Islam and is something the Holy Quran instructs us to do at times of great celebration, like at the start of Eid,* but also every day of our lives.

I know sometimes you get frustrated and upset by the constant queues of people outside the door of our house. They are people who

---

want to talk to me, need my help, or are asking for money. Every morning from daybreak a small queue forms outside our house. Sometimes, before we have even had breakfast, the queue can be a dozen people long. I know you get upset because these strangers never make appointments and they demand so much of my time when you need your mother's time and attention also. Especially in the morning when I am trying to help you pack your school bags and enjoy our few moments of time together before parliament business takes me away. But girls, as frustrating as it can be, please try to understand that I cannot turn these people away.

And this is a lesson I want to teach you. Never turn anyone away from your door because you never know when the day will come that it is you who will need to throw yourself at the mercy of another's door.

With love,
Your mother

ELEVEN

EVERYTHING
TURNS WHITE

Since their initial victory in capturing Kabul, the Taliban had been steadily increasing ground in the north of the country. But the mujahideen were still determined to try and stop them. Areas that had been under the full control of the mujahideen government began to lose pockets to the Taliban. In the middle of a government area a village would suddenly fly the white flag of the Taliban.

Anywhere the Taliban had supporters, the flag would appear. In previous government strongholds—Mazaar, Baghlan, Kunduz—these white flags kept appearing.

But as the Taliban grew in power in the north, they decimated the culture. They banned women from wearing white trousers or even white socks. They saw the wearing of white as disrespect for the color of their flag. But in many northern provinces the common color for a burqa was white. (Only in Kabul and in the south was it blue.) Most of the women in the north who wore the burqa only owned them in this white color, but the Taliban beat them for it. They were beaten for not wearing a burqa and then they were beaten for wearing a burqa in the wrong color. It was insanity.

By now the Taliban was moving swiftly across the country. They took full control of Baghlan and Kunduz. Takhar and Badakhshan were the only two provinces where they couldn't get a foothold.

Once they captured a province they immediately closed the schools and arrested people. It was barbaric. They would torture people without any justice, without any trial, they just made up the rules as they went along. The north, which generally had a more open-minded culture than the south, was in collective shock.

But then some Northern Alliance commanders started to make deals with the Taliban, to try to protect themselves. It was never a meeting of minds—the Taliban were much more fundamentalist in their thinking and their ideas than the mujahideen ever were.

And besides, the Taliban had their power sources overseas. They didn't really need internal alliances. Even some of the former communists tried to ally with the Taliban. But the Taliban usually just used someone for what they could offer, then betrayed them or assassinated them. You were either one of them or you weren't.

By now our once close-knit family was spread out in little units all over the country. Most of my elder sisters still lived in Badakhshan; they had married local village men and never left the province. I missed them very much.

Mirshakay, who had never quite been the same since Muqim's death, decided he'd had enough of Afghanistan once and for all, and wanted to leave the country. His plan was to first go to Pakistan to pick up his second wife and from there onto Europe.

Before he could start to carry out his plan, Massoud and Rabbani's men sent word that he was needed in Takhar province to help establish a force there to fight against the Taliban. So we followed him there and began yet another temporary life in yet another rented house. A few weeks later, Massoud himself came from Takhar to Panjshir to organize his troops, so my brother took this opportunity to ask for permission and safe passage to take his family to safety to Pakistan via Kabul. Massoud agreed.

He took off his uniform and put on civilian clothes as we women hastily threw what we could into bags. Then we took a taxi. It was a balmy, warm spring day.

As we drove along a river we gasped as the Taliban blew up the bridge ahead, preventing people from driving across. The bridge exploded into shards of metal and wood, and the unfortunate cars that were on it were tossed into the air before shattering.

We had no choice but to get out and walk. My sister-in-law had a newborn baby. She hadn't expected we'd need to walk, and she had, perhaps not very sensibly, chosen to wear high heels for the journey. We walked for most of the day. It wasn't a straight, direct path. We had to walk up a rocky mountain, through gardens of rose and mulberry trees, then down to a path that ran along the side of a river. The road itself was too dangerous to walk on because of the heavy artillery shelling coming from either side. That would have made us sitting ducks. At times so many rockets were whizzing overhead we had to stop and take cover in bushes. Occasionally a taxi would take us part of the way. Not official taxis, just ordinary people charging money to drive people. They were risking their lives by doing so, but they needed the money.

One car took us right to the front line, where the Taliban and Massoud's men were shooting at each other. This was the road over the Shomali plains, taking us closer to the outskirts of Kabul. Normally the road would be busy, but no taxis dared to drive this part. We joined crowds who were walking. I laughed at the irony that these same people were the people we'd seen fleeing Kabul the day the Taliban took the city. Now, the temporary sanctuary of quieter towns was the scene of fighting, and Kabul was once again the safer option. Hungry wild dogs ran over the plains, snarling at people. As I stepped over some grass I almost trod on a snake. It scared me as much as the rockets.

In our party there was me, my brother and his wife and children, along with a friend of my brother's and his family. My sister-in-law started to cry. She was in her heels and was struggling to carry her heavy baby boy, Irshad.

I was wearing flat sandals so I offered to change my shoes with hers. For some reason I've always been good at walking in high heels, even in the middle of a battle. It's one of my more unusual talents.

As we stopped to change footwear more rockets flew close by, so we took cover again. I sat under a tree and was enjoying the few minutes of rest. We had found some apples and were hungrily biting into them when suddenly my tree started to shake. Then I heard the sound—whiiiiirrrrrrrr. A rocket was just above my head. I froze. It exploded just feet away from me, taking the tree and all the leaves with it.

It all happened so quickly. One second I was sitting under the tree and the next second I realized the tree was not there. Once again, I had narrowly escaped death.

As we walked on we passed bodies of women and children who hadn't been so lucky when the rockets hit. My brother saw the dead bodies and screamed at us to keep moving.

After two more hours of walking we came to what had once been a popular picnic stop by the river Sayad—an idyllic little stop with a fast-flowing stream and trickling waterfalls.

We were exhausted. The heels were beginning to hurt my feet. A family saw us and came out of their house. They beckoned us inside and offered us tea, bread, and mulberries. These little moments of kindnesses by strangers I will remember forever. They even gave me a pair of sandals to replace the heels.

After we'd refreshed we thanked the family and moved on again. We needed to cross the river now, and the only way over was a handmade, shaky footbridge. It was made of planks crudely held together with wire and string. There were big gaps in some of the planks and the whole thing looked like it could collapse at any moment. One of my brother's bodyguards was holding all the passports and documents for all of us in his pocket. He stood at the edge of the bridge and began to help us across one by one.

He grabbed my hand and urged me to step onto the first plank. It was evening by now, and the wind was so strong it was hard to even stand properly. Holding the man's hand I managed to get over, as did my sister-in-law, still holding the baby. But as she stepped off she lost one of her sandals. She started to cry loudly.

Finally the bodyguard started to cross. But there was no one to hold his hand as he did so. I was watching him as he got to the middle, then a plank gave a little sway and he fell.

We watched in horror, the sickening thought going through my mind that if he drowned, all our passports drowned with him. But this poor guy suddenly resurfaced with one hand above the water. He was holding the passports aloft. Somehow he managed to work his way to shore and my brother dragged him out. He'd managed to keep the passports totally dry. We all fell about laughing, even him.

My brother hugged him and thanked him. This man had always been one of my brother's favorite staff. He was very loyal. Sadly after my brother left the country, his former bodyguard later joined the Taliban. With no income he had no choice. Thousands of Afghan men have joined the Taliban for this reason. They might not share the ideology, but if the Taliban are the only people willing to pay the wages they need to feed their families, then they join.

After walking another 30 minutes we reached a Taliban-controlled area and found another taxi. I collapsed into the backseat and fell asleep. When I next woke up it was dark and the car was driving through the streets of my beloved Kabul.

Mirshakay asked the taxi to take us to his house in Makrorian. His relatives had been staying there for him and they knew we were coming. I can't describe the relief I felt at taking a shower in hot water and eating a proper meal. The simplest dish is so much tastier after having spent the day dodging rockets and bullets in a pair of ridiculous high heels.

Dear Shuhra and Shaharzad,

I love the intimacy we have as mother and daughters.

When I listen to your chatter it reminds me of how much has changed between my generation and yours. You talk about wildlife documentaries you've seen on TV. You show me Bollywood dances that you've learned from your favorite Indian films. You talk about computers and things you've found on the Internet. You have access to the wider world in ways I never did.

I love it when you tell me stories of your friends, even the sad ones. Like the friend of Shuhra's who lives with her father and stepmother. The stepmother treats the little girl badly and Shuhra feel so sad for her friend, she cries.

I love that you have me to share your stories with. I could never talk to my siblings about my life because no one was interested. My brothers had no interest in hearing about me and my dreams and the silly little things that happened to me that day. Maybe the only time they would hear about my school was when I would bring my result sheet saying that I got the first or the second position in the class. Then they would show some pride at their clever sister.

Whenever my friends in school would talk about their birthday presents or invite me to their party, I would always suffer. I always wished that I could celebrate my birthday as well and then tell my friends about it. Sometimes I wanted to lie to my classmates about my birthday and pretend I'd had a big party with music and dancing. But then I was scared that my classmates would ask me to invite them and I couldn't invite them because it would never happen. Celebrating girls' birthdays was not usual in our family.

That is something I wanted to change for you. When it's either of your birthdays we take weeks to plan your party. You have balloons and cake. You even get the privilege of sending the family car to pick up your friends. I love being able to do this for you because I want *you to love celebrations. I want you to celebrate the big things and the small things.*

Know this: Whatever our circumstances, there is always something to celebrate about life.

With love,
Your mother

TWELVE

A TALIBAN WEDDING

Every girl dreams of her wedding day and I was no different.

I always think life is simply a series of important moments. Moments that define us as the individuals we are. And the best moments we cherish all our lives, such as an enjoyable party, fresh grass after the rain, a picnic by a river, an evening spent laughing with loved ones, the birth of a precious child, or graduation from a university.

The day a bride goes to choose her wedding dress should be one of those moments.

But as I put on my coat to go to the bazaar that morning, I felt like a walking ghost.

My sisters and my mother had always taken great delight in discussing what kind of wedding I would eventually have. Over the years they had gossiped and giggled about all of it, from what I might wear, to how my hair would look, to what food we'd serve. In those pre-war days we were a relatively rich family, and so the assumption was always that I would have a big wedding, with people coming from far and wide to see me. When I was a little girl I'd always found this a bit annoying, but now that I was finally getting married I so very much wanted that dream day. I wanted to hear my mother talk about her plans again more than anything in the world. The loss of her was still like a dull, constant ache.

I had also never imagined that the most important day of my life would be taking place under the rule of the Taliban.

Because of their rules, there would be no music, no video, and no dancing. All the restaurants and wedding halls were closed and joyous ceremonies now prohibited. Wherever you live in the world, a wedding day only comes once in your life and you want it to be perfect. I know it sounds so girlish and silly to admit it now, but most nights before the wedding that I cried myself to sleep, I cried for both my mother and my lost moment to shine as a beautiful bride.

Despite the wearing of the burqa now being law, I still hadn't been able to bring myself to buy one. When I did have to go outside I had taken to wearing my mother's old one. Her burqa was far more beautiful and with finer detailing than the blue nylon ones that are so common today. Those blue ones are a Pakistani design, cheap and mass produced. In my mother's era women saw the burqa as a sign of status, and my mother had one befitting her rank as the wife of a powerful and rich man. It was made of green silk with soft folds that rustled gently as she walked, and was lightly embroidered with a fine silver mesh panel covering the face. When it got dirty she took it to a specialist cleaner who steamed and pressed each individual fold into place. For her it was a thing of pride. For me, wearing it felt like shame. Even after my marriage I continued to wear my mother's burqa, thinking that if I must wear one, at least let it be one that reminded me of her.

The day we went shopping my fiancé accompanied us. It was the first time I had seen him in months. The last time I saw his face properly was my last day at the university before the Taliban came to power. The day he came to visit us in Puli Khumri, when my brother had finally agreed to our marriage, I had only gotten to see the back of his head as I hid behind the curtain. That day at the university the mujahideen government had been in control, and he had sported a neatly trimmed small beard. But under Taliban rule his hair and beard were now longer. He didn't look nearly as handsome. Through the hated-burqa I kept sneaking sideways glances at his beard, thinking how much I disliked the look of it on his face. I had this over-powering feeling that Afghanistan was slipping back in time. No more progression, only the darkness of the uneducated men who now ruled our land.

The Taliban had another new regulation: Any woman who goes out of the family home, for whatever reason, must have a *muharram,* a male blood relative, with her. This, like so many of the Taliban's rules, was more akin to Arab culture than our own Afghan culture. In my grandmother's day women didn't go out alone, but these things were changing in Afghanistan with each new generation, as is the natural progression of any culture. But now the Taliban was plunging us back in time.

If they stopped your car at one of the many Taliban checkpoints that had sprung up all over the city, they would interrogate you for your family name, your father's name, and they would ask endless questions until they were satisfied that the man and woman were blood relatives, not just friends. A special department called the Ministry of Vice and Virtue was responsible for making sure people did not commit these crimes against morality. It seemed to me this department saw their day job as beating women.

In the wedding bazaar they were beating women who were, like me, trying to shop for bridal gowns. One poor girl had worn white trousers, which were now banned because wearing the color white was said to be disrespectful to the white Taliban flag. Perhaps this girl didn't know about the ban, maybe she was uneducated and poor, or maybe she had been too scared to leave the house until today. Whatever the reason, I heard someone yell at her in Arabic (by now many Arab fighters had come to join the Taliban and live in Kabul). The men took a rubber cable and held her down on the ground while they beat her legs with it. She yelped in pain. I turned away, biting so hard on my lip that it bled. I was consumed with anger at the injustice of it and at my failure to be able to stop it.

The sound of the Vice and Virtue car is one I will never forget. It was usually a Hilux, a pickup truck. It would drive through the streets, and always there was the music of the Holy Quran blasting from loudspeakers on the top. When they heard the sound of the car, women caught outside would rush to hide themselves. Even for the tiniest mistake or misdemeanor the men would start beating you. Sometimes they would just look at you and beat you for no reason. One day I saw a young girl getting beaten and watched as her mother and sister threw themselves on top of her to try and protect her. The Taliban just continued to beat all three of them. It was truly madness.

On this day there was a group of us, my sister, my fiancé, and his sister. Fortunately they ignored us. We bought the marriage rings, and at least we created one small memory from that. Through the mesh of the burqa I know Hamid could tell I was smiling as I watched him pay for the rings.

With weddings now under such strict rule, most of the shops in the bazaar hadn't bothered to buy new wedding dress stock. So little was available, and I struggled to find anything I liked. I had always imagined a short, puff-sleeved dress, but bare arms were now banned.

Afghan brides wear three or four different dresses for their marriage ceremony. Each one is a different color and represents something different. For my henna night I went for a kind of light green dress. For *nikah*, the first part of the ceremony, people often have a dark green outfit. But I wanted something different, so I went for pink. It was a beautiful rosy pink and it felt like a shot of pure joy against all the misery of the Taliban. Just looking at that dress cheered me up. After nikah the bride then changes again for the reception party. Normally this is a white wedding dress and veil, similar to the styles worn by brides in the West.

A big difference between Afghan weddings and Western weddings is the size. In Afghan weddings the guest list can sometimes run to many thousands. In normal times my wedding would have most definitely been this size. Family and friends would have been invited, but also political allies, supporters, and villagers from Badakhshan. In our culture, and particularly in a political family like mine, a wedding becomes a networking affair.

But because the wedding halls were closed, we had nowhere to host a large party. In our reduced financial circumstances, I doubt we could have paid for it anyway. Even so, my family invited over 1,000 people to my ceremony. In the end closer to 1,500 came, more people than we had invited.

Afghan weddings are also segregated—women and children on one side and men in the other. So we had it in two houses, in my brother's house and in one of his neighbor's houses. The men went to the neighbor's and the women came to ours. The night before the wedding we have a traditional henna ceremony where the bride has her hands decorated with henna. For that we went to a beauty parlor. Normally I loved a trip to a beauty salon, but even that didn't cheer me up. Not a thing about this wedding was my choice or what I would have wanted it to be like; not the quality of the dresses, nor even my hairstyle. I'd done my best, but deep down it all felt so cheap and make do.

The henna night lasts most of the night. Usually it's done a few days before the actual wedding so the bride can rest before the big day, but we didn't have a choice but to do it the night before. The whole night long there was music with what's called *daira*, which is a circle where the ladies sit and sing and play music. So when my wedding day came I was exhausted, having been up half the night. In the morning when I went to the beauty parlor to get my bridal makeup, the women admonished me and told me I needed more sleep because I looked so rough. But in truth, I would not have slept anyway, even if the henna night had been a whole week before.

My wedding was so bittersweet. My mother was dead and my living sisters, who were still scattered across the country, couldn't come. My mother, who had at my birth wanted me to die, had then worked so hard for me to have a future. It was she who had effectively picked out my husband for me, telling me on her deathbed that "this man will be enough for us." Preparing for my ceremony without her there to hold my hand and whisper words of encouragement was as painful as walking on burning needles.

At six A.M. the hairdresser put the rollers in my hair and I nodded off in the chair. I slept there until about 10:30 and then she started to do my makeup. I looked in the mirror and realized I really did look awful, with red-rimmed eyes and a spotty face. By the time we entered the house I was feeling really blue. The other big disappointment was that I wanted to have the wedding secretly filmed with a video camera or a proper photographer. The Taliban had banned video, but some of the video operators still did it anyway. They just charged triple to compensate for the risk. But my brother wouldn't allow it. Some of my brother's friends were these days working in low-level government jobs and he was worried they would report us to the Taliban authorities they now worked for. I have no photographic memories of my wedding, except for a few grainy snapshots friends managed to take with their personal cameras.

I didn't know many of the people at the wedding—they were my brother's friends and their wives or his work colleagues. I started to get a bit angry inside, wondering if they had come just for the chance of some free food. It certainly didn't feel like they were there for me.

For the actual religious part of the marriage—conducted by a mullah— they took Hamid and I and our two witnesses to a separate room. That was when I cried for the first (but not the last) time that day. And of course all my makeup, the only thing making me look a little bit pretty, started to run down my cheeks. I wiped my eyes then forgot myself as I inadvertently wiped mascara over my pretty pink dress. Fortunately after the ceremony it was time to change into the white dress. In the white gown, with its lacy sleeves and long veil, I like to think I looked a little bit more beautiful.

Later in the evening the tradition is that the elder of the family, either a father or brother, takes a cloth containing some sweets and clothes and ties it to the bride's wrist. It's symbolic of sending the new bride to her husband's home. It's a very moving and personal scene. When my brother took the braid and started to tie it on my wrist, I started to cry. He started to cry too. We were hugging each other and crying our eyes out. I think it was more than the moment that got to us. We were crying because of all the people who weren't there, those dead and those killed. My mother, my brother Muqim, my father. We cried for all the family we had lost, for our lost status, our homes, our way of life. In that private few minutes my brother and I hugged and cried in silence, both of us understanding the enormity of loss, the joy of moving forward, and the pain of change.

Eventually he gathered himself and with a stern, "Come now, Fawzia jan," he gently touched the tip of my nose and led me out of the room.

Dear Shuhra and Shaharzad,

Your father was the love of my life. He was more than enough for this "poor girl." In marrying him I was a lucky girl indeed.

Marriage is an important rite in a woman's life, but I truly believe marriage should not prevent her from living her dreams. Rather, her dreams should become those of her husband's and her husband's dreams should become part of hers. This new couple should stand together and make the world theirs.

Sometimes I long to see the day you will get married, but at other times I don't want it to happen, because I know on that day you will stop being my little girls and become grown women. I don't want that to happen too fast.

I hope you will find love one day. Love is important. But then not everyone thinks so. Many people believe duty, respect, religion, and rules are more important than love.

But I do not think these things have to be separate. Love can exist alongside duty. Love thrives on duty. And respect.

With love,
Your mother

THIRTEEN

AN END BEFORE
A BEGINNING

My wedding day marked the next new chapter of my life—as a wife. I had no inkling just what a short and tragic chapter it was destined to be.

My husband lived in an apartment in fourth Makrorian. It was a three-bedroom purpose-built apartment, simple, solid, and functional. He had made a real effort (I suspect with the help of his sisters) to decorate our bedroom nicely. He'd bought new pink curtains, a pink bedcover, and even some pink silk flowers in a pink vase by the side of the bed. It was such a thoughtful gesture, but everything looked so very . . . pink. I had to stifle a giggle.

By the time of my wedding night I'd been awake for 24 hours. Thankfully my husband was also exhausted after such a long day and didn't make demands on me. We both fell fast asleep.

In the morning I awoke first, and for a second I panicked. My eyes opened and I saw a pink curtain with hazy sunlight outside, and I was in a strange bed with a man beside me. For a split second I struggled to work out where I was, then I came to. I was married to Hamid, to the man sleeping next to me. He snored gently, and I smiled indulgently at him as I stroked his cheek. This was the first day of my new life.

Hamid's sister and her two children were also living with us. She had recently been widowed and had nowhere else to go. I was happy about this, thankful for the comforting presence of another woman about the place. She had been a teacher and was an intelligent, feisty woman. We got on famously.

At last I was a little bit content with life. Hamid was the kind, warm man I always suspected he was. We basked in each other's company, we laughed, and we made plans for our future. I hadn't felt a joy like that since the first day I started school at seven years old. Life was finally going my way.

A week after our wedding, we had another ceremony called *takht*. The bride and groom sit under decorations, flowers, and ribbons, and visitors come and congratulate them and give them gifts. That lasts for three days, and the last day is called *takht jami*. That signifies the end of the marriage celebrations.

In my childhood days my sisters and mother would of course regale me with stories of all the riches I would receive on my *takht jami*—a new car perhaps, or a house in the mountains, or a whole ton of gold. But of course, life during Taliban time wasn't so ostentatious. Friends and family came, bringing what they could—a tablecloth, some new dishes, 50 dollars.

About an hour earlier we'd said goodbye to our last guests and Hamid had popped into his office for half an hour to check on things. His sister and I were about to make a cup of tea when there was a knock at the door. My sister-in-law went to open it and there stood bearded men in black turbans.

Mullah Omar, the Taliban leader, had heard my brother was back in Kabul and had an arrest warrant for him. They had been searching for my brother for the past three days and he'd already gone into hiding. The family had not informed me of this because they wanted me to enjoy my honeymoon period.

Now here they were at my door. They barged into my newly married bliss like the battering rams of doom. Without asking they walked into the living room, where I was sitting under flower garlands in all my silly makeup and finery. As they looked at me, all the color drained from my face. I had had enough trouble in my life already to know that their arrival meant the end of this happy chapter already. They barked at us to stay where we were and then went into my bedroom. They started tearing the bedsheets off the bed, the bed where less than a week ago Hamid and I had begun our married adult life together.

It was such an invasion of privacy, of decency, and an affront to our culture. But these brutes didn't care about that. They started looking under the bed and pulling things out of cupboards. They said nothing, they just turned the house upside down, tearing at the nice furniture with their dirty, unwashed hands.

Then they spoke, yelling at me: "Where is Mirshakay? Where is the police general?" They waved an arrest warrant in my face. I felt sick to my stomach as I realized who they wanted. I told them calmly I had no idea. By now they'd ripped apart my house so they knew I wasn't lying. Then my heart stopped again. Hamid!

"Please don't come back from the office yet," I silently willed my husband. "Stay at work, don't come home yet. Please. Don't come home yet."

They left and I listened with bated breath as they walked down the five flights of steps to the door of the main building. With each click-clack of their boots on the stair treads I breathed a little easier—four floors to go, three floors, two. Then on the first floor I heard a door open. I gasped in horror. "No please, please don't let that be Hamid." He was seconds away from danger. He had bounded happily through the front door with a gift of chocolates for me and walked right into them. If only he'd paused to buy a newspaper, chat with a neighbor, or even bent down to tie his shoelaces, he might have missed them.

Angry at their failure to find my brother, they arrested Hamid. He had done nothing. He had committed no crime, but they took him.

I ran down the stairs, screaming. I begged them. "We've only been married seven days, he knows nothing. This is my husband's house, we are newlyweds, we are innocent people, leave us alone."

They simply asked me again: "Where is Mirshakay?"

They handcuffed Hamid. He barely moved or spoke; he was in shock. The flowers he'd been holding for me dropped to the floor. A few neighbors had gathered to watch the scene. Nobody said anything. I grabbed my burqa and followed my husband. Hamid knew better than to tell me to stay at home and wait.

They put Hamid in a red Taliban pickup truck. They pushed me aside, laughing when I tried to get in after him. I flagged down a taxi. The driver wound down the window and said: "I am sorry ma'am. I am sorry sister. Do you have a *muharram* [male blood relative] with yourself?" I snapped at him: "What? Just let me in. I have to follow that car." He shook his head: "You need a *muharram* with yourself, sister. These stupid people, these men you want to follow, if they see you alone with me they will put both of us in prison."

Then he drove away. I followed the pickup with my eyes as it turned down the street and along the main road, then it took a left toward Share Naw (the new town area of Kabul). I was desperate not to lose sight of it.

I hailed another taxi. This time I spoke before the driver had chance to. I begged for all I was worth. "Brother, dear brother, please please help me. Please. They are taking my husband. I need to follow him. I'm alone. Can you please take me?"

He told me to get in. As we drove he spoke hurriedly. "If they stop the car say you are my sister, my name is . . . , I live in . . ." As we drove, this kind man, this complete stranger, downloaded to me all the key details of his life should I, just a random passenger, have to pretend he was my brother. It was so absurd. But the driver's actions were another reminder to me that whatever those in power threw at the ordinary men and women of my nation, Afghan values of decency and kindness prevailed.

They had taken Hamid to the intelligence agency office, a building in the center of town, close to the Ministry of the Interior. I don't know how much money I gave the driver, but I know it was quite a lot. I was just so grateful he was prepared to help a woman despite the risk to himself in doing so. I thought if I paid him well he might just help another woman in the same circumstance. I went to the gate but they refused me entry. Now I took a massive risk. I lied to the Taliban at the gate. I told them that the other Taliban had arrested me but I couldn't go with the men in their vehicle, and so they had ordered me to come into the building. I said if they didn't let me in they'd be blamed. They let me in.

Once inside the main gate I found the prison building. Hamid was standing there, surrounded by two Talibs. Hamid was barely reacting, and I think he was in shock. One moment he was dashing home with chocolates for his new wife, the next he had been arrested. I ran over and grabbed Hamid's hand. I looked directly at the Talibs through my burqa and spoke: "Look, look at my hands. This is bridal henna. You are talking about Islam but you do not act as Muslims. We are just married. If you put him in prison I have no more *muharram*. How should I live? How should I survive? I have nobody to do shopping, to take care of me. I am just a young girl. I am helpless."

I was hoping that I could appeal to their sympathy and that they would let him go. But these were men who remained unmoved by the pleas of a mere woman. They ignored me and they walked Hamid to another gate, with me following, still holding his hand and still pleading.

When they opened the gate my heart sank as I could see hundreds of prisoners inside. Some were handcuffed, some were bound, others were standing, all were crammed into a central stinking courtyard. One of the Talibs took Hamid's other hand. We'd started our new life, it had just begun, and now they were taking him away from me, tearing us apart. I was terrified that they would just execute him with no trial. They had arrested him without charge, so it was entirely possible. I was holding on tight and not letting go. I was begging: "I'm coming too. How can I go alone? I am a woman, I cannot live alone outside. You are a Muslim, how can you do this?"

The Talib answered me in Pashto; he spoke crudely, with the accent of an uneducated village man. "Shut up woman, you talk too much." Then the man pushed me hard, so hard that I fell. I was still wearing my high heels and a fancy dress. It was less than an hour ago that we'd been receiving guests. I fell over into a puddle of stinking water, and Hamid turned his head to try and help me up, but the Talib pushed him in the opposite direction, inside the gates. My last glimpse of my husband was as I struggled to stand up and the gates closed.

With Hamid behind the gates, my thoughts turned to my brother. It was him they had come to arrest. Was he safe? Where was he?

I had no money left for another taxi so I ran as fast as I could in heels across the city and back to my brother's apartment. His wife was there and she told me he was hiding in different relatives' houses. For the past three days he'd been changing places every night so as not to be discovered. Right now she told me he was in Karte Seh, an area west of Kabul that had been badly destroyed during the civil war. I couldn't do anything for Hamid now but I could still try to help my brother.

I went to my relative's house and entered the house rudely. I didn't stop to say salaam or greet the family. I just needed to see my brother with my own eyes. The couple who owned the house are both professors. The husband is a professor at the Faculty of Economics at Kabul University and the wife was a teacher. They had no children. Because female teachers had been banned from working, she was one of the several brave Afghan women who took great personal risks secretly running a school from home.

The room had no sofa, just lots of cushions lining the walls. My brother Mirshakay was lying on a mattress, facing the wall. When he saw me his face registered alarm. It was the first time he'd seen me since my wedding day, when he'd hugged me and wept as I went to my new life. Now we had entered chaos again.

Very quickly I told him the whole story about Hamid and how they were searching for him now. It wasn't safe for him here, they would be searching all of our relatives' houses one after the other. It wasn't safe to take a taxi either. There were Taliban checkpoints everywhere and if they stopped us they might have my brother's photo and recognize him.

We left the house and started to walk. I was still in the blasted heels and my feet were killing me.

This was the first time I'd worn a burqa to walk such a long distance. I was never very good at walking in it anyway, but in heels and with such anxiety it was even worse. I stumbled over what felt like every stone and crack in the pavement. We walked out of the city toward the outer suburbs. We didn't have anywhere specific to go, but we had limited choices. Somewhere too public or central and there would be checkpoints; in the outer suburbs there would be buildings we could hide behind but not so many people. So we headed out. As we walked we chatted. My brother asked me about Hamid, about whether he had met my expectations as a husband. In some ways I was happy to tell my brother that yes, indeed, Hamid had and I was right to marry him.

I told him how Hamid and I had discussed where we would live, whether we should leave Afghanistan. Hamid had suggested a new life in Pakistan. But I'd told him I couldn't; I would not leave while my brother was still in Kabul. Then we'd discussed moving back to Faizabad, the capital city of Badakhshan province, and the place I had first gone to school. Badakhshan was not controlled by the Taliban. My sisters were there and Hamid's family was there, and we both missed the region. So that had been our plan. We would move back to the countryside, where I could teach and Hamid could run his business.

Telling my brother these plans was more painful than the weeping blisters that now coated my heels. All those newlywed dreams and plans were now in ruins.

After fours hours of aimless walking we hailed a taxi. I remembered one of Hamid's relatives, a lady who lived alone with her son. I didn't know the exact address but knew it was fourth Makrorian, near where Hamid and I lived. On the way we passed a checkpoint. We sat inside the car, terrified they would wind the window down and see my brother, but we were lucky. They waved the car past without looking inside.

My brother had met this woman when Hamid's relatives had come to ask for my hand in marriage and she was among them. He had not warmed to her. He said she wore too much makeup and her nails were too long. In Mirshakay's view that was the sign of a lazy woman. But now he had to throw himself on her mercy. I asked around and was pointed to her apartment. I quickly explained the situation and asked if she could prepare a room for my brother for one night. She said yes but she wasn't happy. She was understandably scared—if she had been caught sheltering a non-blood relative she would have been arrested and taken to the Ministry of Vice and Virtue. I felt awful putting her in that position but I had no choice.

I left my brother there and walked home. By the time I reached the house my feet felt like they were on fire, sweat caked my eyes and ears, and my hair was like a mattress of caked grease on my head. I threw the wretched burqa up and off my head, ran into the bedroom, and wailed with frustration.

Dear Shuhra and Shaharzad,

Loss is one of the hardest things for any human being to bear.

But loss of those we love is a part of life and a part of growing and no one can be protected from it. Perhaps you are reading this letter because I've been killed and you've lost me. We know one day that will happen, we've discussed this and I want you to be prepared for this inevitability.

Losing a home, as we did many times during the war, is also a horrible thing. Losing a home is hardest on children. It's something that has happened to millions of poor children in Afghanistan. Be aware of how lucky you are to have a house with a warm fire, a nice soft bed to sleep in, a lamp to read by, and a table to do your schoolwork on. I know it doesn't sound like much, but not all children have this.

But perhaps the worst thing that can happen to any woman is to lose yourself. To lose sense of who and what you are or to lose sight of your dreams is one of the saddest things.

These last three are not inevitable life losses but are forced on us by those who don't want us to dream or succeed. I pray you will never lose your dreams.

With love,
Your mother

FOURTEEN

THE DARKNESS
PERVADES

I was half mad with worry and fear. My brain was racing, thinking of anyone who might be able to help me. All night I barely slept, trying desperately to think of a plan.

In the morning as I stood in front of the mirror brushing my teeth, an idea came to me.

I remembered a friend who told me she had been teaching embroidery to the wife of a Taliban official. I threw on the burqa and ran to her house. She listened, wide-eyed with shock and sympathy, as I recounted what had happened to Hamid. We didn't know if it would do any good, but she said she would take me to their house and make the necessary introductions. We walked there together across the eerily quiet roads of this once bustling city. A few cars and taxis spluttered noisily into life, the early morning sun dancing in the dust of empty street stalls and boarded-up shops. I caught my reflection in the grimy window of an empty photography shop. I saw a dejected-looking woman with hunched shoulders in a blue burqa. For a second I didn't recognize it was me looking back at myself. The burqa had stripped me of so much identity I didn't even know myself.

Startled by the strangeness of that sensation I peered into the shop. It was long deserted. Faded photographs lined the walls, young men posing next to backdrops of waterfalls and posing like Bollywood actors; babies holding aloft balloons, smiling toothlessly at the parents who would have been standing just behind the camera trying to make them laugh; little girls in lacy dresses and ankle socks grinning shyly; brides in white veils standing proudly next to besuited husbands. I stared at the images, wondering what had happened to all those smiling faces. Who were they? And where were they now? By the time Taliban rule came to Afghanistan a third of our original population of 18 million was dead, killed in the fighting. Another third were refugees overseas. Only 6 million of the original 18 million remained. Were all the faces I was staring at dead? And where was the owner? All photography was now banned by law of the Taliban. With his livelihood gone he might have just closed the door and found another way to survive. Or he may have continued to work in secret, breaking the Taliban law. He could be in prison right now. With Hamid. The thought of the mystery photography studio owner lying next to Hamid in a cell brought me back to reality. My friend touched my arm gently and we walked on until we reached the Talib's house. He lived in a gated apartment block. A little boy played outside the front door. A scent of boiled mutton wafted out.

The man was there with his wife, a pleasant woman with green eyes who seemed to share her husband's sympathies for our plight. They welcomed us into their home and gave us hot green tea. He said he would try to help and he would go and make enquiries as soon as the official offices opened that morning. I was frustrated, but not ungrateful. I was surprised that a Taliban, any Taliban, could show humanity. This man was trying to help me when he didn't know me and didn't have to do so. That man changed my thinking about many Taliban. I realized that just because he didn't share my ideals or my politics didn't necessarily make him a terrible person. Many Afghan men aligned with the Taliban because of a shared ethnicity and culture, a sense of shared geography, or just out of economic necessity. It was the same then as it is today. If the Taliban pays a salary in a village with no jobs, what is a poor man to do? And of course many Afghan men, particularly in the southern cities like Kandahar or Helmand, agree with the more hardline aspects of Islamic culture. While I disagree with such, I have always had a strong understanding and respect for the many different views, ethnic groups, languages, and cultures that make up Afghanistan. Not many people know that over 30 languages are spoken across the country. For me that diversity is our strength. Or at least it is a strength during peaceful times. In wartime those ethnic divisions are our greatest weakness and the main reason people murder each other senselessly.

As we left the Talib's house he kindly walked us to the gates of the apart-ment block, but he made it clear he wasn't sure he could do much. On the walk home I began to prepare myself for the worst: news of Hamid's execu-tion, or a life sentence based on false charges. I didn't want to think about it, but I knew I had to be ready to face what was very likely to be bad news. I tried not to think of Hamid being dragged, hands tied, into the prison courtyard to be shot. Or lying in a filthy, freezing prison cell, emaciated; slowly going mad with hunger and cold. The thought of it was enough to drive me insane, too.

I arrived home, preoccupied with my tortuous thoughts, when a familiar face emerged from the bathroom.

There Hamid stood. Water was still glistening on his hollow cheeks, drop-lets hanging off his beard.

I thought I was dreaming. Or that I'd lost my mind.

My husband was standing in the hallway smiling at me as if it was the most normal thing in the world. He moved toward me uttering my name, his weak legs faltering beneath him. I rushed to him, embracing his skinny frame before he could fall. His arms were like sticks around me, bony and thin. Their normal masculine strength had been stolen by the abuse meted out by his jail-ers. The unexpected emotion of his sudden appearance was too much for us to bear and we both sobbed with relief. Hamid, my Hamid, was home.

I made him some breakfast of eggs and sweet tea, and he lay down to rest. I was exhausted from the rollercoaster of emotion but I had no time to rest myself. Without warning they had chosen to release Hamid. But now that he was released they would surely renew their attempts to imprison my brother. We had to find another house in which to hide him. Fast.

I remembered a woman who used to go to my English class. She lived nearby, only a few blocks away. She was a very tough lady. She had a bad leg, which had made it very hard for her to walk, and since her husband died she struggled to take care of her two daughters. They weren't a political fam-ily, but were just ordinary people trying to survive in the craziness that had become Kabul. No one would look for Mirshakay there. I knew their house would be a perfect place for him to lie low until we could work out a way to get him out of the country. I put my burqa on and ran to her house.

It was a very modest home, made all the worse by the shortages of the war. A few spartan rugs lay on the living room floor. There were very few luxuries, and I guessed that what few they had possessed were long since sold to buy rice, cooking oil, and gas to fuel the stove. The woman limped around her living room, ushering me to take a seat as she ordered her oldest daughter to make tea for us. I explained that I wanted my brother to stay with her but that it might be dangerous for her if the Taliban caught him there. Her tone immediately became a little offended. Not that she was angry that I should come into her living room and make such an outrageous request, but rather, in a very Afghan way, she was angry that such a request was even necessary. Of course he could stay—what a silly question!

I finished my tea and rushed to collect Mirshakay. We gathered a few clothes and some extra food together—I knew the lady would probably feign offense if I took food, but she was already taking a great risk hiding my brother. An extra mouth to feed would stretch her meager resources to the limit. We returned to the lady's house. It was imperative I went with my brother—not because he didn't know the way, but rather because the surest way to arouse suspicion would have been for a strange man to enter the house alone. A man and a woman in a burqa looks like a social visit, while a man by himself looks like a morality crime in progress and would surely set tongues wagging locally, which would trigger a visit from the Taliban.

The woman and her family were very kind to Mirshakay and I think he was able to relax a little. He stayed in that house for ten days. After that we decided things had cooled down enough for him to move back to my house. It was still too dangerous for him to move home with his family. As it was the Taliban harassed his wife often, dropping by uninvited and announced, threatening her with quiet voices of menace: "Where is your husband? When did you last speak to him? Tell us." He was a hunted man and they watched for him daily.

In the end his wife became so scared she also moved into my house.

Hamid and I were still newlyweds—we should have been enjoying our new life together, but I was so busy running the house that it was hard for us to snatch more than a few moments of quiet together. I suppose young wives all over the planet have romantic ideas of how those first few months of marriage will be, but for me, and I think for a lot of other women, they soon discover that the realities of adult life begin to overtake the girlish notions of marital bliss. At first I was quite resentful of the intrusion on what was supposed to be one of the happiest periods of my life, but mostly the resentment was short-lived and my sense of duty would take over. Also, this was my brother, whom I loved dearly. I would remember how kind he had been to me as a child, and how much of an influence he had on my life. In those moments I would feel guilty at such selfish thoughts. Now was my time to take care of him and his family. I knew he would do the same for me, no matter what the risks or hardships.

Mirshakay was determined to flee Afghanistan. It was the only way to guarantee his safety, even though it meant a life of uncertainty as a refugee abroad. For the next three months he didn't trim his beard, but instead he let it grow long, thick, and dark. After a while we barely recognized him. We prayed the Taliban wouldn't recognize him either.

The plan was to get a taxi to Torkham, the busiest border town into Pakistan. It's close to the famous Khyber Pass and lies on the edge of Pakistan's Federally Administered Tribal Areas, a region ruled by tribal elders where Islamabad doesn't have any great measure of control. Most of the people who live in that region are Pashtu, Afghanistan's largest ethnic group.

But the Pashtu people of this border region are also famous for their wonderful hospitality. They are people who would die for you if you were their guest, but kill you without regret if you offend them. Historically Pashtu occupy an area encompassing Southern Afghanistan and Northern Pakistan, an area known as Pashtunwali. For centuries the Pashtu have come and gone freely over this frontier. To them, the border is merely a line on a map, not a reality. In Afghanistan the border between Afghanistan and Pakistan has still never been formally recognized. It's known as the Durand line, and is even today one of the greatest tensions between the Pakistan and Afghanistan governments. The Afghans refuse to recognize the line. The foreign forces, the Americans, and NATO, who are fighting Al Qaida, claim this loose border is home to thousands of Al Qaida fighters. Pakistan denies this, but does little to control fundamentalism in the area.

The Pashtu codes of honor are so strong that even when American bomber planes have pounded the area looking for Bin Laden or his sympathizers, the local villagers refuse to reveal their whereabouts. Bombs may rain down on the villages but "honored guests" will never be betrayed. I realize it is hard for people in the West to understand this. But the locals simply cannot and will not change. These ancient codes of honor are what Pashtunwali is founded upon and how it operates. The codes create an unbreakable rule book and a way of life that has remained unchanged in hundreds of years and is as immovable as the jagged mountains. They far outweigh any laws or commands laid down by formal governments. To go there is to step back in time 500 years. Understand that, and you begin to understand the area. Fail to understand that, as successive governments and foreign forces have done, and you will always be defeated.

In the year we were planning my brother's escape, 1997, Afghans didn't need a visa to enter Pakistan across the main border crossing, unlike nowadays. My brother was hoping he could slip across the border unnoticed amid the noisy chaos of trucks, traders, and travelers that flocked through Torkham on an hourly basis.

Mirshakay had arranged for a taxi to come collect him early in the morning. I was rushing around helping him get ready to leave—organizing food for the journey, some naan bread and hard-boiled eggs to sustain him, while his wife packed his suitcase. There was a knock at the door and before I had time to stop and think I opened it wide, expecting to see the driver. Two black turbans stood in the doorway—Taliban. They pushed their way into the apartment, waving their guns. Everybody froze. There was no time to react, and nowhere to hide. We exchanged looks—this was it—we were caught.

The two men were openly triumphant as they grabbed my brother, forcing him to the floor. The larger of the pair—both looked like they were only in their twenties—jammed his knee hard into the small of my brother's back, making him yelp with pain. The other, in an act of barely concealed spite, grabbed Hamid by the neck and pushed his head toward the living room floor. Hamid was still very weak from his time in prison and the Talib pushed him around like a ragdoll. They were laughing and jeered at my sister-in-law and myself as they dragged and shoved our men into the hall and down to their pickup truck. As they went my brother shouted at me not to follow them and to stay at home. Even in a moment as bleak and desperate as this, his male pride could not allow the disgrace of a woman coming to the jail to try to get him out.

At the police station my brother managed to persuade a guard to smuggle a note to the family. It contained instructions for us contact an old colleague of my brother's who held a senior position at the Ministry of Defense during the communist years and was now working for the Taliban government. In communist times this man had been a general, now he was a senior

Taliban military advisor. My brother hoped this man might be able to pull some strings to get both he and Hamid out. The note included an address for an apartment near the airport.

Once again, it was a brutal waiting game. For once my strength left me and I lay on the bed for two days, paralyzed by frustration and fear. Hamid had been taken from me again. But this time it was not only me he'd left behind. It was also our unborn child.

Three days earlier I had learned I was pregnant. Like many new mothers I had my suspicions when I started being very ill and vomiting in the mornings. A visit to the doctor confirmed what I had suspected. Hamid and I were delighted, of course. But the excitement we felt was tempered by the turmoil in our lives. There are perhaps few things as worrying as being a first-time mother in a time of war. In war everyday survival is a battle in itself and only the strongest survive. Was it fair to bring a helpless infant into that kind of hell? Perhaps not.

But I also knew that life goes on despite the bullets and bombs. And in some ways the desire to celebrate life and creation, however bad the circumstances, is an intrinsic part of the human spirit. I was scared, yes, but I also thought it would be wonderful to have something as precious and positive as a newborn child to focus on.

But despite the joy I felt, it was clear from the outset that this was not going to be an easy pregnancy. Afghanistan has one of the highest maternal and infant mortality rates in the world. A lack of health resources and a cultural reluctance to openly talk about gynecological and pediatric care means doctors can be hard to find, and the few that do exist are badly trained. Families often resist seeking medical attention for a woman until there is absolutely no other choice and it's clear she will die otherwise. But by then it's often too late to save either the child or the mother. Working in these conditions takes great skill, patience, and dedication. Some of Afghanistan's best doctors were women. I'm sure women everywhere feel more comfortable being treated for health issues of a personal nature by someone of their own gender. For a long time I wanted to qualify as a doctor myself and join their ranks.

However, the Taliban had banned women from working; a decree that completely depleted Afghanistan's medical staff. And then in a further twist of insane cruelty, they banned male doctors from treating women. Even for a common cold a male doctor was not allowed to prescribe a female so much as an aspirin. So women doctors weren't allowed to work and male doctors weren't allowed to treat females. The result? Hundreds of women died unnecessary deaths during Taliban rule. They died because they caught the flu, because they had an untreated bacterial infection, because they had blood poisoning, or a fever, or a broken bone, or because they were pregnant. They died for no sane reason, but simply because these brutal men who ran the country thought a woman's life was as worthless as a fly's. These men who claimed to be men of God had no sanctity for one of God's greatest creations—woman.

My morning sickness was really bad. And it wasn't just limited to the first few hours of the day. I can joke about it now, but at the time, trying not to vomit into the face covering of my burqa was no laughing matter. I hope no other young mother ever has to learn to pull up the hood of their garment, tilt their head forward and aim for the gap between their feet—all while fighting the natural urge to drop to their knees.

For three months I vomited most of what I ate—it was a burden I could have done without. Especially on the day when I took my brother's letter and set off to find the house of his former colleague who was now a Taliban. My brother knew it was a long shot asking this man for help, but long shots were all we could cling onto right now.

I was feeling very sorry for myself when I entered that house. But as my eyes adjusted to the gloom I realized I still had an enormous amount to be thankful for. Sadly, most Afghan people are desperately poor, but they are also immensely proud, taking pride in their home however simple it is, and always offering food, tea, and sweets to guests. Perhaps that is why I was so shocked by the terrible state of the living room. The floors were filthy and had clearly not been swept or washed in a long time. I wanted to take the carpets outside and give them a good dusting. The walls needed wiping and I wanted to throw the windows open wide and let in some light and fresh air to clear the musty smell that filled the house. The lady of the house greeted me. That was when I realized she was just a very simple woman who had never been taught any better. Even her ability to greet a guest into her home was stilted and awkward, from her speech to her manners to the very way she carried herself. Looking around the room I scanned a row of dirty faces, her children and other members of the extended family, each face more grubby than the next. That at least explained the smell.

I couldn't find anywhere clean to sit, but having found the least dirty spot I squatted down. I felt desperately nauseous. I kept my burqa on even though I was indoors and prepared for a long wait. I was becoming familiar with dealing with the Taliban now. The first rule was patience. I was told the man would speak to me in 20 minutes, but I was prepared to wait all day if necessary. It seems strange now, but I was far less worried about Hamid than before. The fact that he was in prison with my brother and not alone was a big comfort. I knew they would both draw a lot of strength from each other, no matter what terrible things were being done to them.

I sat, waiting, idly watching the woman clean the river of black and green snot that was oozing out of a young boy's nose. We made small talk, but it was difficult. I found it hard to be civil sitting there in a filthy room, in a filthy house, waiting for a filthy man who is now one of the key security advisors of my country's government. What sort of nation can you create when even your own home is filthy and the women and children who live there are trapped in ignorance? What hope for Afghanistan, I thought, while these ignorant uneducated people are in power? And then I shivered with horror. The realization had come to me. If this was the family living room of a senior Taliban advisor, then what must the Taliban prisons be like?

When the man finally appeared he looked rough and disheveled like the rest of his family, not the man of power and authority I had expected. I explained the situation of how Hamid and my brother came to be in jail. The man was not unpleasant and told me he remembered my brother well. He listened patiently and made assurances that he would get them released. He asked me if I would wait while he made some phone calls in private, then excused himself. I made myself as comfortable as I could on the dirty floor and sat back to wait. The smell had gone now. My nose must have become accustomed to it.

When the man eventually returned the news was not good. With a sigh he looked at his filthy hands and told me it would take time to get them out. He promised he would keep monitoring the situation and would contact me with any news. His tone had the sort of half-baked sincerity of someone who felt obliged to help, but did not really want to, and certainly was not willing to go to any great lengths to do so. This worried me. I walked home dejected. Hamid was still so very weak. He'd only just begun to recover from his first incarceration. The air was getting cold and crisp now. We were well into autumn and the winter snow was already settling in the mountains around the city. Soon Kabul itself would be covered with snow and temperatures would drop as low as 5 degrees Fahrenheit. I could imagine Hamid and my brother huddling together for warmth on the freezing prison courtyard, each of them only wearing the clothes they were arrested in. No warm jacket, no thermal vests, no woolly socks. I bit my lip hard to stop the tears flowing as I thought of Hamid's toes freezing and turning blue. I didn't know how much more my husband's fragile body could take. His mind was a fortress of strength and intelligence and could sustain whatever tortures they threw at him. But every person has a physical breaking point. In the freezing grip of the night air, air so cold it hurts to catch your breath, I knew Hamid's breaking point would be fast approaching.

Early the next morning I was in my usual position—doubled over the toilet being violently ill. But today my morning sickness seemed to have another cause. It had snowed in the night. As I dashed from my bed to the bathroom I glanced out a window to see the rooftops below covered in a sparkling white fresh blanket. Had Hamid and my brother stood all night in the snow? Or were there two more dead bodies in the prison yard, fused together by the layer of ice that now covered them?

I dressed and hurried to the Talib's house, slipping and skidding along the icy streets that had turned into treacherous skating rinks. My burqa provided an extra layer of warmth, but it also left me struggling to make out the frozen contours of the road and limited my agility, so that each time my feet took off in a direction of their own choosing I would throw one arm out in front of me for balance and to break my fall, while the other went low around my waist, to protect my unborn child should I hit the ground.

Something had changed at the house when I arrived. The smell was still there, but I could see somebody had made an effort to sweep the floor, and the children's faces were smeared where a dirty cloth had been rubbed over them in an attempt to clean them. The man was different too. He smiled widely at me, showing blackened teeth.

"I want you to teach my children English," he said. It was a request, not an order. But not a request I had any choice to refuse.

"Of course," I said. "Perhaps they could come to my house. There is room for them to play and I can teach them better there."

This seemed to please him, which was good because I really didn't want to spend any longer in that home than was absolutely necessary. I needed to keep him happy, but part of me was also encouraged on a deeper level. If I could teach children such as these even a little something of life beyond these grubby walls then perhaps there was hope for my country after all.

I left the house feeling optimistic. The man had spoken little of my beloved prisoners, but the talk of English lessons and the changes I saw in the house were all the encouragement I needed to know that he was going to help us.

Later that night a fist banged on my apartment door. I cracked it open, cautiously. Hairy knuckles shoved it back hard into my forehead and I reeled backward. Two dark eyes beneath heavy brows and a black turban stared hard at me. But I wasn't afraid. In fact I barely noticed the Talib's face, because standing next to the Talib were Hamid and Mirshakay. He shoved them both hard through the doorway, like a spoiled child who had been forced to share his toys. He muttered some impotent threats as I closed the door on his face and launched myself into Hamid's arms. My sister-in-law squealed her way across the living room and flung herself against her own husband. The former communist general-turned-Taliban with the filthy children had in fact been as good as his word.

We wasted no time. A taxi was arranged—it would pick us up the following morning. We had to get to Pakistan. The men were free, but it was not enough to rely on the whims or good graces of the Taliban. They were just as likely to change their mind in a heartbeat and re-arrest them. That was a risk we couldn't take.

The next morning we squeezed into the waiting vehicle. Hamid, myself, my brother and his wife and their baby. Hamid sat on one side of the back seat, I was crushed next to him in my burqa, next to me was my brother, tucked in the middle where we hoped no one would recognize him, and his wife next to the other window. A family friend, yet another retired general, had kindly offered to help us. He was an ethnic Pashtu. He rode in the front passenger seat. If we ran into problems we hoped his stature as a general could help us, and failing that, his ethnicity would also lend some weight at both the Taliban checkpoints and once we got closer to the border. To travel with us was an act of pure generosity. It still amazes me when I think of all the friends and neighbors over the years who risked themselves helping us. It's one of the reasons my door is never closed to those who need my help today. My Islamic faith teaches that each good turn done to us must be repaid by doing another good turn.

The taxi driver chatted nervously, trying to assure us his taxi was sturdy and reliable. I wasn't convinced but Mirshakay had been insistent that we all go to Pakistan with him this time. And I agreed. After all the tensions of the previous weeks I felt I needed to get out of the country, even if it was just for a week. It was also a good opportunity for Hamid to get some medical attention. This second time in prison had left him even weaker. It was almost as if I could see his health deteriorating before my eyes. I was still suffering morning sickness and for most of the journey I carried a bowl beneath my burqa to vomit into.

It was a terrible journey. We were squashed and uncomfortable, and all of us were on edge, expecting at any moment to be stopped and detained at a Taliban checkpoint. The general was unflappable, keeping up a steady banter with the gunmen each time we encountered them. Being Pashtu—the same ethnic group as most of the Talibs—meant they were more relaxed when they heard their mother tongue being spoken in a familiar accent. His natural authority demanded respect, and even the bravado of the young Talibs wilted in the glare of the general's old soldier demeanor.

"You may pass, Uncle."

My heart heaved a sigh of relief each time I heard those words, but when we crossed the border at Torkham my spirits soared. The car erupted into laughter as we entered Pakistan. You could feel the freedom. The fearful oppression of the Taliban had been lifted. And with it, a huge weight was taken from each of us.

By 4 o'clock that afternoon we were in the southern Pakistani city of Peshawar. From Peshawar we boarded an overnight bus to Lahore, the ancient city of kings. There was my brother's house and a warm welcome from his first wife and her parents, who had been living there. That night we ate chappali kebab, a wonderful local dish of ground beef mixed with pomegranates and red chili, washed down with Coca-Cola. It tasted as divine as any meal I had ever eaten. It was the first meal I'd eaten in months that wasn't tainted by the poisonous coating of Taliban rule.

It was wonderful to be in Lahore. For the first time since our wedding Hamid and I were able to go out to cafes and relax and enjoy ourselves as a perfectly normal young married couple. Lahore is a truly beautiful place of centuries-old tiled mosques and winding bazaars. Hamid and I walked around for hours, sightseeing and simply enjoying walking next to each other and breathing the same air.

The city was so functional and clean after the turmoil of Kabul. Where much of my city's great buildings had been destroyed in the civil war, in Lahore I marveled at the historic architecture. Between the sixteenth and eighteenth centuries Lahore was ruled by the Mughals—an Islamic Indian dynasty of emperors who controlled much of the Asian subcontinent. The Mughals were famous builders, for example, the Taj Mahal was built by the Mughal emperor Shah Jahan. And in Lahore they created many of the city's most notable landmarks, including the spectacular Lahore Fort and the Shalimar Gardens, both of which are now UNESCO World Heritage sites. I was three months pregnant by that stage and still not feeling very well. Hamid was also fragile from his two terms of brutal treatment by the Taliban. But for a few short days we drew emotional and physical strength from the tranquility of Lahore. Tranquil is an odd word to use to describe a bustling Pakistani city of almost five million people, but tranquil is how it felt after all we had been through.

After a week in Lahore we got word that our Afghan president Rabbani was in Peshawar. He had been deposed by the Taliban, but as far as we, and the rest of the world, were concerned, he was still Afghanistan's legitimate leader. Rabbani's ambassador still represented Afghanistan in the United Nation's General Assembly. Only Saudi Arabia and Pakistan had recognized the Taliban as the official government. My brother had once worked for Rabbani at the interior ministry and knew him well. On arrival in Peshawar he made contact, and he and Hamid were invited to Peshawar to meet with the president. They went readily, wanting to pay their respects and to hear our president's plans for regaining control of our country.

Burhanuddin Rabbani, like my family, was from Badakhshan. He and my father had been friends and occasional rivals, and we respected him deeply. He had been a key voice against the rise of communism in Afghanistan during the 1950s and 1960s, and during the Soviet occupation he organized military and political resistance from Pakistan.

When President Najibullah fell from power after the communists were defeated, Rabbani was elected to replace him. Most recently, Rabbani was tasked by current Afghan president Karzai to lead peace talks with the Taliban.

But in September 2011 he was killed by a suicide bomber with explosives hidden in a turban. The mujahideen government of the time was very factional and divided. These divides then pitted Rabbani and Ahmed Shah Massoud's forces against those of Generals Dostum and Hekmatyar, and launched the civil war.

There were a lot of people at Rabbani's compound, and both my brother and Hamid returned from their meeting very excited. They were convinced Rabbani was the key to a stable Afghanistan—although with the Taliban firmly in control it was hard even for Rabbani himself to envisage how that might happen. I was pleased by their sense of optimism. It was infectious, and from the safety and calm of Lahore I found myself entertaining thoughts that perhaps all was not lost for Afghanistan.

We were all so excited by the prospect of Rabbani regaining his rightful role of president that Hamid and I decided, almost on the spot, that we should return to Kabul immediately. Apart from our newfound sense of optimism, Hamid's widowed sister was alone in Kabul with her children and Hamid and I wanted to be there to support her. My brother decided it was too risky to return and that he would stay in his house in Peshawar. Leaving my brother and his wives was awful because I had no idea when or if I might see them again. But I was a married woman now and my rightful place was with my husband.

Winter was closing in, and the snow was getting heavier. As we retraced our journey back to Kabul the landscape through the high mountains of the Khyber Pass had become white and crisp. Perhaps the jagged rocks were like the Taliban, and the fresh snow was a new beginning for Afghanistan—covering their hard, unforgiving ways. I certainly hoped so.

Hamid and I crossed back into Afghanistan without incident and were soon back in our apartment in Kabul. A week away had refreshed me enough to enjoy being in my homeland again. Even under Taliban rule, I never lost my patriotism. This was my Kabul, my Afghanistan.

It was the beginning of Ramadan, and like all observant Muslims we fasted between sunrise and sunset. We were up before dawn for sahaar, the substantial breakfast eaten while still dark to sustain us through the day's fasting until after sunset. Typically, we would eat early and then go back to sleep for a little while before morning prayers.

Hamid and I had just returned to bed when there was a knocking at the door. Hamid went to answer it—we thought it was a neighbor coming to ask a favor or something similar. I heard voices, then Hamid's footsteps on the floor as he came back to the bedroom. His face was ashen gray and he looked like he was going to be sick. He asked me for his coat. The Taliban were at our door. They had a car waiting for him outside. Hamid had no choice but to go with them. I wanted to rush to the door with him, to beg the Talibs to leave him alone, to leave us alone. We had come back to Kabul in the hope we might have an ordinary peaceful existence. And now here they were taking him away again.

Hamid was his usual dignified self. He gently ordered me to stay in the bedroom. I was dressed in my nightgown and not properly attired to be pleading with strange men, even on the doorstep of my own home at 5 o'clock in the morning. It wasn't clear what they wanted with Hamid. There were no charges. They just told him his presence was required and he was to go with them. I heard the door bang closed. I lay back on the pillows sobbing, clutching the unborn child in my belly, and once again wondering what would become of us.

I knew of a man from my own province of Badakhshan who now worked with the Taliban. I found his address in an old notebook. He had a job in Puli Charkhi Prison. Built in the 1970s, it was notorious for the brutal torture of inmates during the Soviet occupation. I didn't know where the Taliban had taken Hamid, but we were running out of people who might help us. You can really only ask someone to intervene once on your behalf or it becomes too dangerous for them, so it was impossible to go back to any of the people who had helped us previously.

I didn't know this man very well, but I hoped the fact that we were from the same region and that he knew who my father might make him more sensitive to my pleas. Donning my burqa, I slipped into the cold morning air and went in search of him.

Puli Charkhi is about six miles outside of Kabul. I walked out of the city suburbs as they faded away into small villages and then nothing but a few mud houses here and then only dusty desert tracks. It is not a place a woman should be walking alone, and especially not in those days. The tracks appear to lead to nowhere, then suddenly the prison rises out of the earth, razor wire and the guards' bayonets glinting in the sunlight. The walls have a medieval feel, imposing stone watchtowers and rough, mud-plastered walls. It is a terrifying place known as the Alcatraz of Afghanistan because escape is impossible. I entered the guard house and explained the situation, asking for an audience with the man from Badakhshan. A guard went away to ask. He returned with a one word answer. "No."

"What kind of Badakhshani was he?" I asked back. Didn't he have any *gharor* (pride) that he would not even allow a wife to ask about her missing husband?

I hoped the accusation might sting the man into action. I was a newly married Muslim woman, and as such it is considered culturally inappropriate that I should be left alone without any support. The guards looked ashamed and promised to take the message back to their boss. He still refused to see me. I could see why. I had chastised him in front of his men and he probably felt humiliated. I was told to go home and follow up my enquiries by coming back a few days later.

I walked all the way home again on an empty thirsty belly with a kicking baby, and still with no idea about where they had taken my husband.

I got home at lunchtime in a foul mood. One of Hamid's elderly relatives had died recently, and my sister-in-law and I were expected to attend to pay our condolences. I really didn't want to go, but family duty and honor dictated that I must. I don't remember much of the afternoon. My mind was wrapped up with worry about Hamid. As I sat quietly on a carpet lost in my own thoughts, an elderly man approached me. News of Hamid's arrest had spread quickly, even though it was only a few hours since his detention. The old man's dark eyes conveyed sympathy, and his long gray beard danced as he whispered to me that he had news of Hamid's whereabouts. According to one of his relatives—he didn't offer who or how this person came by the information—my husband was being held by the Intelligence Service Number 3. They were the most dangerous of all the intelligence wings. Their job was to root out dissenting political voices and make them go away. I was terrified for Hamid, but at least I knew now where he was.

Every day for a week I went to the intelligence offices and every day was turned away by sneering guards. On the seventh day I was allowed inside to see my husband. His naturally slim frame was gaunt and hunched. He had been repeatedly beaten and was in too much pain to strand up straight. His dark features were silhouetted against his unnaturally white skin, his eyes sunken and cheekbones protruding.

We sat at a rough wooden table and whispered to each other. I tried to hug him, but a Taliban prison is no place for affection, even between a husband and wife. He told me they had forced him to stand outside all night in the snow, while by day he endured endless interrogations and beatings. They asked him: "Why did you go and see Rabbani? What was the purpose of the meeting? What is your connection with Rabbani?"

President Rabbani was guarded by Pakistani security agents from the ISI—Inter-Services Intelligence. It was long suspected many of the agents had sympathies with the Taliban, but here was elegant proof. The Pakistani agents had clearly been feeding the Taliban the names of Rabbani's visitors, including Hamid, and presumably my brother as well.

As I was leaving the prison a senior Talib came to me and asked: "How much is your husband's release worth? $2,500? $5,000?"

They obviously knew by now Hamid was not political. They could beat him all day and all night and he wouldn't tell them anything. He couldn't because he didn't know anything. But his detention still created an opportunity for them to profit. I would have given them whatever I had but I didn't have any money. We weren't that rich, not cash rich anyway. And even if we could arrange finances from Pakistan via my brother, the Taliban had effectively ruined the banking system, so transferring money or borrowing large amounts of cash was now impossible. I just could not pay it. Something I will forever feel guilty about.

Hamid was now getting very sick from all the abuse he was suffering. He was half starved and frozen to death. What started as a cold entered his lungs and became more and more serious. The lethal combination of his failing immunity and being in close proximity to a lot of other very sick prisoners without anywhere to wash meant he developed tuberculosis.

I prepared a letter pleading for his release and planned to give it to the executive board of the Intelligence Service. In it I told them about Hamid's innocence, and the fact he now carried a communicable disease that threatened the health of the other prisoners. I delivered it myself to the office of a career bureaucrat. He wasn't a Talib—but rather just an ordinary bespectacled man seemingly a little bemused and baffled by his latest masters. Given his age I imagine he'd served the Russians, the mujahideen, and now the Taliban. Different bosses for the different ages of Afghanistan.

He held out his hand and took the letter from me and I burst out the story of Hamid, his illness, and our recent marriage. I wanted to gain his sympathy so that he might present the letter to the board with greater urgency.

He peered through his glasses as I stood on the other side of the partition in my burqa. He looked down at the letter, saying: "Sister, who wrote this letter for you?"

"I did," I said. "I am a medical student and just want to get my sick husband out of prison."

"Your husband is lucky," he said. "He has a wife who cares for him and is educated. But sister, what if they put me in prison? Who will take care of me? My wife is not educated; who would write the letters for me?"

He let out a long dramatic sigh and put the letter underneath a pile of other letters, probably written by other desperate relatives. "Go now sister, I cannot promise. But I will do my best to take your letters to the executive."

With tears stinging my eyes I left his office. Hamid's life and liberty was just another letter underneath a hundred other letters. I knew it had little chance of being delivered by the bespectacled bureaucrat.

I walked home in the snow. As I climbed up the stairs to our apartment, I felt that my home without my husband was as empty as my stomach. As I entered the apartment, Hamid's sister Khadija ran to greet me, asking if I had any news about his release. I had no answer for her. I went straight to my bedroom and lay down trying to hold back the tears. I dozed off to sleep. Hours later, the sound of a mullah calling *iftar* (the evening meal that breaks the fast) woke me up. I lay back and listened: *Hai Alal falah, Hai Alal falah!* Feeling hungry, I got up and went to the other room, expecting to see Khadija and her children about to eat. But she was feeling as low as me and she had also slept the day away. No one had prepared any food. I felt a pang of guilt. This was Hamid's home, and I was his wife. In his absence, it fell to me to keep the home running and look after his family. After all, it was the fault of my family that he was in prison at all. I went out to buy some rice and a little meat and came back to cook it. Khadija came into the kitchen fussing over me, telling me I was pregnant and should rest. She took the knife from my hand and took over the job of cutting the onions. We continued to cook together in companionable silence. It was a cold winter night in Kabul, snow was falling thickly and the city was silent with both fear and boredom.

I turned to Khadija with tears in my eyes. "I'm so sorry, jan [dear]. I feel all I have done is bring trouble to your family. I wish poor Hamid had never wanted to marry me. I have brought all this pain on him."

She put down the knife, wiped away an onion tear and took my hand. "Well, Fawzia, he is a strong man. And prison will only make his character stronger. You should not be sorry, you should be proud of him. He is a political prisoner, not a criminal." This was the first time we had discussed the reasons why Hamid was in jail, and I was amazed she could be so calm and balanced about the situation. She had every right to be resentful of me and my family. Khadija has always been a woman I admire; she was strong, intelligent, and reasonable. I was so touched by her tone, I couldn't reply because the tears choked my throat. I carried on stirring the rice pot and tried to convey my thanks with a silent look.

She hugged me and then ordered me into the dining room to find a date or a piece of fruit to break my fast with, telling me I needed to put my baby's health first.

I went and sat alone in the dining room, memories of my childhood starting to flicker across my mind. Long forgotten and half hidden until now, they came to the surface because of my melancholy mood. I recalled *iftar* at the *hooli* back in the days when my father was alive. A traditional napkin, like a large tablecloth but for the floor, would be laid out in the center of the room. Local village women made the napkin by hand with delicately woven threads. It had the most beautiful vibrant colors, stripes of red and orange created by natural dyes made from mountain plants and flowers. Mattresses and cushions would be placed around the edge of the napkin, and everyone would sit cross-legged on them to eat.

The napkin would be piled high with nutritious and delicious fast-breaking foods such as *bolani* (a tasty flatbread filled with vegetables), *manto* (parcels of steamed mincemeat with onions and yogurt) and *qabuli pilau* (rice mixed with raisins, lentils, and carrots).

My elder sisters would all rush to prepare the meal, usually finishing minutes before the fast ended and the hungry hordes of family members descended. All the family would sit together (apart from my father who was either away or sitting with his guests)—all the wives and their children, my half brothers and sisters. We would sit and eat, talk, and laugh. I was only a very small girl then, but I used to love those moments. It was a time when everyone relaxed and shared stories of the day. My heart ached to think of those pre-war days when we were a whole family untouched by grief and loss. I missed my mother and my brothers and sisters so much. I yearned to be back there again, an innocent village child whose only preoccupation was stealing chocolates or dressing up in a pair of wooden shoes.

My thoughts were broken by Khadija entering the room with a plate of steaming *pilau*. I smiled gratefully at her. Her presence was a reminder that I wasn't alone: Hamid's family was also my family now. Khadija's children ran in to join us, and my heart gladdened as we all tucked in.

Every day, I tried to visit Hamid and on the rare occasions I did get to see him he put on a very brave face and pretended he was being well treated. He didn't want me to worry. But I could see the signs, whether it was the uncontrollable trembling that had developed in his hands or the bruises on his increasingly thin face. I pretended to believe him and tried to be a dutiful wife, knowing that to confront him with the evidence of his abuse would only make life for him even harder to bear. I think the pretense that he was hiding his ordeal from his young pregnant wife helped give him the strength to endure it. Instead we would spend those few precious moments together talking about the ordinary events of family life, as if he had just come back from a conference, or a sales meeting, or some other mundane event that husbands and wives everywhere take for granted every day. It was easier to pretend that this was just our ordinary life—as if nothing was strange, or scary, or out of place. Some people will tell you denial is wrong—perhaps it is—but when you are being tossed in the stormy seas of helpless despair, denial can become the tiny raft that you cling to madly. Sometimes denial is the only thing that keeps you afloat.

I decided to make another attempt to persuade the Badakhshani man who worked at Puli Charkhi jail to help us. After the long and tiring walk to get there, I was relieved when this time he invited me into his office. I told him that Hamid was innocent of any political crime, and that he was being tortured and would soon die if he wasn't released. But again it was to no avail. He said there was nothing he could do for us. I started to cry. He let out a long sigh, then reluctantly promised me he would try to talk to the guard in charge of Hamid's section of the prison.

It was a Friday afternoon, a day I could usually gain access to meet Hamid. Khadija put on her blue shuttlecock burqa and I the black Arab-style *niqab*, and we walked to the prison together.

As we waited at the gate, the guard went inside to call Hamid.

As he did so, he left the door open and I was able to peek inside the main building. I watched as a second young guard, barely out of his teens, washed his hands and feet for the ablutions required before Islamic prayers. The first guard approached him and the man asked in Pashto, "*Sa khabara da?* What is up?"

The guard replied, "*Hamid khaza raghili da.* Hamid's wife is here."

The young man put down his water pot and started to walk toward us. I turned away so they didn't see I had been watching.

Some other men walked past and I heard them speak in Urdu, the most widely spoken language in Pakistan. They weren't prisoners, and I can only assume they were Pakistani Taliban sympathizers working in our prisons. I took Khadija's hand, hoping the young man might have good news about Hamid's release. He walked straight up to us and asked, "*Hamid khaza chirta da?* Who is Hamid's wife?" I stepped forward, holding my *niqab* across my face with my left hand. "I am."

Without saying another word, the man bent down, picked up a stone from the ground and threw it at my head. I recoiled in shock.

"You woman. You complain to your Badakhshanis about us? Who are you to do this? Go, get out of here, woman." For a few seconds I was too shocked to move. I started to speak, to try to explain that I had only been trying to free my innocent husband. The man picked up a second stone and threw it again. It just missed my head, and as it did so I moved my hand protectively, giving the man a glimpse of my painted fingernails.

He sneered and spat at the ground. "Look at your nails! You are a Muslim yet you have the fingers of a whore."

The blood rushed to my cheeks in anger. I wanted to tell him that he had no business judging or commenting on another man's wife. I was a Muslim woman unrelated to him, so he had no right to talk about me. He was the bad Muslim, not me.

Khadija could read my thoughts and stepped forward to stop me. The man grabbed another stone and threw it. "Get out of here, woman." Khadija grabbed me and we half ran, half walked back to the gate. Once at a safe distance, I turned and said to her loudly, so they could hear me, "These men are not Muslims; they are not even human beings." The man waved another stone at me menacingly and then turned to go back inside, cursing and swearing with words no decent Muslim I know would ever use.

Then, the awful reality of what had just happened hit me: I had been insulted and my attempts to speak to the Badakhshani in Puli Charkhi had backfired badly, which would now make things even worse for Hamid.

I started to shake and cry loudly under my *niqab*. Khadija also cried. Luckily we managed to find a taxi driver who was prepared to break the rule against driving female non-relatives. I don't think I trusted my legs to walk; I was shaking too much from a combination of anger, fear, and pure humiliation. Once home, I threw myself on my bed and howled.

That evening, Khadija and I reached the awful decision that it was safer not to try to visit Hamid for a while. We feared it would only make things harder for him and lead to more beatings. The guards had decided his wife was an insolent whore for trying to protest his imprisonment and for wearing nail polish. I was furious with the Badakhshani from Puli Charkhi. I suspected that not only had he chosen not to help us, but he had deliberately caused trouble for us.

The fact was, I hadn't even complained to him of prison conditions. I had spoken only of Hamid's illness and his innocence.

That night, my last hopes for Hamid's release died.

For two weeks I didn't attempt to see him. I didn't want to be insulted or humiliated by those guards, and I feared that even if they did let me see him I'd break down and cry in front of him. The last thing he needed was to worry about my being upset. But by the following Friday, I could bear it no longer. I needed to see my husband.

I also needed to ask him something important. As a married woman, I needed his permission to travel and I had decided that I wanted to go to my brother's in Pakistan to give birth. I couldn't bear the thought of delivering my first baby in Kabul, where the Taliban had banned all female doctors from working and male doctors from treating women.

Khadija insisted on coming with me for safety, and as we approached the prison gates I was a bag of nerves. I wasn't very optimistic that they would let me see him. I stayed a few paces back, while Khadija approached the guard and asked for Hamid. He disappeared, then came back accompanied by the same young guard who had thrown stones at me. I kept quiet, and so did Khadija, expecting a rock to come flying at my head at any moment. He looked straight at me and ordered, "Come close, woman."

Slowly I inched forward, promising myself that if he threw another stone at me, I would throw it right back at him.

"Show me your left hand," he ordered. I said nothing and I didn't show him my hand, instead hiding them both under my *niqab*. The man was coarse and rude and, in my eyes, totally unfamiliar with the Afghan custom of showing politeness and manners at all times.

He laughed as I hid my hands and said, "I am telling you. Don't put nail polish on your fingers anymore. If you do, you are not a Muslim."

I glared at him through the safety of my covered face. He dared to tell me I wasn't a Muslim, but then permitted himself to comment on the makeup worn by another man's wife! "Why do you wear it? Tell me," he ordered.

I replied as calmly as I could. "We have been married for only four months. It is customary and cultural for a new bride to wear makeup and nice clothes for the first year of marriage. Surely as an Afghan man you know this?"

He laughed a mocking and guttural laugh, showing a hint of his yellow teeth as he did so. "I see. So do you want me to release your husband?"

I didn't know what to say. I assumed he was just mocking me. I answered, "What is his crime? He has committed no crime."

The guard shrugged his shoulders and said, "Go, and come back with a male relative. Bring a man who is prepared to show me evidence of property. If the man will use his property as a guarantee that your husband will not attempt to leave Kabul, then I will release him."

I didn't say a word but turned and ran out the gate as fast as my legs could carry me. Khadija ran after me. We didn't know if he meant it, but we knew we had to try. We stood looking at each other, two women standing on the streets of a male-dominated world gone mad. We didn't know who we could ask or what to do next. My brothers had all left Kabul, and Hamid's family were mostly living in Badakhshan.

Then I remembered a cousin who owned a shop. We ran across the streets to get there. We reached it, both panting and out of breath, only to find it closed. In our excitement, we had forgotten it was Friday, the day of prayer and rest.

I didn't want to give the prison guard the chance of changing his mind and losing this possibility of releasing Hamid. We ran back to the prison. The guard was sitting on a chair enjoying the sunshine. I was pleased to see he looked relaxed.

I didn't want to go close to him in case I made him angry again.

So Khadija went and explained the situation. He stood up, not saying a word to her, and went back inside the prison for what seemed like hours but was in reality only a few minutes. Then he reappeared with Hamid and another, even younger-looking guard. Then he spoke.

"Hamid can go with you and this man will go too. If you can bring a letter back from a neighbor or friend, then I will release him."

He ordered a Taliban driver with a Hilux pickup truck to take us.

We all got in. I dared not look at Hamid for fear of the guard, but I sneaked a sideways glance at him and saw he looked white as a sheet and on the verge of collapse.

The young Taliban who was accompanying us told us he was from Wardak province. He seemed kind but very young, and I doubted he had any power or influence in the prison. I was terrified none of the neighbors would be able to help us and he'd drive Hamid straight back to prison. Dusk had fallen by the time we drove into Makrorian.

Khadija recalled that one family among our neighbors owned their apartment; she didn't know them very well but we had no choice but to approach them for the guarantee. She went to talk to the man while Hamid and I and the young Talib went upstairs to wait in our apartment. It was emotional agony. Hamid was sitting in his own living room, but I couldn't even talk to him and at any second he might be taken back to prison.

I was still wearing my *niqab* but I noticed the young Talib was looking at my face, trying to read my eyes. I was scared and looked down. I think he saw how sad and scared I was. He was a native Pashto speaker but he spoke to me kindly in broken Dari, the language he knew Hamid and I spoke. "Don't worry, sister. I too am newly married, only twenty days. So I understand your pain. Even if you don't find a guarantee, I will leave Hamid here tonight and will come again tomorrow to get the letter."

He risked the wrath of his superiors by making that offer. It was another one of those surprising acts of random kindness when least expected. Hamid and I both thanked him.

We all sat and waited in silence for Khadija to return.

I heard male voices in the corridor of our apartment. I went out and saw half a dozen male neighbors. They smiled and said how happy they were that Hamid was being released. All of them told me not to worry; they would collectively offer Hamid his guarantee.

I was so grateful to them that I could do nothing but cry. They went into the room and Hamid hugged them all. Two of the neighbors who owned property signed the letter of guarantee, which stated that Hamid, an engineer, would not leave Kabul and would attend appointments at the Interior Ministry whenever the Taliban required it. Failure to do so would result in the two men forfeiting their property. It was an awfully big risk for our neighbors to take, and once again I was amazed at the generosity some people show to others at such times of war and conflict.

I took a small lace handkerchief I had recently embroidered and gave it to the young Talib as a gift for his new bride. He thanked me sincerely. I wondered how this kind and sweet young man had come to join the Taliban's ranks. He was so unlike the rest. It seemed like years before the kindly neighbors left and I could finally be alone with my husband. He looked like a ghostly shadow of himself. Khadija and I tried to make him smile and told him jokes; he started to laugh and as he did so, his breath caught and he coughed. A terrifying, hacking cough that refused to stop. Khadija and I looked at each other, grim-faced. Hamid had tuberculosis. The cough was a sign of worse to come.

Dear Shuhra and Shaharzad,

There will be times in your life when all hope and strength leave you. Times when you just want to give up and turn your face away from the world. But my darling daughters, giving up is not something our family does.

In those early days of my marriage when your father was arrested I wanted to give up myself. Perhaps if I had not been pregnant and felt Shaharzad kicking in my belly, I may have done so. But knowing I was about to give a new life meant I had to fight even harder for the life I had. I also remembered my mother, your grandmother. Imagine if she had given up after my father died. Imagine if she had taken the easy route and married a man who didn't want us and placed us in an orphanage or neglected us. She never would have done this because giving up was something that woman did not know how to do.

Imagine also if your grandfather had given up when the central government had told him it was not possible to build the Atanga road pass. If he had given up think of how many lives would have been lost on the mountains. By refusing to give up and building the road, he saved countless lives over the years.

Thank God I have both of their blood in me. Because of them giving up is not something I can do, either.

And you, my dear daughters, come from that same blood, too. If there comes a day in your life that the fear takes hold of you so hard and it squeezes the fight out of you, then I want you to remember these words: Giving up is not what we do. We fight. We live. We survive.

With love,
Your mother

FIFTEEN

BACK TO WHERE
I BEGAN

Three months after his incarceration began, Hamid was released. He had been beaten senseless, manacled, and left outside for days in the wind, rain, and snow as a punishment, and he contracted a fatal disease. And for what? Nothing. They had charged him with nothing.

It was the beginning of spring 1998 and the heavy snows of winter were thawing fast as each day got progressively warmer. It was a welcome relief to feel the sun again. It was good for Hamid, too. He was still very sick and coughed constantly.

By now I was almost seven months pregnant and my baby was very active, kicking and wriggling inside me. I was having trouble getting a good night's sleep with my unborn child testing her growing strength and Hamid exploding into coughing fits at regular intervals throughout the night. He was too ill to work and the medication the doctor had prescribed didn't seem to be making much of a difference for his condition.

Despite the sun's growing rays Kabul felt very oppressive. Taliban rule in the capital was absolute. We lived in constant fear that the Taliban would show up at our front door and drag Hamid back to prison. It was more a question of when, not if, they would come to detain him again.

But those times in prison had taken such a toll on Hamid's health that a fourth detention would most certainly be a death sentence. We knew we had to flee beyond the control of the Taliban. Pakistan wasn't really an option. Hamid became a target for the Taliban after Pakistani spies reported his visit to President Rabbani's compound, so we feared he would also be followed there. We decided to return to our home province of Badakhshan. General Massoud and President Rabbani's forces still held out against the Taliban in this northern stronghold. Even the might of the Soviet war machine couldn't defeat the mujahideen there, so we felt hopeful we could find some genuine refuge. But getting there was fraught with danger.

Hamid was prescribed six months of medication and we set off. It was a difficult journey in any circumstance, across rough tracks and winding mountain passes, but now it was fraught with the danger of the Taliban, too. Hamid's health and my pregnancy made us even more vulnerable, and it was a measure of our desperation to get away from Kabul that we even considered traveling at this time. The city that had once been a safe-haven now felt like a prison overrun by sadistic guards.

I packed a few belongings for the journey—mostly wedding gifts and things that reminded me of my family. I wanted to take the few precious photographs of my mother and my murdered brother Muqim and hide them beneath clothing in the bottom of a suitcase, away from prying Taliban eyes. But I knew the risk would be too great. If the Taliban found them they would be destroyed, and as much as I wanted those pictures with me, I dared not take the risk.

My sister-in-law, Khadija, was determined to stay with her children in Kabul. I argued and pleaded with her, but she would not be budged. I think she felt she owed it to Hamid's brother to stay in Kabul and raise her children. She had become such a close friend it was hard for me to leave her in the house, but I respected her decision to stay. Perhaps if I had felt as though there was even a chance the Taliban would leave us alone I would have stayed, too. But there was no chance of that and Hamid and I were living on borrowed time. Sooner or later some Taliban administrator would review the list of all the people they had detained and released, and decide once again to send more fanatical young men to re-arrest Hamid out of mere suspicion. Their attitude seemed to be: "He's bound to doing something wrong. Let's arrest him, torture him, and then he will tell us." Of course, if you torture someone for long enough they will tell you anything. And if they don't, then by Taliban logic they died guarding some terrible secret. Ordinary people were being imprisoned for the most trivial of so-called offenses. When Hamid was in jail he spoke to taxi drivers who had been arrested for taking unaccompanied female passengers. Ironically, although the driver would be thrown in jail the woman in question often got far worse for "tempting" the driver. The Taliban's rules were often as unique as the man holding the gun. Their arbitrary nature and enforcement created an environment of paranoia in which it was safer to stay at home rather than risk breaking some new law. It was terrifying and infuriating at the same time—these men thought they were ruling my country, when all they were doing was ruining it. And all their actions were done in the name of Islam, which they used as a political catchall to silence their critics. You don't like the way we treat women? You're un-Islamic. You want to listen to music? You're un-Islamic. You disagree with our justice system? You're un-Islamic. What do you mean we are misinterpreting the Quran for our own purposes? That's un-Islamic. These uneducated men had a two-dimensional view of the world that seemed to be firmly anchored in the dark ages, and that's exactly where they were determined to take my country, too. So as much as it pained us, we felt we had no choice but to leave Kabul.

We left the city early one morning, creeping through the city streets as dawn broke over the mountains, the springs in the taxi creaking over every bump in the road. Our plan was to drive east, following the path of the Kabul River until we reached an area called Surobi. The Taliban had control of Southern Afghanistan and the capital Kabul, but they didn't control certain sections of the north of the country. Once outside the city, their influence extended only a few hundred miles to the north of Kabul, where General Massoud's Northern Alliance forces had so far managed to keep them at bay. But to get to them we had to find a way through the battle lines. One that wouldn't get us killed or draw too much attention to ourselves—the Taliban were suspicious of people going north and worried that they were spies.

Surobi is a small town in a lush valley surrounded by lakes that from as early as the 1950s have provided much the of capital's erratic supply of electricity. It's a relatively short drive, only 43 miles, but the valley saw some of the heaviest fighting during the civil war, so even by the standards of hardy Afghan travelers the road was in an appalling state, full of potholes and craters. That meant we had to drive at walking speed most of the way, nose to tail with all the other traffic. Beyond the edges of the gravel road the earth was embroidered with a deadly latticework of landmines. During the past 20 years over ten million landmines have been littered across Afghanistan. To this day these evil weapons maim and kill our population, and the majority of the victims are children.

Occasionally frustrated or fatigued drivers would stray from the safe middle road, sometimes without consequence. Other times their vehicle would erupt in a geyser of smoke and flaming metal. The largest landmines are designed to destroy 60-ton armored battle tanks—driving a rusting 2,000-pound sedan onto one is like holding a dandelion in front of a screaming jet engine. The most terrible scenes would occur when a gung-ho bus driver would try a short cut. Sadly, he would be the first to die in the blast, which would usually rip the wheels and the entire front of the vehicle away. The terrified and shaken survivors would then face an awful choice as the flames from the explosion grew in intensity. Either perish in the blazing wreck of the bus or leap out a broken window and take their chances in the mine field. There really only was one choice, but it was a life-and-death gamble that not all of them won.

The road to Surobi passes over arid dusty plains outside the capital and passes Bagram Airbase. Today Bagram is the main US military base in Afghanistan, but even then it was already a huge installation, having served as the Soviet's center of air force operations.

The expanse of valley soon gives way to steep and rocky mountains and the road cuts its way through the narrow gorge.

Once we got to Surobi our car turned north toward Tagab. The road from Surobi to Tagab got even worse. This area is just under 100 miles northeast of Kabul and saw some of the heaviest fighting during the Soviet area. The road had been heavily bombed, or blown up by the mujahideen to prevent the Red Army advance, and when we got to Tagab I was a little shocked by how many of the simple mud houses were in ruins. Many of the people there were living among the rubble, sheltering in whatever part of their house still stood.

Hamid and I were very anxious. So far we had managed to get through the Taliban checkpoints without any problems. The next leg of our journey would be more difficult. Tagab marked the end of the Taliban front line in this part of the mountains. There was a lot of military equipment and large depots that appeared to be full of fuel for the tanks and trucks, and ammunition for rifles, artillery, mortars, and rockets. Tired-faced young men stood on guard and the traffic backed up as we neared the main checkpoint. Hamid and I stiffened. This would be where our escape succeeded or failed. We were worried that Hamid's name might be on a Taliban watch list, and that his presence here might be enough to cause the Taliban to arrest him again. As the line of cars and trucks crept forward I could see nervous men and their wives in burqas being ordered out of their vehicles and made to present their luggage for inspection. Fervent young men with black turbans rifled through open bags and suitcases, tossing neatly packed clothing and treasured personal possessions on the ground. One stood up suddenly with a whoop of excitement, holding a video tape aloft like a trophy. This was contraband. A woman lurched at the cassette as the Talib dangled it out of her reach. She was wearing a burqa but I could tell she was young. I imagined she, too, was a new bride, torn between her anger and frustration at the injustice being dished out by her tormentor and the fear she felt knowing that by protesting she was in danger of inviting more serious consequences. Her husband stayed a few paces behind, murmuring at his wife to stop. He would not let himself restrain his bride, knowing her actions were just, but neither could he challenge the Talib and condone her dissent. The gunman pushed her hard in the chest, his hand lingering on the outline of her bust, which showed vaguely beneath her burqa. She recoiled in shock for a moment before rushing back toward the Talib, fueled by anger at the sexual assault. He just laughed and groped her once more before ramming his shoulder under her chin and knocking her to the ground. For a moment she lay there stunned, and as she got onto her hands and knees the young Talib dropped the black plastic video cassette on to the ground in front of her and brought his heel heavily down upon it, smashing the brittle case. The woman didn't utter a word, but elevated her head so she could better see the cruelty and pointlessness etched on the man's face. He grinned at her theatrically and scooped up the spilled entrails of tape. He let the coils of plastic unspool between his fingers as he walked backward, watching her for any reaction. Turning to a tree, he hurled the tangled remains high into the branches, where the ribbon tumbled through the leaves. Her head fell forward, sobbing as her husband stooped to help her up. The Talib's dark eyes blazed triumphantly, clearly pleased by another so-called moral victory. The branches of the tree glistened in the midday light, filled with the innards of dozens of similar tapes. This was clearly a game played out on a regular basis.

My decision to leave the photos of my family at home hurt at the time, but I was thankful now that I had. I hurriedly began unloading our luggage from the car, while Hamid quietly asked some other men where we could hire a horse and a guide. Our plan was to go through the narrow mountain passes and strike out northwest to an area called Jabul Saraj, which was not under control of the Taliban. Effectively our plan was to loop west through the mountains and around the front lines of the fighting, rather than take the most direct but also most dangerous route north.

I was worried they would take our passports and tear them up, but when it was our turn to face the Taliban checkpoint, the armed men didn't actually pay us much attention. Their friend's game with the newlyweds had put them in a good mood, and apart from a quick search of our luggage they let us pass largely unbothered.

A woman a little further back in the queue was not so lucky. It was obvious she was from a Northern province because she was wearing a white burqa. The Taliban turned on her for daring to wear such a garment, beating her with sticks and lengths of wire cable. I wasn't looking forward to the horse ride, but after what we had witnessed I couldn't wait to be away from these terrible, inhuman men and in the comparative safety of the hills beyond.

At more than seven months pregnant it was a struggle mounting the horse that Hamid had managed to hire. But with his help and my natural desire to escape what I had just witnessed I managed to get on. Hamid walked beside the animal, and I felt very strange as we left the Taliban behind. It was as if my life had been diverted to some strange parallel universe where my country had regressed half a millennia. Here I was, an educated, ambitious young woman, with her educated, urbane, intellectual, and loving husband. As a couple Hamid and I were what I felt the picture of future Afghanistan should be, yet here I was dressed in a burqa riding on horseback as my long-haired and bearded husband walked beside me through the mountains. This Taliban ideology threatened to shackle my country in the Dark Ages.

But beneath this fear I also had a powerful sense of optimism. The Taliban didn't represent the true spirit of the Afghan people I knew and loved so well. The Taliban were an aberration, a disease that had taken hold after so many years of sickness brought about by war and suffering. As we climbed through the mountains, fording streams and negotiating narrow paths, I felt the weight of their oppression begin to lift. With each cautious step it seemed to get lighter, until finally, after several hours of hard trekking, we made it to Northern Alliance lines.

Not that there was any great accompanying fanfare when we got there. We simply arrived at a small town, at which point our guide turned to us as if to say: "Here we are." People went about their business in a very ordinary way.

We arranged for another car, which would take us to Jabul Saraj. It was just a few hours' drive but it really was like entering another world. The markets were thriving and full of shoppers. Women were walking and talking to men without the strict supervision demanded by the Taliban, and the restaurants were busy with diners. Hamid and I checked into a hotel, which in Kabul would have been an impossibility but here felt incredibly normal.

As I stood in the foyer of the little hotel I felt enormously overwhelmed by the events of the past year. Life under the Taliban had changed me in ways I hadn't really understood until now. I wasn't the same person I had been—my confidence had evaporated and the daily fear had exhausted my reserves of strength. I stood there quietly, like a good Taliban wife, whereas once I would have been organizing our check-in, inspecting the room, and making sure the porter brought in our bags. Now I was passive, just waiting for my husband to make all the arrangements. It saddened me to realize how much I had changed. Even as a little girl I was a great organizer, it was something my mother would always comment on when we talked about stories of my childhood. The Taliban had taken that confident little girl and determined teenager and turned her into a diminutive, cold, scared, and exhausted woman beneath the invisibility cloak that was her burqa. I couldn't bring myself to talk to the hotel manager or the owner who waved his greetings cheerily. My attitude toward men had changed. They were cruel and not to be trusted, merely existing to exploit women at the first opportunity. And this terrible shift in my attitude had been done in the name of Islam, but it wasn't an Islam I recognized. This division between the sexes was not an Islam of peace; it was born of fear and suspicion, not respect as I had been raised to believe.

My mother came from a much more conservative generation, yet even she enjoyed the kinds of liberation and empowerment that were being denied to me and hundreds of thousands of other women under the Taliban. She was allowed to visit her family when she wished and was given the responsibility of managing my father's businesses in his absence, of supervising his cattle herds on their annual journey to the higher pasture. Yes my father beat my mother, but as wrong as it seems now, it was normal for the time and in the village culture. But I know he truly respected her. The Taliban had all and more of the violence toward women, but none of the respect.

There was a huge silence inside me. Until now I hadn't even noticed it. Little by little it had grown, caused by the visits to the prison, the reality of watching women get beaten on the streets, the public executions of young women just like me.

We went up to our room, which was typical of Afghan guest houses: small, with a mattress on the floor. I was in a strange mood, with the emotion of being free of the Taliban churning up feelings I had buried deep for a long time. Hamid was in good spirits and almost danced around our little room with a boyishness I thought had been crushed out of him by those frozen nights in the prison yard. His enthusiasm was infectious, and I finally allowed myself to relax. Taking off my burqa, I threw it in the corner of the room—casting it aside—and with it, some of my cares. Looking at the crumpled and dirty burqa in a heap, I wanted to jump on it and grind it into the floor.

"Put your scarf on, my darling," Hamid said. "We're going out."

The words seemed so strange that for a moment I felt as though he had just dared me to do something very naughty, like we were mischievous children plotting to do something they know they shouldn't.

That's when the wave of euphoria washed over me. I could. We could. Go out on the street, like a normal couple. And I only needed to cover my hair, not my face. My pregnant belly was very large, but to this day I can't recall my feet touching the stairs as we scampered outside like a pair of giggling teenagers.

The wind on my face was like the kiss of freedom. My scarf covered my hair in full and my clothes were modest in accordance with the teachings of Islam, yet without my burqa I felt strangely naked. I began to think about how much the Taliban had damaged Islam. These were men who acted in the name of Allah, but they didn't respect the God they claimed to represent. Instead of following the Quran, they placed themselves above the teachings of the holy word. They believed they, not God, had the right to become the moral arbiters, deciding what was righteous and what was forbidden. They had hijacked and corrupted Islam, turning it into a tool to pursue their own selfish purposes.

The following morning we took a small bus to Puli Khumri, the capital of the Baghlan province. Afghan buses can be a very chaotic. Hamid and I had already gotten aboard, and we were waiting for the rest of the passengers to finish saying goodbye to friends and relatives, or argue with the driver, or try to stack an extra piece of luggage onto the already overflowing roof. Nearby a street hawker was selling Ashawa panir—a type of cheese that is a regional specialty. Like most pregnant women I had a very good appetite and I asked Hamid to go and buy me some. Like a kind husband should, he dutifully indulged my request. The bus was nearly ready to depart when he climbed back aboard, out of breath but clutching a small white cheese—mild and chewy and not unlike mozzarella. It's a favorite ingredient in many Afghan family picnics. However, despite Hamid's chivalry in dashing out to buy the mother of his child some cheese, he hadn't remembered to get raisins. These are the traditional accompaniment to the cheese because they help bring out the flavor. I didn't want to seem ungrateful, but I was a little disappointed. The bus was beginning to move and there was no time to go back and get some. I was resolving to enjoy the cheese despite the absence of raisins when a sharp knock at the window startled me. I spun around expecting to see the black menace of a Taliban turban. Instead, I was greeted by the kind eyes of the elderly cheese merchant.

"Here sister," he said, passing a small plastic bag to me. "The man forgot to get the raisins."

It was a simple act of kindness, from one human being to another. Under the Taliban we would have been considered criminals. Yet here it was—courtesy, good manners and respect. Nothing more, nothing less but it was so unexpectedly touching my eyes pricked with tears.

That incident put me in a much better mood and I enjoyed the spring landscape. The mountain peaks were beginning to cast off their wintry jackets of snow, while the new growth of grass and flowers further down the slopes sprouted toward the sun's rays. It gave me a sense of hope for my country. No matter how cold and cruel the Taliban might be, I felt that they too, one day, might melt away like the snow.

At Puli Khumri we went to stay at the home of another of Hamid's sisters and her husband. This was the couple who had come to my brother's home once to negotiate the marriage proposal, and I liked them very much. But I was mindful I had a lot to live up to. Their neighbors all knew their brother Hamid had married this girl who cost $20,000, an enormous amount of money. They would all be curious to see me and assess me. And that brought with it an enormous expectation that after months of stress, days of travel, and only weeks away from childbirth I couldn't help but feel I was struggling to live up to.

Hamid's sister was kind. She knew exactly how I felt and had already begun to make preparations for a bath. By that I mean a bucket of water heated over the cooking fire, but I can tell you that when you are exhausted and caked in dust and sweat, pouring enamel jugs over your head from a bucket of what had hours earlier been pure mountain water amounts to an experience as indulgent as any five-star hotel spa imaginable.

With each splash I scrubbed away the stress, the strain, and the filth of my life under the Taliban. Days previously I had left Kabul accorded no more value than that of a dog. With each soaking I regained a little more of my humanity and a little more of my self-worth. All I had to deal with now was the scrutiny of the neighbors, and as self-conscious as I might have felt, the terrible rule of the Taliban had also given me an inner strength I was only just beginning to realize. The fact is I wasn't the young and naive bride I hade been not so long ago. Now I was a wife who had negotiated with fundamentalist tyrants, I was an expectant mother who had climbed mountains, and I was an idealistic and hopeful woman who was finally beginning to find the firm ground of maturity beneath her feet.

However, when I emerged the neighbors made it clear from their faces that they didn't think Hamid had gotten his $20,000 dollars worth. They barely bothered to conceal the raised eyebrows and pursed lips. I can only imagine what they said about me once they went home.

Once we were alone Hamid laughed about it. He kissed my forehead gently and told me not to care what people said or thought. We had each other and that was all that mattered.

After a night's rest we continued our journey north. When we got to Talakan we had to hire a jeep because floods from the winter snow melt had washed out parts of the road to Kisham. From there we would have to go by truck to Faizabad, the capital of my home province Badakhshan. This wasn't the news I wanted to hear. Traveling atop a truck is the lowest form of transport in Afghanistan and usually the preserve of the Kuchis (the country's small gypsy population). And the spring melt had caused havoc with the roads here, too. I asked Hamid to see if he could find us a car, but despite his best efforts, there were no small vehicles going to Faizabad.

I was horrified when I saw the truck. I was an educated city woman of high breeding, and this was a lorry normally used for transporting goats. To-day it was piled high with sacks of rice. If I had been offered this vehicle to escape Kabul I would have gladly climbed aboard, but now that I was safe and regaining my confidence my pride was getting the better of me. Hamid gave me an ultimatum: This was the last truck going to Faizabad and if I didn't get on it we would be stuck in Kisham. I had no choice but to swallow my pride and get aboard. I had put my burqa back on, for warmth and to protect me from the dust as much as for any reason, but even with the anonymity it af-forded, I spent the next four hours with my head tucked into my knees, in case we should pass somebody I knew. Occasionally I would look up to enjoy the view, but the shame of being seen swaying on top of that goat truck always got the better of me and I would bury my head once more.

The road was incredibly steep and rough. As we crawled our way up one hill the driver lost traction and came to a halt. But when he tried to use the brakes he discovered they didn't work. They had become overheated on the downhill sections, and the truck started rolling backward toward the river. That gave me cause to look up, and we were gathering speed toward the icy clutches of the fast-flowing floodwaters. Hamid, myself, and the other pas-sengers perched on the rice sacks all braced ourselves for the expected colli-sion into river. A mental image of the freezing water clawing at my sodden burqa, dragging me under, smashing me against the rocks, filled my head. I closed my eyes in sheer panic, fingers digging into the rice sack as if it might offer some protection. The tires of the truck skidded backward, fighting to gain a hold on the slippery gravel as we bounced and lurched amid shouts and screams of passengers and driver alike. Suddenly we stopped, just yards from the water's edge. I turned to Hamid, whose hand was being crushed in my adrenaline-fueled grip. We turned to each other and laughed a relieved, nervous laugh. The driver tooted the horn in feeble celebration as cries of "*Ahamadullah*" ("Praise be to Allah") rang out. My knees felt weak as we climbed down from the truck. I was glad to back on my own two feet, any thoughts of social embarrassment purged from my head by the near-death experience.

The truck wasn't going anywhere. The brakes were cooked and it was beginning to get late. Besides, as close as I was to Faizabad, the last thing I wanted to do was to get back on top of the truck. Instead I walked around the rocks on the river bank, drinking in the landscape. I was free of the Taliban, free of the threats of beatings, free of their persecution of Hamid, free of the burqa if I chose. That night we slept on top of the truck. I didn't care anymore. Tomorrow I would be in Faizabad, sleeping underneath the mountain skies of my home province.

Dear Shuhra and Shaharzad,

*When I was a young village girl and desperate to go to school
I felt so dirty and rough. I had so few clothes—I always wore my
wellingtons and a big red scarf that I trailed in the mud. I normally
had a runny nose with snot dripping off it, too.*

*Today it makes me smile when I look at you two dressed in
your fashionable clothes and worrying about your hairstyles. You
two have grown up in Kabul, our capital city, and you are properly
sophisticated city girls. If you saw me as I looked at your age, you'd
probably recoil in horror.*

*I know when I take you home to Badakhshan these days, you
sometimes find it hard to fit in because the village children look so
different to you.*

*But girls, the one thing I do not ever want you to be is a snob. We
came from a poor village and we are no better than these children in
their rags. Negative circumstances may take either one of you back
there one day.*

*And remember this. The place you come from will always
welcome you back.*

*With love,
Your mother*

SIXTEEN

A DAUGHTER FOR A DAUGHTER

Hamid and I settled into Faizabad life quickly. I was delighted to see all my relatives again. All of my full sisters, my mother's other daughters, had married local men and never left. Many of my half brothers and sisters had also stayed behind when war broke out. I hadn't seen any of them in years and was delighted to be reunited with them. My sisters hadn't even known I had gotten married or was pregnant.

Faizabad itself became a haven for me, just the way it had when as a small child we'd fled there from the mujahideen. I had forgotten what a beautiful city it is, highly elevated with fresh air, its old bazaar of mud-plastered shops, and a clear turquoise river running right through the center of the city.

We rented a house and Hamid was able to run his finance business. He also started teaching at the university. I was able to relax and prepare to give birth. I was as nervous as any first-time mother and had no idea what to expect from labor, except that it was likely to hurt. The hospital in Faizabad wasn't hygienic and I knew I'd rather give birth at home than on a wire-framed bed with a paper-thin mattress in the dirty public ward the hospital offered.

It was July 8, 1998, when my first-born daughter made her entry to the world. I'd been invited to lunch at one of Hamid's relatives but I felt so sick I could barely touch my food. At three o'clock I went home and by 10 P.M. my little angel was born.

The labor was relatively short but it was tough. I had a female doctor friend with me but no pain relief. In our culture it is really hoped a woman will give birth to a son first, it's almost expected. But I didn't care what I had so long as my baby was healthy. After the baby was delivered she was taken from me to be washed and dressed in swaddling clothes. No one had yet told me the sex.

Then Hamid was allowed to enter the room. In most Islamic societies it is not normal for men to be present during the birth. He came over the bed and stroked my hair, smoothing the perspiration from my forehead. He spoke softly: "Daughter, we have ourselves a daughter."

He genuinely wasn't bothered he didn't have a son. Our baby was a perfectly formed 9.9 pounds of delight, and we were both overjoyed. She looked like Hamid, with thick black hair.

In the days after her birth when, like all new mothers, I struggled to learn how to breastfeed and deal with sleepless nights and exhaustion, I became very reflective. As I stared at her tiny sleeping form I prayed so hard for a better world for her, a better Afghanistan. I didn't want her to know any of the discrimination and hate that women suffer in our country.

As I held her to my breast I had this sense that she was my world now. Nothing mattered but her. My clothes, my appearance, my own petty and selfish desires all just melted away.

I had to argue with my family to be allowed to breastfeed immediately. In Badakhshani culture there is a tradition of not starting to breastfeed until three days after the birth. The people believe that something bad is in the milk in those first few days. Of course, the opposite is true. In those first few hours breastmilk contains colostrum, something essential for a child's immune system.

Without food in those first few hours the baby gets weak and cold. And of course, if a woman doesn't start to express her milk straight away she's at greater risk for infections like mastitis or of not being able to express milk when the time comes. This misperception about breastfeeding at the start is yet another reason why maternal and child mortality is so high in my province.

Because I had studied medicine at the university I knew the truth, but I had to argue with my sisters so they wouldn't prevent me from feeding her. They tried so hard to stop me, shouting at me that I was hurting my baby by feeding her so soon. I tried to explain to them that it was good for her, but they just looked at me accusingly, as if they thought I was being a bad mother.

In their eyes, years of tradition and being told the same thing far outweighed whatever their sister may have learned at the university.

But my sisters were kind to me in other ways, forcing me to stay warm and wrap up in blankets (even though it was July and was baking hot), cooking me my favorite foods to keep my strength up, and forbidding me from doing housework. But the joy of the baby was tempered by the acute agony of missing my mother. I wished so much she had lived to see her granddaughter. She'd have known that another one of us had been born, another woman of strength and determination had entered the world.

Six days after her birth we were so proud of her that Hamid and I threw a big party to celebrate. We invited half the town and we had music and a video camera; we had everything we weren't allowed to have at our wedding. I think in some ways that party became the proper wedding day we'd never had. It was a genuine celebration of our love and our new little family unit.

Hamid and I found a house of our own and I decided to teach again. I rented a big house with three rooms and advertised myself as an English teacher. Within a month I had 300 students, ranging from young girls to male doctors, students and teachers. I didn't have a lot of teacher training, so I ordered audio and visual material from overseas. These things had never been used in Faizabad before and my school got a reputation as a modern professional place of learning. I couldn't believe my luck. I was earning a good income, around 600 dollars a month, running my own business and doing something I loved. I had my baby in the classes with me and the students loved her, and some of them became close friends of mine. For the first time in my life this was real, proper independence.

I still wore my burqa daily, but what was strange was that it no longer bothered me. There was no Taliban rule in Badakhshan and no law forcing me to wear it. But culturally most women seemed to do so; my students all wore them. It was important I got respect from people for the sake of my school, so I decided to wear it, too. I didn't mind it because it was my choice to wear it, and it wasn't imposed on me.

The only blot on the happy landscape was my husband's health. He had also found a teaching job at the university that he also enjoyed. But he struggled. The chalk dust from the blackboards got into his lungs and made his coughing worse.

But generally life was good. Then, when Shaharzad was just six months old, life took another unwanted twist.

I got that familiar nauseous feeling again. I was pregnant.

I was devastated. I didn't want another child so soon. My school was running successfully, I had my friends and my life. I didn't want a baby.

Hamid gave me permission to have an abortion. Abortion was not legal (and is still illegal in Afghanistan today), but there were doctors at the hospital willing to carry out the procedures. I went to see one of them and was shown all sorts of suction machines that they used to carry it out.

But I was too afraid by what the machines might do to my insides. So the doctor suggested giving me an injection to induce miscarriage. I don't know what was in the injection but I allowed them to inject the needle into my arm. No sooner had they done so than I panicked. I had changed my mind. I jumped up shouting: "No, no, I can't do this. I want my baby."

I was terrified that it was too late and the injection would work. I clutched my stomach and talked to the tiny embryo inside me, willing it to live, telling it I was sorry. Just like my mother before me I had wanted a child to die, only to realize later that I would do anything to keep it alive.

Hamid stayed at home, battling the issue out with my sisters. They had been truly horrified by my desire to abort a child. They screamed at us, telling us we were breaking God's code, that it was against Islam. And they were right to say that. I cannot defend my initial decision to do it, other than to say I really didn't think I could cope with another baby at that time. Hamid understood this and that was why he had supported me.

I came back from the hospital still pregnant. My eldest sister was still there with Hamid. She was overjoyed I hadn't aborted the child, but she was so disgusted I'd even considered it she could barely look at me. Hamid just held me in his arms and whispered that it was going to be okay. I wasn't sure he was right. I had no idea how it was going to be okay. But I also knew now that it wasn't my unborn child's fault we were where we were. My duty was to her as a mother.

My youngest daughter Shuhra knows the whole story. My sister told her when she was about six. Sometimes she uses it to tease me. If I'm telling her off or asking her to tidy her room, she places her hands on her hips and looks at me squarely with a mischievous glint in her eye. "Mother, you wanted to kill me, remember?"

Of course she knows full well that I am then wracked with guilt and she gets away without cleaning her room.

The pregnancy continued but it was hard. I was breastfeeding Shaharzad, which tired me, and I was standing in the classroom teaching from 8 A.M. until 5 P.M. The Taliban were also encroaching. They took control of Kisham, the border town of Badakhshan. We were terrified they would get as far as Faizabad. If they did so Hamid and I decided we would try and flee to the mountains and make our way back to my father's village in Koof district.

At one point Taliban fighters were only 15 miles away. I stood outside my school listening to the familiar sound of heavy artillery and watching as the men of the city boarded trucks, volunteering to go fight the Taliban alongside the mujahideen army loyal to the Rabbani government. Part of me wanted Hamid to join them, but then I told him not to go. He was a teacher, not a soldier, and he didn't even know how to use a gun. Besides he was too weak to fight anyone. Many of the young men who got on trucks that day never came back. But they were successful in keeping the Taliban out of Faizabad and succeeded in pushing them back.

In the middle of all this Shuhra decided to make her own entrance to the world. I had a terrible labor that lasted for three days. My sister and a female doctor friend were with me. Hamid stood waiting outside. This time he wanted a boy. I already had given him a girl, now I really was supposed to produce a boy. His family, my family, our neighbors, our entire culture of boys before girls, expected it thus.

But I failed to deliver them the son they wanted. Instead my second daughter Shuhra came kicking and screaming into the world. She was tiny and red faced, just five and a half pounds, which was a dangerously low weight. When I saw her I was reminded of how I might have looked when I was born. I was the baby that was described as ugly as a mouse. The same description could be said of Shuhra. She was wrinkled and bald and red and screaming nonstop. But as I looked at her my heart filled with so much love that I thought it might burst into hundreds of pieces. Here she was. This little girl who was almost not born, whom I had shamefully almost killed, here she was alive and screaming and looking just like I had.

I was overjoyed but Hamid was not. This is Afghanistan, and sadly, even the most liberal or modern-thinking man is affected by hundreds of years of culture. And that culture dictated that I had failed in my biggest duty as a wife by not giving Hamid a son. This time the cruel gossip and innuendo got to him.

I think somebody a made a joke to him about the $20,000-dollar girl being a bad value. Perhaps he had heard these jokes at his expense so many times over the years that he was just sick of it and something snapped inside.

He didn't come into my room to see me for almost nine hours. I lay back on the pillows with Shuhra in my arms, waiting for him and unable to understand where he was. She was so tiny she almost disappeared into her swaddling clothes and I could hardly hold onto her.

When he finally came in, Shuhra was asleep in a crib next to me. He refused to look at me. When Shaharzad was born he had burst into the room excitedly, stroking my hair and cheek as he gazed in wonderment at his child. This time he offered his wife no tender touch or reassuring words. His angry face said it all. He looked into the crib and at least managed a wan smile at his sleeping baby daughter, another of Afghanistan's "poor girls."

In the weeks that followed I found it difficult to forgive Hamid for how he had treated me the day she was born. I knew he was only behaving like countless other Afghan men and within the confines of a culture that makes boys more important, but I had not expected it from him. He had always been so supportive in the past, taking pride in his ability to fly in the face of the gossips and the patriarchy.

Perhaps I had expected too much from him. But I felt disappointed and badly let down.

His coughing kept me and the baby awake at night so he moved into a separate room. That marked the end of our physical relationship. We never again shared a bed or any sexual intimacies.

But despite my own upset at him over this, I was aware of how lucky I was that he was such a wonderful, tender father to his girls. He loved both of them openly and deeply, and if he was still angry at not having a son, he never once let that show to his daughters. For that I was grateful.

By now he was barely strong enough to teach, and he cut down his days at the university to just two a week. The rest of the time he stayed at home and looked after Shaharzad. She has wonderful memories of a father who sang to her, played games with her, let her play dress up with him, and even allowed her to make him up as a bride and put ribbons in his hair.

Hamid was everything to me and he was an extraordinary Afghan man. In many ways he was very ahead of his time. We were in love when we married, deeply in love. But I suppose the years together, the trials and tribulations of his imprisonment, and his illness just meant that over time we grew apart from each other. The casual intimacy, the laughter, the joy of being in the same room and sharing secret glances had gone. I think it's probably a sad truth, but over time that happens to couples all over the world, wherever and whoever they are. We forget to take a moment to listen to what our partner is trying to say to us, we jump too easily to harsh words and impatience, and we fail to make the special little efforts that we used to. Then one day we wake up and our intimacy and love is gone.

Up until she was about six months old I was desperately worried Shuhra would not survive. She was so tiny and frail I was scared that even washing her would give her a fever. I was also terrified and wracked with guilt that the medicine I had taken to try and abort her had affected her development somehow. If she had died I don't think I would ever have forgiven myself. Like my mother before me I felt my denial of her then gave me an even greater debt of duty to her now.

Gradually she grew stronger and put on weight. And as she did so she became all the more funny and clever. Today she is the brightest, cheekiest, and sometimes naughtiest little girl that ever lived. I see myself and both of my parents in her. She has my father's wisdom and my mother's wit and strength.

She also wants to be president of Afghanistan when she grows up. Thankfully she is far removed from the image of a "poor girl."

A couple of weeks after she was born I had received a part-time job offer to manage a small orphanage. I didn't want to return to work so quickly, but with Hamid sick we needed the money. I left Shaharzad with her father and wrapped baby Shuhra in a big scarf that I tied around me. She would lie quietly against my breast, hidden under the burqa. I would attend meetings with my baby hidden this way and people wouldn't even realize she was there. She didn't complain and rarely even made a noise. I think she was just happy to be alive and to be snuggled so close to her mother. I carried her at work like this until she was five months old and became too heavy. I think it's one of the reasons she's so secure and confident as a child today.

As Shuhra and Shaharzad blossomed and grew, Hamid was dying before my eyes.

He was losing weight almost daily. The skin on his once handsome face had turned dark, almost like a translucent layer of black coated it. His eyes were bloodshot and he coughed almost constantly, and he was beginning to cough little bits of blood.

When Shuhra was three months old I was asked to take part in a medical survey of the province for an aid agency called Foundation for Children. The survey meant joining a team of 60 nurses, doctors, and support staff to travel across 12 remote districts assessing the medical and nutritional needs of the people. It was an incredible offer and the type of community outreach work I had dreamed of doing when I had wanted to be a doctor. Despite the bad timing with a new baby and a dying husband I couldn't turn it down. Hamid understood this and gave me his blessing to go.

I almost didn't, though. It was a grueling trip for anyone, let alone someone with a tiny baby. It would be hard to find clean water or proper washing facilities and we would be traveling across remote and barely accessible mountain tracks. The journey was to take in many of the country's Ismaili communities—devotees of Shia Islam's second-largest sect. In Afghanistan they predominantly live near the Takjik border. Our trip would also take us to the wild and rarely traveled Wakhan corridor—a finger of land that connects Afghanistan with China. It was created during the so-called Great Game—the nineteenth-century period when the Russian and British Empires were wrestling for control of central Asia—and it served as a buffer between the militarized ambitions of the British Lion and the Russian Bear.

Despite my reservations I knew I'd regret it if I didn't go. Good opportunities rarely present themselves at the perfect moment, that's just a fact of life. And I felt I could play a real part in the success of the survey.

As we set off, I was reminded of the trips my mother used to make each year, driving my father's cattle herd out to graze the spring pasture. She would sit proudly upon her horse, still wearing her burqa, and go off on her annual adventures complete with a caravan of donkeys, horses, and servants. I remember sitting on the horse in front of her feeling so small in the large mountainscape but so important in our mission. As we set off across rugged tracks on our survey I felt a similar emotion, only this time it was me with the baby on my lap.

That trip changed my life.

We visited some of the most remote places in the region. Places I have never been able to visit again. The levels of extreme poverty we found crystallized once and for all my political awakening. I knew my calling was to help.

We started the survey in January. It was so cold that people were actually using fresh animal dung to keep their babies warm while they slept. Their biggest fear was that their children would freeze to death, so they thought they were helping their child. They had no idea that the dung could cause disease or infection. Hygiene was nonexistent, children were barefoot in the snow, and most of them were malnourished.

By night we would eat and take shelter in the religious leaders' houses. That would usually be the largest house in the village with running water and a drop toilet, literally a large, deep hole in the ground. That was similar to the house I had grown up in, and although the Western doctors on our survey found it hard, for me it was reassuringly familiar.

But community leaders aside, the other villagers lived in a poverty I had never seen before, even as a child. Often we would find a one-room house with an entire family living inside, the animals in one corner and a toilet in the other. And when I say toilet I don't mean the traditional hole in the ground, or even a bucket—just a corner of the room with feces piled high and babies crawling around all over the room. It was shocking. I tried to explain the dangers such poor hygiene posed, but the reality is, it would fall to the husband to dig a proper latrine a safe distance from the house. Digging latrines—even ones that might save his children's lives, is sadly often more than the Afghan machismo of these uneducated village men could bear and they didn't like to lower themselves by doing it.

I tried a different approach: "Doesn't your good Muslim wife deserve her dignity being preserved when she performs her bodily functions?" But sadly, the indignity suffered by a woman defecating in the corner of the living room, or outside in full view of her neighbors, is outweighed by the male indignity of providing such a facility. Having seen all that, it makes me understand even more why Badakhshan province has the world's highest infant and maternal mortality rate.

In Darwaz, one of the poorest of all the districts, the women told me they have to go out at four o'clock in the morning in the snow to feed the animals. Sometimes the snow can be as much as three feet deep. No one helps them, and then when they get back in they have to cook the bread on an open fire and prepare the food for the family. It is more than a life of domestic drudgery. It is a life of hard labor. The men, too, work hard, going out into the fields at 6.00 A.M. and not returning until after dark, trying to grow enough crops in summer to last the family and the animals throughout the winter. It was a wake-up call to remind me how poor and marginalized these people are.

Seeing their suffering triggered something of an epiphany about who I was, where I had come from, and what my calling in life was to be.

We were in an area called Kala Panja, one of the Ismaili communities. We'd been invited to have dinner and stay the night at the house of the local leader. I had never met him, but he greeted me like an old friend. It was slightly embarrassing and my colleagues were beginning to laugh at me when he revealed the reason. He had known my father. As we sat he told tales of my father. He talked of a hard-working, dedicated man, one who did all he could to bring changes to the poor. He smiled at me and said: "Now Miss Koofi, I see you sitting here and I see you are the same as your father."

It was the first time in my entire life anyone had likened me to my father and I flushed with pride. As I sat in the room surrounded by elders, doctors, and villagers, all people coming together to try to make a difference, I was transported back in time. To a time when my mother ruled her kitchen, and servants and brothers stood in a line to hand out piping hot pots of rice to that mysterious room where my father met with his guests. As a child I had yearned to enter, to see what happened, to know what discussions took place in that mysterious secret room.

I smiled to myself as I realized the mystery had lifted now. Those meetings my father had were actually just like the one I was in now. They were simply dinners with delegations of aid workers, doctors, engineers, and local elders. How many nights had he sat and dined and discussed plans and projects and ways to bring development to his people? How many meals had my mother cooked for visitors like this? I sat there barely engaging in the conversation, lost in my thoughts and feeling secretly thrilled to be here, to be understanding such a critical part of my father's life.

In the morning when we left the man gave me a gift of a sheep for my baby Shuhra. Wakhan sheep, short and fat, are famous for their tender meat. The other Afghans on the trip were jealous and teased the man: "Where is our sheep? Why did you give it to Miss Koofi?"

But he just smiled and said: "It's a gift for Miss Koofi's father. I am honored today to have hosted his daughter and his granddaughter. And to see how his daughter has grown like him." Once again, the man's words made me flush with pride.

As we traveled the districts I met more people who had known my father. And I gained a deeper understanding of the political role my family had held. I had only been hired as a translator on the medical survey, not a senior role. But people heard my name and thought I was somehow here representing my father, that the Koofi family were once again back in Badakhshan mobilizing communities.

Villagers started to come and seek me out personally, presenting problems to me. I tried to explain to them I hadn't organized the survey, I was just a low-level helper. But they kept coming, and they came with problems unrelated to the survey, like a salary problem or a land dispute. I found it a little unnerving and overwhelming. But at the same time I had a growing sense of purpose and determination. And of belonging.

Here, with my father's political legacy, with my mother's personal values and my baby at my breast, I realized I wanted to be a politician. I don't even know if "want" is the right word. It was what I had to be. It was what I was meant to be.

The survey took six weeks. Shaharzad was only 18 months old and I missed her terribly while I was away. Hamid was more than happy to take care of her because in his heart I think he knew his days were limited and I think he enjoyed those few weeks of bonding, just him and his beloved daughter.

After the survey ended I went back to my job at the orphanage. This further mobilized me.

The children all had different stories. Terrible stories. Some had lost both parents, others had a parent who remarried and refused to allow them in the house, others had been placed there by parents too poor to feed them. It was heartbreaking and I wished I could have taken every one of them home with me. I spent the first three months of the job interviewing them about their backgrounds and organizing their individual histories into a database. There were 120 students, 60 boys and 60 girls. Despite the sadness of the children's stories the orphanage was a happy place. I was able to take both my daughters to work with me. Baby Shuhra stayed quiet, hidden under her scarf, and Shaharzad played with the children. I still see some of those same children every once in a while. Some of them are at university now and I still try to help them as much as I can.

But things really changed for me when a few months later the United Nations opened a UNICEF office in Faizabad. I applied for and got a job as children's protection officer. It was a small office and I was effectively the second in charge. Working for the United Nations was a big step up for me. And the job was tough. It involved working with children and internally displaced people (people who had lost their homes during the fighting).

Part of my job was to network with youth and civil society organizations. One of them was called the Badakhshan Volunteer Women's Association. In my spare time I volunteered for them, trying to fundraise and organizing things like micro-credit for women wanting to set up small businesses. I was also involved with a team that planned annual International Women's Day celebrations every March 8. International Women's Day is not celebrated everywhere and certainly isn't celebrated all over Afghanistan, but in Badakhshan we recognized it as an important symbol. We traveled to the villages giving gifts and organizing a Mother of the Year contest. It was a way of giving the village women a sense of pride about who they were.

We organized a big day of events in Faizabad and it was there in 1999 that I made my first ever public speech. I talked about how women were treated and how the civilians were treated in Kabul during the civil war. I spoke freely, angrily about the strength and power of Afghan women, how during all the atrocities of the civil war, when they had seen husbands and sons murdered and suffered rape and torture themselves, they didn't lose their strength or their pride. I called them the unstoppable Afghan women.

Although the Taliban controlled the rest of the country, they didn't control Badakhshan. Rabbani's government was still very much in control. Rabbani was a former mujahideen and many people thought my speech went too far in blaming the mujahideen for torture. In those days people didn't want to criticize the mujahideen, something that's true even today. These were the men who saved us from the Russians, so to criticize them for anything is seen as unpatriotic, almost treasonous. I admire and am proud of what the mujahideen did in defeating the Russian invaders, but there is also no denying that in the civil war years that followed they were responsible for many barbaric acts committed against innocent civilians, including my own family.

There were a few pursed lips and shocked silences among disapproving government officials when I spoke of this. But afterward many ordinary people, teachers and doctors and community volunteers, came up to me and told me what a good speech it was. I was finding my voice. And I was finding my rightful place.

Hamid was getting weaker and weaker and in a desperate attempt to stave off the inevitable I spent most of my wages trying to source new medical treatments to help him. My sisters were harsh with me, they told me not to bother wasting my money and to face the fact that he was dying. But this was the man I loved. Just as I could not sit back and wait when he was in prison, I could not now sit back and calmly wait for him to die. And this man was so supportive to me in those days, so happy to see his wife succeeding that I felt I owed it to him to keep him alive. After Shuhra's birth our physical relationship died, but in some ways our love came back. I think he felt guilty for his treatment of me for giving him a second daughter and so he worked even harder to prove to me that he was completely behind my work. When I came home in the evenings he always made a point of asking me about my day, persuading me to share my problems and work worries with him. I felt for him, he was in so much emotional pain. After all those years of waiting for me, of persuading my brothers to allow us to marry, the result was a slow descent into death. With sorrow in his eyes he once held my hand and told me it was like having a dish that you'd wanted to taste for so many years. A dish you'd dreamt of eating every day, a dish you could taste and smell in your imagination. When this dish was finally served to you, you had nothing to eat it with, no spoon or fork, so all you could do was look at it.

Part of my job involved traveling to Islamabad in Pakistan for conferences. I would fly to Jalalabad in Southern Afghanistan and then across the Torkham border pass, the same drive Hamid and I had taken with my brother for that brief happy week we had spent in Lahore before he was arrested for the final, third and fatal time. I loved the trips to Pakistan and they gave me a chance to buy Hamid more medicine. But arriving in Jalalabad, which was in Taliban control, was horrible. I hated seeing them and hated the way they snarled at me when I showed them my United Nations identification.

I was scared of them even though I knew I was under UN protection and they couldn't do anything to me. I would walk off the plane and straight into a waiting UN vehicle. But I felt their stares as I walked past them. I used to repeat a little mantra to myself to calm myself down: "You're UN now. You can work. You can deliver. They can't stop you."

One day I was about to board the plane to Jalalabad when I was stopped by Afghan security officials. They told me that Rabbani government officials had told them my husband was a suspected Taliban and I was a security threat. I was incredulous and enraged. I said: "Thank you so much. My husband was in prison for three months just because he met Rabbani in Pakistan and now you are telling me he's a traitor?"

Later on I discovered that someone, I don't know who, had given the intelligence services false information about us deliberately. It was another reminder that your enemies can be hidden everywhere and that in Afghanistan gossip can be deadly.

Badakhshan was the only place in Afghanistan not under Taliban control where women could work, and I was the only Afghan woman in all of Afghanistan working for the United Nations. It was high profile and of course that came with certain dangers. Pretty much all of Faizabad now knew who I was and what I did. Many people were pleased for me and pleased to have the UN presence. For others I was a constant source of scandal and gossip. Even my direct boss couldn't get his head around having a female deputy and used to tell me to close the door so I couldn't be seen if he had male visitors to the office.

There was a mosque close to our house and one Friday afternoon the mullah started preaching about women working for international organizations. He was preaching about it being *haram* (forbidden) and said no husband should allow his wife to do this. His view was that women should not work alongside non-believers and that any salary was also *haram*.

On this day poor Hamid was sitting in the yard playing with Shaharzad. He says he managed to laugh as he sat there listening to this. His wife was the only woman in the entire province working for an international organization so it had to be me the mullah was referring to. There was Hamid babysitting his daughter while I worked. Of course, our roles are much more common today. Not only in the West but also in Afghanistan many younger men of the modern generation take a much larger role in sharing childcare duties, and in many households both husbands and wives work. But back then we were almost unique.

When I got home Hamid told me he chose to laugh at the mullah's sermon and then went inside, so he didn't have to hear it all. But I was desperately upset at what had been said. Perhaps it was easier for the mullah to try to turn an entire community against one family, rather than speak to my husband man to man about what he perceived to be an errant wife's behavior?

Ironically, when I became a member of parliament (MP) a few years later this very same mullah came to ask for my help. He was also a religious teacher and had been kicked out of his job and he wanted me to intervene with the Ministry of Education. Back at the time when he preached against me he would never have come to me for help, but years later even a man like that could accept that women now played a role in government and society. That is why it is so important to have women in public and governmental roles, because by doing so people's views can slowly change.

The United Nations was a wonderful organization to work for and were very helpful to me at that difficult time. Sometimes I was able to take the kids and Hamid with me to Pakistan. One time I took him to the Shafa Hospital, which is one of the most famous hospitals in Islamabad. He received a different type of new medicine there but the prescription was $500 a month—$3,000 for six months. I managed it for six months but after that my salary just couldn't cover the expense.

I suppose I was still in denial about him dying. He was so young. It was early 2001 and he was only 35 years old.

By now the fighting between the Northern Alliance and the Taliban had almost stopped and there were rumors the UN Security Council was about to recognize the Taliban as the legitimate government of Afghanistan. That was something that many Afghans found terrible to accept. It seemed that the world couldn't see what we saw, nor could it see the danger the Taliban presented. In the spring of 2001 Ahmed Shah Massoud went on a political trip to Europe on behalf of the Rabbani government. He was invited by then European president Nicole Fontaine to address the European Parliament in Strasbourg. He used his speech to warn of the emerging threat of the Taliban, and the imminent large-scale threat of an Al Qaida strike on Western targets. During his brief visit to Europe he also traveled to Paris and Brussels, where he held talks with European Union Security Chief Javier Solana and Belgian foreign minister Louis Michel.

He carried with him the hopes of many Afghans. And we were pleased to hear via BBC radio that he was well received. His message was simple and clear. The Taliban, and the Al Qaida fighters they were sheltering, were a growing threat—not only to Afghanistan but to the world.

In a personalized message to then US President George Bush, Massoud warned: "If you don't help us, these terrorists will damage the US and Europe very soon."

But the West's political leaders did not heed his warnings in time.

There was very much an air of sad resignation among my friends in those days. It really felt like the Taliban was here to stay forever. For 14 years we fought the Soviets and now we had to fight this new and strange form of Islam. And if the United Nations did recognize them as the government that meant the Rabbani government that ruled in Badakhshan would become the illegal government. On a personal level I would have almost certainly lost my job.

At the same time that General Massoud was in Europe, a lot of foreign delegations came to Badakhshan to meet Rabbani. He had since returned from Pakistan and was based out of Faizabad. It was clear the United Nations was now actively trying to broker peace and some kind of agreement between the Taliban and the government.

It was September 9, 2001, a sunny autumn day. I had just got in the UN car and was on my way to a displaced persons (IDP) camp. I was supposed to be monitoring the children's play activities. When I got there everyone was crying. The lives of these IDPs was truly awful—they lived in tents with no sanitation but they never lost their spirit and would always smile and joke. But now they were all in floods of tears. A young man told me why. Ahmed Shah Massoud had reportedly been killed. My head spun and my knees buckled underneath me. It was just like the sensation I had when my mother died when I thought I was falling out of the sky. The hero of our nation could not be dead, he couldn't be.

Later on that night we got more details of the story on the BBC. The situation was still very confused as to whether he was dead or just badly injured, and certainly on the ground there were wild rumors. But over the course of the coming weeks and months the picture became clearer. Two Arab extremists posing as television journalists detonated a bomb that was hidden inside their camera as they interviewed the famously cautious Massoud. One died in the explosion, and the other was gunned down by Massoud's men as he tried to escape. Massoud was badly injured in the blast and died while being flown by helicopter to a hospital. Police in France and Belgium later made a string of arrests and convicted a number of Al Qaida–linked North African men for providing the killers with forged documents and cover stories. It seems Osama Bin Laden had correctly judged that following his network's now infamous terrorist attacks on the United States two days later, Washington would naturally turn to Massoud's Northern Alliance to capture or kill him. Indeed, they did. But the Northern Alliance would have to go into that battle without their great commander.

I can only liken it to the day in America when President Kennedy died. Americans of that generation always say they remember exactly where they were when they heard the news. It was the same for us Afghans when Massoud died. Even Shaharzad, who was just a tiny girl of three, remembers that day.

For many, Massoud was the hero of the mujahideen, the man who had led the battle against the Soviets. He was a skillful tactician and a brutally efficient soldier. His victories earned him the title "Lion of the Panjshir." But for many of the younger generation, like me, who had been damaged by that war, his real heroism began when he started to fight against the Taliban. He was so often the lone voice speaking out and warning against the extremism they carried with them. He warned the world about the terrorists and he paid for that with his life.

To this day I struggle to understand how the West ignored his message that Islamic terrorism was a threat to the world. He told them that if we don't stop it now, stop it today in Afghanistan, tomorrow it will come to their borders. He tried to explain that he was a Muslim—a strong Muslim—but the Islam the Taliban propagated was not one he agreed with nor one that represented the culture or history of the Afghan nation. He had five children, four daughters and a son. All of his daughters were educated and he often spoke about that. He tried to educate people that Islamic values do not prevent a woman from being educated or working. He knew the Taliban was creating a negative image of Islam around the world and he tried to counter this.

He was such an inspiration to me. He taught me that freedom is not a gift from God. It is something men must earn.

When he died I felt Afghanistan had lost all hope.

Just 48 hours later Massoud's warnings about Islamic terrorism came horrifically true. The twin towers of the World Trade Center in New York were attacked, along with the Pentagon in Virginia, while a fourth airliner crashed into a field in Pennsylvania, killing 40 passengers and crew along with four hijackers, taking the total number of Al Qaida victims that day to 2,977 people. Innocent people.

The world had woken up to the warnings too late to save these poor people.

And many more innocent lives, mostly in Afghanistan and Iraq, would be lost in the so-called war on terror that now followed.

Dear Shuhra and Shaharzad,

It saddens me so much that many people in the world have a negative view of our country and our culture. The reality is there are many people who think all Afghans are terrorists or fundamentalists.

They think this because our country has so often been at the heart of the world's strategic battles—wars over oil, the cold war, the war on terror.

But beneath this is a country of great history, of enlightenment, of culture. This was a land where our own warriors built great minarets and monuments. It was even a land where early Islamic kings allowed other faiths to build their own monuments, such as the Buddhas of Bamiyan. It is a land of mountains and skies that never end, of emerald forests and azure lakes. It is a place where the people show hospitality and warmth like no others. It is also a nation where honor, faith, tradition, and duty know no bounds. This, my dear girls, is a land to be proud of.

Never deny your heritage. And never apologize for it. You are Afghans. Take pride in this. And make it your duty to restore our true Afghan pride to the world.

This is a big duty I ask of you. But it is one your grandchildren will thank you for.

With love,
Your mother

SEVENTEEN

THE DARKNESS LIFTS

On September 11, 2001, I was sitting at my desk when a colleague ran in clutching a radio. We listened in shock at the news that the twin towers had been attacked.

I had tears running down my face as I thought about all those people trapped inside that building. We had no skyscrapers in Afghanistan and I had never seen a building so high it touched the sky, so I could only imagine the terror of being unable to get out of a burning building.

For the first time I felt a strong connection between what was happening in Afghanistan and what was happening on the other side of the world. For me the whole story was like one big jigsaw puzzle. It was a puzzle that had been coming together for years. Now someone somewhere had placed the final piece on the board. And the world was shaking with shock.

Bitterly I thought that at least world leaders would now finally recognize that Ahmed Shah Massoud's warnings had been right when he said terrorism would come to their borders.

What I didn't expect was such a quick response from the world. Many Afghans would disagree with me on this, but I personally believe very strongly that the United States was right to send troops into Afghanistan to topple the Taliban.

At work, a barrage of emails started to come in, warning international UN staff to leave Afghanistan and all local staff to stay in their main office and not travel within the country. My boss was from another province and went to be with his family, so I was left to manage the office alone.

It was a very difficult time because we had been setting up a back-to-school campaign in which thousands of boys and girls who were past school age but who had missed an education because of the war or the Taliban were invited back to finish their studies.

UNICEF, in cooperation with other organizations, provided the children with temporary school tents, stationery, and books. It was exhausting but hugely rewarding to know that I was helping to ensure that these young people an education.

We had also been planning a big polio immunization campaign all over the province. For two months, alone, we managed to implement the immunization campaign for children and we managed to keep the schools open. I was still the only Afghan female UNICEF staff member inside Afghanistan, and now I was also the only one managing the office.

In America the investigation into who carried out the 9/11 attacks quickly identified the hijackers, and then traced their activities back to Al Qaida sources. Washington demanded that the Taliban government hand over Osama Bin Laden. The Taliban refused.

On October 7, 2001, less than a month after the attack on the World Trade Center, the United States launched Operation Enduring Freedom. American and British warplanes and cruise missiles struck Taliban and Al Qaida targets across Afghanistan. At the same time Massoud's Northern Alliance soldiers began to push south toward Kabul with the aid of their new-found air superiority, but sadly without their key general.

The West was hoping for a quick, clean removal of the Taliban and the death or capture of Osama Bin Laden and his deputy, Ayman Al-Zawahiri.

It was a simple plan: US and British airpower would devastate Taliban forces, while new types of bombs would blow apart whole mountainsides to kill Al Qaida fighters in the caves where they hid. On the ground the Northern Alliance and other key forces, again predominantly from the north, would mop up what the bombs had missed.

Some of these men took to their task with a chilling enthusiasm. We occasionally heard news of the atrocities against Taliban forces, such as hundreds of Taliban prisoners being burned alive. Whoever an enemy is, such gross inhuman abuse in war is always wrong. In some of the villages that had been oppressed by the Taliban, people grew brave and began pelting them with stones and telling them to leave.

I knew that not all the Taliban had been bad. Some of the low-level people in their ranks were just people trying to survive. And hadn't I even been helped by some of them? Like the old man who didn't even know me but had helped me to get Hamid out of prison one time. I was sad these individual men were getting killed, but I was thrilled the Taliban's theocratic regime was being destroyed and this dark period of Afghan history was coming to an end.

I didn't mind that it was the United States and a host of other foreign nations leading the fighting. Many Afghans dislike the help of non-Muslims because they are infidels (or non-believers). But I didn't see it that way. I had never really considered the Taliban proper Afghans anyway. They were always controlled and led by other nations. I remember when I had lived in Kabul seeing the entire of neighborhood of Wazir Akbar Khan taken over by the Taliban's "guests": the Arabs, the Chechens, and the Pakistanis. Hearing their accents and seeing their wives dressed in black niqabs (the Arab style face and head covering), I'd had the sensation that Kabul was no longer under Afghan control but had become an Arab proxy city, like Riyadh in Saudi Arabia or Doha in Qatar.

And some of the Taliban's worst atrocities had foreign connections. When the Taliban attacked an area north of Kabul called the Shomali plains, they did so with such ferocity that the land is still known as the burning plains. During one battle they killed thousands of men, and then they deliberately burned all the trees and crops before bulldozing the remains into the ground. This totally annihilated the population's chances of future survival. Destroying crops and other scorched-earth tactics are things I associate more with Arab countries, rather than Afghanistan. And it is most definitely not something the Taliban would have been clever enough to have thought of themselves.

After that they went from house to house forcing all the young girls and women outside. The last time people saw these women they were being herded into trucks and cars. The local suspicion was that they were taken to countries like Pakistan, Saudi Arabia, and Qatar and forced to work in brothels. And of course many of the foreign fighters took these women as forced wives. No one can prove these local suspicions are true, but too many of these things happened for me not to believe them.

So when non-Afghan forces were involved in the Taliban's defeat I was grateful for their help. I was just so very pleased they were no longer going to be running my beloved country. One by one the provinces fell from Taliban control. In Tora Bora, which had been believed to be Bin Laden's hideout, the fighting raged for weeks. Then suddenly it was over. The Taliban were gone.

The men who had tortured my husband and destroyed my chance of a happy marriage were losing their power, just as my poor husband Hamid was losing his own final battle with his health.

BEING THE ONLY FEMALE STAFF MEMBER at the UN in the country made me the subject of much curiosity. Journalists constantly visited my office wanting my advice on stories they could write—something that was hard to find time for because of all my work responsibilities.

My workload meant that I was out until late most evenings, and this made for problems at home. Hamid was sick and he needed me. I wanted to be with him, but I also wanted to be doing this essential work for my country. Usually, Hamid was supportive and didn't mind when I worked long hours, but by now he knew he didn't have long left and he resented the time I gave to my job over him. I was completely torn emotionally, which only added to the stress.

Some days I was literally running from one meeting to the next, with no time to eat. I was still wearing my burqa, even during the meetings with foreign officials and aid workers. Then one day, the provincial governor suggested I take it off. He said it was okay. These people needed to see my face to communicate with me. After that, I stopped wearing it at work.

It was a hard time, but I learned so much, not least about my own ability to lead and to implement. As I gained the trust of both local people and my international colleagues, more trust and responsibility came my way. I knew I really had found my calling.

In the weeks and months that followed Afghanistan was a country transformed. The air of optimism in Kabul was so potent it was almost as if you could put out your tongue and taste it.

Overnight hundreds of refugees started returning home. Those who had fled Afghanistan at various points during the last few years, be that during the Soviet era, the civil war, or Taliban rule, felt safe enough to return. Afghan investors who had made money overseas came home and started planning new businesses, hotels, banks, even golf courses and ski resorts.

The country was still on its knees economically, of course, and most people were living in truly abject poverty. In all the major cities basic power supplies like electricity had been destroyed and few people still had access to clean water. Many people returning found their homes had been destroyed or taken over by other people. Unemployment was rampant and food short-ages massive as the country struggled to return to a semblance of normalcy. It was chaos but it was a chaos that for the first time in a long time was forward looking.

The UN office expanded massively. Funds were coming in thick and fast from all over the world, and the race was on to distribute them where they were needed most.

I needed to spend time with Hamid so I took a month's leave and came to Kabul.

I tried to re-admit myself to Kabul University so I could continue the medical studies I had been forced to abandon when the Taliban banned women from higher education. But I was told too much time had passed for me to pick up where I left off. But in reality I think I was denied the chance because I made the mistake of taking Shuhra with me to the interview. The admission officer made it clear to me he did not approve of mothers going out to work. I was upset they wouldn't admit me, but I had bigger concerns. Hamid was coughing up blood almost every hour.

I took him to Pakistan again, to the same doctor who had prescribed the $500-a-month medicine. The doctor gave us the devastating news that because Hamid hadn't been taking the medication continuously his tubercu-losis had developed a resistance to it. The condition was now so serious that doctor said he could do nothing. He advised we try a hospital in Iran that was experimenting with a new technique. I gave Hamid the money and he went alone. I returned to Faizabad. Hamid stayed in the Iranian hospital for four months. Our contact was limited to a few phone calls, but he sounded upbeat and said he was feeling better.

Back in Faizabad things were changing at the government level. A demo-cratic constitution had been debated and agreed upon at a national *loya jirga* (tribal council). For women the future was looking brighter than it had in years. Hamid Karzai had been declared interim president of the country until formal elections could be held.

Human rights activists who had been persecuted under the Taliban were now working openly to create civil society and women's movements. But of course Badakhshan was no longer the seat of government, and the central power base had moved back to Kabul. Suddenly I felt isolated and provincial. I wanted to be part of the action. So I applied for and got a job as a UNICEF women and children protection officer based in the capital. Fortunately UNICEF provided at-work daycare so I was able to take the girls with me. It was busy work and I thrived on it. I became deputy chairperson of the staff association and was expected to travel the country overseeing projects. I recall one trip to Kandahar, a city that had been the spiritual heartland of the Taliban. When I arrived, the community leaders I was working with barely spoke to me. These were conservative men who had been Taliban supporters. In a few short months they'd gone from Taliban rule to the indignity of a woman turning up and telling them what to do. Gradually I won them over and after a few days we were all cooperating as if we'd always worked together. Even today I stay in touch with some of them and they visit me when they come to Kabul. I truly believe that people change their opinions only from first-hand experience. And opinions on gender can and do change, even among the most conservative men.

Hamid came back from Iran and initially I was thrilled by how much he seemed to have improved. But within a few weeks he was back to square one: He couldn't walk more than a few yards without coughing up thick globules of blood again. It was heartbreaking to see. The disease is transmittable and whenever he started to cough he would put his handkerchief over his mouth and order the girls to leave the room. He was terrified they might catch it. We were living back in our old apartment, on the fifth floor of the Makrorian buildings. He was essentially housebound because walking up and down the stairs was too difficult for him. We had long since ceased being able to have any physical intimacy, but he was still a good husband as much as his health allowed him to be. The illness had not destroyed his mind and he had great problem-solving capacities. Whenever I had a bad day at work or couldn't figure out how we were going to implement a new project he would always be on hand with advice or a sympathetic ear. Even now he was my rock.

After a few weeks he needed a check-up so we flew to Aga Khan University Hospital in Karachi, one of Pakistan's most modern hospitals. He was too weak to walk and I had to push him through the ward in a wheelchair. He was so thin and gray by now that one of the nurses assumed he was my father.

We stayed overnight in the hospital. I slept by his side just as I had done with my mother in the days before she died. The following morning the doctor gave us the news. It was too late. His lungs were now like leathery shoe soles, not essential organs. His medicine was so strong the side effects made his whole body sick and he felt very nauseous. He said he wanted to stop taking it. It was summer 2003 and the sun seemed to perk him up. Now that the medicine wasn't killing his appetite by making him vomit, his hunger returned. He started to eat proper meals again and the color returned to his cheeks. I had a week's leave from UNICEF and wanted to spend every moment of it with him. It was Wednesday and I had decided to prepare a chicken broth for him. He hadn't slept well the night before and was tired. I was trying to force him to eat the soup but he barely had strength to lift the spoon. That evening both my sister and his sister, my sister-in-law, came to visit.

He was chatting with them and as I watched I noticed how very handsome and fresh faced he looked. It was as if the illness had lifted from his face, and suddenly he was the old Hamid again. I joked with him: "Hamid my love, you are kidding me aren't you? I think you are teasing me, you are not sick. How can you look this good?"

He laughed too, but when he did so his breath caught and he started gasping for air.

We carried him to his room, and I had to turn my head away so he didn't see me cry. It was late and I lay down in the other room with the women for a while, but I couldn't settle. I went into Hamid's room and lay down next to him. I took his hand and we both started to cry. I was thinking back to the first week of our marriage when we were so happy, when we were planning our future together. We hadn't asked for much yet all we had been given was sadness and sickness.

The girls came in to the room. They'd dressed up like little Kuchi (gypsy) girls and started to sing a song for their father. It was their childish attempt to cheer us all up. It was beautiful and it was heartbreaking. They twirled and spun veils over their heads, singing: "I'm a little Kuchi girl, look at me dance." After they sang they asked Hamid to kiss them, but he refused because he was scared of the risk of transmission. He wanted so much to kiss his little girls goodbye but he couldn't. I was still trying to force food into him, begging him: "Please have this mulberry, please just try a little more soup. Just swallow one spoonful."

I was exhausted and started to nod off. My sister came into the room and told me to go rest. I didn't want to leave him but he insisted. He was still joking with me: "Fawzia, your other supervisor will look after me. She will make sure I keep eating my food and my fruit and keep breathing. Go rest for a little while please."

I went and lay down with the girls on their bed, holding them tight, wondering how these little creatures would live without the love of their father. About an hour later I heard a scream. I will never forget it. It was my sister screaming his name. I ran into the room just in time to see him take his last breaths.

I shouted in terror: "Hamid, no. Please don't go yet." When he heard me he opened his eyes to look at me. Just for a second our eyes met: Mine were full of fear, his were calm and resigned. Then he closed them again and he was gone.

Dear Shuhra and Shaharzad,

When your father died Shuhra was exactly the age that I was when I lost my father.

A bitter irony that I wish fate had not repeated across the generations.

In the first days after your father died I blamed myself for this. From an orphan mother came orphan daughters! I had tasted the bitterness of not having a father. I knew how difficult it would be for you in our society. I knew that you would not only suffer not having a father but you would suffer not having a brother as well.

But just as my mother helped me find strength and encouraged me with enough strength as if she were two parents, so I have had to do the same for you.

You only have me. But know that I love with the might of a hundred parents.

And know your father would be so proud of you today if he could see you growing up into the beautiful young women you are.

When I listen to you talk about your futures my heart bursts with pride. Shaharzad wants to be a rocket scientist and Shuhra wants to be president of Afghanistan. That's for this week anyway. Next week you will probably change your minds again. But I know that what will never change is how high you are both aiming. And you are right to aim high, my darlings. Aim for the stars. That way if you fall you land on the tops of the trees. If you don't aim high then all you see is the bottom of the branches.

I can't give you your father back. But I can give you ambition, decent values, and confidence. And these are the most precious gifts from a mother to a daughter.

With love,
Your mother

EIGHTEEN

A NEW PURPOSE

Hamid died in 2003. My life felt empty, bereft, all love and laughter stolen from it. For two years I worked like an automaton in my UN role, but mentally I was lost. Aside from looking after my daughters, I felt purposeless. I didn't socialize. Weddings, parties, picnics—none of the things I used to love interested me anymore. My days followed the same routine: wake up, go to work, take the girls home for dinner, play with them, bathe them, put them to bed and then get back onto the computer and work until midnight.

I lived for my daughters, but as much as I loved them I needed more from life. I needed a sense of being. Remarrying was out of the question. Despite my family gently suggesting it to me, I had no desire to do it. Hamid was, and remains to this day, the only man I have ever wanted to marry. To remarry would be to betray his memory. I still feel this as strongly now as I felt it in the weeks after he died.

But politics became a husband of a different kind. Politics was in my blood and I believe it was my destiny. God wanted me to live for a purpose and what greater purpose can there be but to improve the lot of the poor and bring pride to a nation torn apart by war?

In 2004 Afghanistan held its first ever democratic elections. Back in the 1970s when my father was an MP, King Zahir Shah had promised to bring more democracy and there had been similar elections for local MPs, but that process was derailed by the Russian invasion and then the war. Now, 30 years later, it was happening and the country was elated.

Hamid Karzai had been interim president since the fall of the Taliban in 2001. He was still a popular figure and was elected in a resounding landslide victory. There had been fears that this election day would be marred by violence but it passed relatively peacefully.

It was a chilly autumn day with a thick fog swirling through the streets. Hundreds of thousands of people came out to vote. In some polling stations a sea of women in blue burqas lined up to vote beginning at four o'clock in the morning. It was an extraordinary moment for Afghanistan and despite my grief the significance of it was not lost on me. I think that was the first day I allowed myself to feel emotion since Hamid died.

President Karzai had initially promised women's rights, civil society, all the things I believed in. After his first victory his attitude changed and he has become much more focused on appeasing the hardliners, but back then he was like a breath of fresh air. Sadly the landslide victory he secured in 2005 was not repeated in 2009. He won that election, too, but amid allegations of widespread fraud. It was another reminder that in my country everything can change for the worst in four short years.

In 2005 it was announced that parliamentary elections would be held in order to select the members of parliament who would each represent the different districts and provinces of Afghanistan.

My family decided the Koofis should reaffirm their political history and be part of this new generation. One of us had to stand.

There were a lot of inside negotiations within the family about who should run.

My brother Nadir Shah, the son of Dawlat bibi, one of the two wives my father had divorced, also wanted to stand.

Nadir had been a respected mujahideen commander and was already a district leader in Badakhshan, so understandably he believed he was the person best placed to represent the family.

I disagreed. But I didn't know if any of my other brothers would even consider my case. I called my brother Mirshakay. As a child Mirshakay had been one of my father's favorite sons. My father used to lift him up on his horse with him and allow him to sit at the front of the saddle. He used to look down at me from the horse with a snooty, proud expression. I was torn up with jealousy. I so wanted to be allowed to ride my father's horse, too, but a daughter would never have been given that treat. As we grew older

Mirshakay became one of my biggest supporters. He had moved to Denmark during the war, but he and I remained close and spoke at least once a week on the phone. He listened quietly as I made my case and told him why I was the best Koofi to be an MP. He hung up the phone, promising me he would talk to the others.

The family was split and the debate raged for a few weeks. It was almost like an internal election within the family. But to my surprise by the end of it most relatives supported me and Nadir was persuaded not to stand. The family decision was that only one person could stand for election; to have two siblings standing against each other would have created too much disharmony between us all.

I wanted it to be official so I asked all my brothers to sign a document affirming that I was the sole Koofi family political representative. I wished my mother had been there to see it. I suspect even she wouldn't have believed it was happening. In my childhood my father didn't even speak directly to his daughters and no one bothered to celebrate the girls' birthdays, that's how far down the scale we girls were. But here we were, only a generation later, electing a woman as the political leader of the clan.

I don't think my family is alone in accepting change this rapidly. I truly believe change in gender attitudes cannot be forced on a country by outside forces, however well meaning those forces are. Change can only come from within and it begins with individual families. I am living proof of this.

Several of my brothers and half-brothers didn't believe I stood a chance of winning. My father had married all but one of his wives for their political usefulness. In doing so he had created a local empire of allies, networks, and connections. But my brothers thought these old networks had been too badly destroyed during the war and Taliban years, and that no one would remember the Koofis anymore. But I had traveled to the villages in my work with the UN and knew that wasn't true. Many people I had met remembered my father and the respect for our family was most definitely still there.

Furthermore I was confident in my own networks. In the four years I had spent living in Faizabad with Hamid, I had volunteered for women's groups, taught over 400 students English, visited internally displaced peoples' camps, and set up sanitation and school projects. People knew me there. My friends were civil society leaders, teachers, doctors, and human rights activists. This was the new Afghanistan I was part of and felt I could represent. I was still

only 29 but I had also lived through Soviet occupation, civil war, and the
Taliban.

And for me the issue was much wider than only gender and women's issues. Men suffer just as much as women from poverty and illiteracy. I wanted
to promote social justice for all, tackle poverty and the root causes of poverty,
and in doing so move Afghanistan out of the Dark Ages and into its rightful
role in the world. It didn't matter if those prepared to join me in that struggle
were male or female. I am the child of my mother, the epitome of the suffering and endurance of so many Afghan women. But I am also the child of my
father, the very model of a committed and dedicated politician. Both of my
parents have been major influences on my life. And it is both of them who led
me to this great calling.

I went to Badakhshan to start campaigning. Within a couple of days the
news had spread that I was to run. I set up an office in the center of Faizabad and I was thrilled when I began receiving phone calls from hundreds
of young people, both boys and girls, volunteering to campaign for me. The
youth wanted change and they saw me as the candidate to bring it. My office
was buzzing with vitality and optimism.

The days of campaigning were grueling. We didn't have much time, and
had very limited funds and a massive geographical area to cover. My days
began at 5:00 A.M., and more often than not I faced a five or six-hour journey
across dirt roads to reach a remote village or town before nightfall. Then back
again to Faizabad the following day and a different town the day after.

I was exhausted but determined. And I was elated by the reception I
received. In one village women came out to greet me, singing and playing
a *daira,* a small drum-type instrument made of goat skin. They sang and
clapped and threw flowers and sweets at me. I already knew for sure I would
win the women's vote because I spoke a lot about the issues that mattered to
them—maternal mortality, lack of access to education, child health. In some
areas of Badakhshan women work just as hard as men and are out in the
fields from dawn to dusk. Yet they still don't have the right to own property. If
their husband dies then the property is often passed to another male relative
instead of to the wife. To me that's wrong.

And I understood these women and admired them. My life was radically
different from theirs. I dressed in the latest fashions and used a computer;
they came to greet me with filthy hands and had never read a book. But I had

grown up in the same way as them. My mother's life was just like theirs. I understood their daily struggles and respected them without patronizing them. I know many people in the West will consider these women to be nameless, faceless victims, but I don't see it like that. They are proud, strong, intelligent, and resourceful females.

Convincing male voters, especially the older ones, was harder. In another village I was supposed to give a speech in a mosque, which was the largest building in the place and the only reasonable location. But the speech almost didn't happen because some of the elders didn't want me to go inside the mosque. I had to sit in the car while the local men and male members of my campaign team debated it. When they finally decreed I could go inside I was so nervous I forgot to say "In the name of Allah" when I started my speech, a very silly mistake on my part. I expected a hostile response after that. But as I talked I saw some of the old men at the back were crying. They were wrinkled gray-haired men in turbans and traditional long striped coats, and they had tears streaming down their cheeks. After I had finished they told me that they had known my father and that hearing me speak had been a reminder of the passion and sincerity he also used to put in his speeches. Hearing them say that made me cry, too.

I didn't wear the burqa when I was out campaigning because I needed to look people in the eye and communicate with them. But I did make sure to wear respectful and extremely modest local clothes, a long baggy dress over loose trousers. The same type of dress one of our neighbors had once used to hide my six-year-old brother from his would-be assassins.

As the campaign rolled on, so did my levels of support. In one extremely remote district called Jurm, I was thrilled to arrive and find a convoy of over 70 cars waiting for us. Both elders and young men sat waving Afghan flags and my campaign posters. This wasn't an area I knew particularly well and one that my father hadn't represented either. But they supported me because they really cared about the elections. They were interested in the democratic process and wanted to make their voice heard by selecting their own local leader. It is often said by critics of the United States that America has forced democracy on an unwilling Afghanistan and that it is pointless to have democratic processes in such a feudal country. I strongly disagree with that criticism. The United States has supported democracy in Afghanistan but has not forced it upon us. Afghanistan has had democratic traditions for centuries, whether that is selecting *arbabs* (local leaders) or the tradition of elders voting on local issues at *loya jirgas* (local councils). Voting for national government is only a step further on from that. And I had no doubt that the people I met, even the illiterate and poor, wanted this chance to vote for change. Who in the world would not want to vote if it was safe to do so and they were given the opportunity?

As I drove around the province it was a strange feeling seeing my poster and picture staring down at me. It adorned cars, shop windows, and houses. I began to feel a sense of rising panic. What if I let these people down? What if I couldn't justify their belief in me? What if I couldn't deliver the services they badly wanted?

At night I would be wracked with self-doubt. I was afraid that I would win this time, but then lose all trust by the next elections. The thought of losing the trust of these nice old men with the honest faces or the women who grabbed me with calloused hands and told me my struggle was their struggle tormented me.

People liked me but only because they needed someone to help them.

But realistic delivery is one thing. Convincing people I wasn't able to make them rich or wave a magic wand was another. One woman asked me if I could make sure she was given a free house in Kabul. She really believed I could do that for her. But I had to explain that that is not an MP's job, at least not an MP who doesn't believe in corruption.

As the campaign wore on I got more and more excited. Dawn broke at 4:00 a.m. and with it my day began. Most days I didn't get to bed until after midnight. I got as many as 200 calls a day from people wanting to ask me questions or offering to volunteer. The whole thing just took on a momentum of its own.

I remember one man who rang me and told me none of the women in his family, his wife or his mother, had voting cards because he had not given them permission to vote. But that these women had all been urging him to use his own vote to vote for me. He had no idea who I was or what I represented so he called me up to ask. He was so traditional, a man who would not let his wife vote but who did respect her view enough to bother to find out about the candidate she liked. He reminded me a little of my father. At the end of the conversation he promised me his vote. I hope in later years he let his wife vote, too.

Some of the calls were hostile. I had several men, complete strangers, call me and tell me I was a whore for running for office. Some simply screamed down the phone at me, telling me to go back home and leave politics to the men. Others told me I was a bad Muslim and should be punished. I tried not to let these types of calls upset me, but of course they always do.

In one town we visited the house of some of my mother's sisters. As a child I used to love visiting these relatives because I remembered the women as super glamorous, particularly one aunt who always wore makeup. Their house then had been noisy and warm, and I remember being smothered in hugs and kisses and the scent of perfume. Now the house was silent. Only two old ladies survived and living with them were several children. The children were assorted relatives who had been orphaned. It was so sad, a house of widows and sad-eyed children. One boy, about nine years old, stood out to me. He had lovely deep brown eyes that reminded me of my brother Muqim, the brother who had been murdered. I asked who he was and learned he was the grandson of my mother's favorite brother. That was the brother who had once galloped his horse back to our house after learning of my father's beatings and offered to take her away if she wanted to leave. He and his children had all been killed in the war, leaving only this little boy named Najibullah. I couldn't leave him there in that house of sadness, so I offered to take him home with me. Today he's a lively teenager and he lives with Shaharzad, Shuhra, and me in our house in Kabul. He goes to school and is excelling at his studies. He's wonderful with the girls and is a great help to me in the house.

Thirty-six hours before the election I still had two districts to visit, both of them a five-hour drive away in opposite directions. The rules dictated that all campaigning must cease 24 hours before voting began. I don't how we managed it but we made it to both districts. In one of them I was touched to find that my local campaign had been led by my Uncle Riza, the father of Shannaz, my father's seventh and last wife (and my half-brother Ennayat's mother). All these years later and here he was supporting me and helping me. He was a very old man but he was still sprightly and insisted on walking everywhere with us. We ate dinner and spent the night at his house. It was another reminder of how powerful and strong the tendrils of the extended family system can be. The poor man had lost most of his children, including Shannaz, in the war.

But the district I had been both dreading and longing to visit the most was my ancestral home of Koof. I hadn't been there since I was four years old. That was the day my mother grabbed me and my siblings and we ran for our lives along the riverbank while being chased by gunmen. Going back had dredged up all those old feelings of fear and loss. As our car bumped along the precipitous tracks and over the plain where my father had been murdered by the mujahideen I felt an ocean of pain wash over me. This was where my family began and where it had been destroyed.

I could barely breathe by the time we reached the village. As we drove through the main track that wove its way through the houses, the same track my father had ridden down in procession each time he took a new wife, the reality of the war was all too devastatingly clear.

The spring where we had played as children was now almost dry. The once fresh clear water that had gushed and gurgled was now just a trickle of brown. My mother's gardens and orchards, which had been her pride and joy, were dust. In her day the gardens had shone with seasonal color—greens in the spring, pink berries and blossoms in summer, fat red and orange pumpkins and peppers in the autumn, and brown nuts and purple vegetables in the winter. Now there was nothing, just the branches of a few dead trees poking into the sky like twisted skeletons.

The hooli—our house—was still standing, but only just. The whole west wing including the guest house had been destroyed. The huge pear tree that stood in the center of the yard was just a stump. It had taken a direct hit from a rocket during the war. This tree had witnessed so much. It was where I hid from my mother when I'd been naughty, where my father had hidden his weapons and where my sister and sister-in-law had been whipped with rifle butts by mujahideen for trying to steal my father's guns.

My father's suite of rooms, the Paris Suite, was still there. The gaily painted murals on the wall were still visible. This was the room where my mother and father laid together as man and wife, where I had been conceived, where my mother had washed my father's dead body, with half his skull missing, to prepare him for his funeral. I touched the cold plastered walls with my hands, tracing what I could of the patterns. Those murals had been my father's pride and joy. In his eyes they were just like the ones from the palaces of Versailles, only better.

Finally I plucked up the courage to go into the kitchen. This was the room where my mother had reigned supreme. The room where we slept on mattresses we rolled out nightly, where she told me and the other children stories of faraway lands and kings and queens, where banquets and feasts were prepared. In here we had watched the rain and snow fall and the sun rise and set from the high window set into the wall. Once upon a time I thought the whole world was in that view from the window.

I took a deep breath and walked in. My knees nearly gave way underneath me. It was almost as if I could see my mother bent over a pan of rice, ladle in her hand. I could smell the meat cooking, feel the warmth of the open fire in the center of the room. For a moment I was five again and there she was. I felt her. Then she was gone and I was left alone. Just me, the adult Fawzia, standing in a room that no longer seemed to contain all the world. Now I cried and laughed as I realized how tiny it was, just a mud room with a tiny window looking out onto a single range of mountains. Not the world at all.

I sat in the kitchen for a long time, watching through the window as the day turned to dusk and a crescent moon surrounded by twinkling stars became visible. No one disturbed me. They knew I needed that personal communion with her.

Next I needed to feel my father. I left the hooli by the back entrance and climbed the hill where he had been buried. His grave had the best view of the mountains, a 360-degree panorama of his own paradise. I knelt down beside it and prayed. Then I sat with him and spoke to the grave. I asked him for guidance and wisdom to help in this path of politics. I told him I knew he'd be shocked that it was one of his daughters and not a son who had chosen to continue the family business, but I promised him that I wouldn't let him or his memory down.

By now it was getting cold and dark and one of my mother's friends, a lady who had been one of our servants, came to call me down. She cried and shook her head sadly at my father's grave and told me not a day went by without her remembering my parents. She said my mother had been a woman who knew only kindness and saw no difference between rich and poor and that my father had been an often fearsome man but one who was determined to improve the lot of his friends and neighbors, whatever the personal sacrifice to himself.

She stroked my cheek and looked me straight in the eye: "Fawzia jan, you will win this election and take your seat in the parliament. You will win it for them. You will."

It was not a statement of confidence in my abilities. It was an order. I had to do it. The Koofi political dynasty was about to rise once again.

Dear Shuhra and Shaharzad,

Politics has always been at the core of our family. Over the generations it has shaped us, defined our lives, how we live, even who we marry.

I have always shared the family love of politics but I never thought it would be the career I chose. I wanted an education and I wanted to be a doctor and heal people.

I never wanted a life in politics.

But it seems it was always going to be my destiny. And in some ways your father's arrest was the start of my own politicization. When he was arrested I could not, would not, sit at home and wait, doing nothing. I had to gather resources, find allies, try and see the bigger picture and work with it.

I was tired of being told to stay back quietly and not to dishonor the men. Where was that getting us? Nowhere.

I had an education and I had a voice, and I was determined to use it to save my husband.

That same voice and desire to save those in trouble is still what guides me through my political life today.

Perhaps my failure to save your father is an even greater motivation. Every injustice I can help solve as an MP perhaps makes up a little for what I could not do to save his life.

With love,
Your mother

NINETEEN

A MOVEMENT
FOR CHANGE

On election day the mood was jubilant. My sisters had been mobilizing female voters, arranging free transport to take them to and from the polling stations. We didn't care who the women wanted to vote for, whether it was me or another candidate, we just wanted to make sure the women with voting cards actually got a chance to use them. My sisters were dressed in their burqas so people didn't know who they were, but they came to the office excitedly and told me virtually all of the women on the transport said they were voting for me.

I knew I was going to win by then but I was still tense. This is Afghanistan and anything can happen. I also worried I might get killed. But in some ways I was more worried about what would happen after I won, and about how I would cope with the expectations and the pressure.

The polling stations opened at 6 A.M. One of my sisters had hired a car and wanted to visit as many polling stations as possible in order to check that there was no cheating or fraud, a problem that blights almost every Afghan election. She rang me from the first polling station. She was shouting, actually screaming: "Something is wrong here, the election staff are supporting a candidate; they are not neutral. They are telling people who to vote for!"

I called some of my contacts in the electoral commission and asked them to send monitors. A Western member of staff went to check the situation and then called me back to say everything was fine. But of course no one would commit fraud openly in front of a foreigner.

Then I got a call from another district to say the same thing was happening there. One of the candidates was the brother of a local police commander and all the policemen in that area had been ordered to go vote for him. My campaign office kicked into action. They started to call all the journalists we knew—the BBC, the local Afghan radio stations, anyone we could think of. We had to get the message out that we knew they were cheating because that was the only way to stop it.

My half-brother Nadir had wanted to stand for election himself and had been very opposed to my candidacy. I think he was more opposed because he didn't think it was a job for a woman rather than being angry at not having won the family selection. If another brother had won against him he'd have been happier. Earlier in the campaign he had allegedly been furious every time he saw my face on a poster, even ripping some of them down. But on this day his family loyalty took precedence over his resentment. He spent the day driving to some of the most remote polling stations to monitor them, and when the roads were too bad to drive he got out and trekked. He had not wanted me to stand but now that I had he most certainly was not going to allow his little sister to lose because of fraud.

At the end of the day all the ballot boxes were collected and brought to Faizabad. They were locked overnight and counting started the following day. My volunteer campaign team was so scared that election staff might tamper with the boxes overnight that two of them decided to spend the night outside the election offices. They had no blankets with them but they stayed there the whole night. I was so touched by the dedication these young volunteers showed me.

The counting process took two very long weeks in total but all early indications were that despite the fraud I would win the seat.

I felt the tension lift and was able to finally get some rest. That evening I was enjoying a dinner with friends when my brother Mirshakay rang me from Denmark. He was crying and sobbing hysterically. His eldest son Najib had drowned that afternoon.

My brother had two wives. His second wife was with him in Denmark but his first wife had opted to stay in Afghanistan. Najib was the son of the first wife and the only child she and my brother had together. He was a lovely kind young man and had been part of my campaign team. He'd worked so hard for his Aunt Fawzia. The morning after the election he'd gone with friends on a picnic and decided to swim. The current took him by surprise and swept him away. I struggled to believe what I was hearing. Why did every happy event in my family have to end with a tragedy or a death?

The counting process took two weeks. Toward the middle of the first week we became aware that some of the election commission staff were cheating. They had been seen removing ballot papers with my name on them and not counting them. One of my supporters actually saw it happen with his own eyes. He was furious and began shouting: "Look she is a woman and she is risking her life to stand. Why don't you count her vote? We are the young generation and we want her to lead us." The argument escalated so violently that the police were called.

Fortunately the police chief took the allegations seriously and ordered a recount of several boxes while they watched. On the recount I received 300 extra votes just from a few boxes. They most certainly had been cheating.

At the end of the count I had won 8,000 votes. The candidate who came next won only 7,000. As a female candidate I was part of a quota system designed to ensure at least two women from each province entered parliament on reserved seats. I had only needed 1,800 votes to fulfill the quota, but I would have won anyway, quota or no quota. I have mixed feeling about these quota systems. I can see why quotas are important in male-dominated countries like Afghanistan, where women might need extra support to enter politics. But I also feel it can stop people from taking us seriously. I want to win people's votes on an equal playing field.

By the time confirmation came that I had won, I was aware that politics had changed my life utterly. Privacy was a thing of my past. There was now a constant stream of visitors at my door, asking for my help on everything from employment issues to illness. It was overwhelming.

And without a husband it was even harder. Most other MPs have a partner to help them manage daily life and deal with guests. With Hamid gone it was just me. The girls were upset because I wasn't able to put them to bed every night like I had before. I felt guilty and torn and wondered if I had made the right decision. Like working women all over the world I wondered if I had selfishly put my own ambitions ahead of my children. But then I thought back to my father. Had it been so different for him? Didn't he also feel guilt at leaving his wives and brood for weeks on end because of his job? It was the price we had to pay. And I consoled myself by trying to remind myself that part of the reason I wanted to work for change was so that my daughters had a better country to live in.

But then the smears and rumors started against me. And I really realized just how hard it is to be a woman in a man's world. My opponents, angry at my victory, started a series of viciously untrue slanders. They ranged from the suggestion that I had a rich businessman boyfriend in Dubai who had funded my campaign to the fact that I had lied about my achievements on my resume. But the most hurtful of all was that I had divorced Hamid in order to stand for election and had lied about his death. According to this particularly nasty rumor Hamid was alive and well and living in a mountain village.

I was still grieving so badly for my husband that the allegation that I had lied about his death made me shake with rage. How dare these people speak filth, pure hurtful filth like this? It is nothing short of disgusting. Unfortunately I was not alone in suffering this. Most female politicians had suffered similarly vicious untrue rumors against them. And they were more than just hurtful, they were downright dangerous. In Afghanistan a woman's reputation and honor can mean her life. And my opponents knew that.

It was a crazy period of adjustment. On some days I had 500 people come to see me. At times people had to sit in corridors because there was no room. They all wanted to know what my policies were, what I was going to do for them. I had to sit and talk to everyone individually, explaining the same thing over and over again. It was clear I couldn't go on like this, so after a few weeks I managed to get a little more organized and hired staff to manage an appointments system.

In October 2005 the new democratic parliament opened after 33 years of conflict. On the day of the opening ceremony I was beside myself with joy. The streets were closed to traffic because of the risk of suicide bombers trying to disrupt proceedings. But people still came out onto the streets to wave flags and dance the Attan, the national dance.

A bus came to take all the female MPs together to the parliament and as I drove past the dancing citizens I felt such joy in my heart. We passed a big poster of president Karzai and Ahmed Shah Massoud and I started to cry. I really felt that I was part of a new Afghanistan, a country that was finally leaving violence behind and embracing peace. Whatever personal sacrifices I was making now, it would be worth it to achieve this.

For the first time in my life, I had a sense of pride and maturity and a feeling that I could change things. I had both the power and a voice to make a difference. I was so very happy, but I still couldn't stop crying. Since Hamid died, I rarely cry. I've been through so much in my life: my father assassinated, my brother murdered, my mother dying, my husband dying, our house being looted. I've cried so many tears over the years that these days I have no tears left. But on that momentous occasion, I think I cried the whole day long. Only this time, they were tears of happiness.

I had never been inside the parliament building until that day and I was almost overcome with excitement at the thought that this was my new place of work and my office. Under the new postwar system of governance that had been decided for Afghanistan, the National Assembly was created as the national legislature. It is a bicameral body, composed of the lower house called the Wolesi Jirga (House of the People) and the upper house known as the Meshrano Jirga (House of the Elders). I was one of sixty-eight women in the lower house and twenty-three women in the upper house. The lower house is made up of 250 members elected to five-year terms directly by the people, in proportion to the population of each province; a quota requirement of two women from each province was instituted to ensure women got elected. In the upper house, one-third of the members are elected by provincial councils for four years, one-third are elected by district councils of each province for three years and one-third are appointed by the president. Again, there is a quota to ensure female representation. Finally, there is the Stera Mahkama, the Supreme Court, which constitutes Afghanistan's highest chamber in the judicial system. The Stera Mahkama is made up of nine judges appointed by the president to a ten-year term, with the approval of the parliament. Judges must be at least forty years of age, have a degree in law or Islamic jurisprudence, and be free of any affiliation to a political party.

As I looked around the room, I realized some of my fellow MPs were former presidents, ministers, governors, and powerful mujahideen commanders—all now sitting in the same room as women like me.

King Zahir Shah, the former monarch who had promised to bring democracy so many years ago and the man whom my father had served, was also there. He was a very old man now and had lived in exile in Europe, but he made this one last historic trip back home.

The national anthem was played and we all stood up. More national songs were played, including one called "Daz Ma Zeba Watan" (which can be roughly translated as "This Land Was My Ancestors"). It's one of my favorite songs and sums up how I feel about my country. The lyrics go like this:

> This is our beautiful land
> This is our beloved land
> This land is our life
> This Afghanistan.
>
> This country is our life
> This country is our faith
> Our children say this when they are crawling
> This is the land of our grandfather
> This is the land of our grandmother.
>
> It is very dear to us
> This Afghanistan.
> I sacrifice myself to its rivers
> I sacrifice myself to its deserts
> I sacrifice myself to its streams.
>
> This is the land that we know
> My heart is made bright by it
> This Afghanistan
> Our heart is made bright by it
> This Afghanistan.
>
> This is our beautiful land
> This is our beloved land
> This land is our life
> This Afghanistan.

As I looked around at my fellow new MPs, I felt I could see all of Afghanistan in their different faces. There were men in big turbans and long coats, intellectuals in smart suits and ties, young people, old people, women, people from every different ethnic group.

This is what democracy means to me. People with different views, cultural beliefs, and experiences coming together under one roof in order to work alongside one another for a common aim. After so much bloodshed and tears, it was a beautiful thing to see and even more beautiful to be part of it.

After the music and pomp of the opening ceremony was over, it was time to settle down to business. I was determined not to be dismissed as "just a woman," so from day one I spoke up about issues and quickly gained a reputation for being both outspoken and capable. I also made it clear I would work professionally and cooperate with everyone. There were many men in the parliament who were opposed to the women MPs and did their best to intimidate us. They also tried to belittle any male MPs who showed us support. One male MP was shouted down in a debate on education after he backed the view of a woman. Other male MPs started to heckle him and derided as a "feminist."

I've gotten used to those things now. The atmosphere in the Afghan parliament is loud and often almost verging on violence. A tug of the beard is an ancient way to tell someone they have offended you. Some days an awful lot of tugging goes on. I decided that showing hostility or shouting back in these situations would achieve nothing. Instead I tried to create an atmosphere of mutual respect. I listened politely to opposing views and tried to find common ground wherever I could. Democracy is about fighting your corner but it is also about learning to accept that sometimes you just have to agree to disagree.

But at the same time I made a vow to myself to never lose sight of my principles and values. If you always go along with the popular flow then you are lost and lose sight of what you believe in. What I believe in is promoting human rights, striving for gender equality, and alleviating poverty.

Sadly some of the female MPs found the process too much. To this day I still haven't heard some of them utter a single word.

All the new MPs had to put our hands on the Holy Quran and swear allegiance to the country. We promised to be honest to Afghanistan and be honest to the people of Afghanistan. When I put my hand on the Quran to swear I felt the wave of responsibility wash over me.

Given the rampant levels of corruption in my country today it seems not all of my colleagues took their vow of honesty seriously.

The next day, the debate began for the election of leadership positions, such as speaker, deputy speakers and secretaries, which are highly important senior political positions in the house. I had already made some good friends among other MPs, such as Sabrina Saqib, who had the proud honor of being the youngest member of parliament. I told her I wanted to run for the position of deputy speaker. My feeling was that I risked nothing by doing so and that even if I lost, the very act of running would ensure that the new female voices were being heard at the most senior level in the legislature.

Sabrina was supportive and agreed that it would be good for all the women if I stood, but she warned me that I was unlikely to win and would face a great deal of opposition from some of the men. She also feared I wasn't well known enough yet and did not have other big-name MPs supporting me.

I then talked to my family, who also urged caution. Nadir, the brother who held the local political role of district manager in Badakhshan's Koof district, was totally against it. He said to me: "Fawzia jan, it was more than enough for a woman to become an MP. You should not be more ambitious. If you stand for speaker, you will lose. That would not look good for the political reputation of our family. Politics is not just about you, Fawzia. It is about the political dynasty of our whole family."

Those words stung, but I understood what he was trying to say. Traditionally politics in Afghanistan is seen as just winning a battle or gaining power, not as a genuine means by which ordinary people can use their voice to demonstrate their will. In the past, if a member of one of Afghanistan's political families lost in an election, it damaged the reputation of the whole family. But that was a risk I was prepared to take. This was a much bigger battle for me. It was a battle to serve the people of my country.

Finally, I talked to Shuhra and Shaharzad. Here, I got the best reaction of all. Shuhra was only six years old and Shaharzad seven. Shuhra, in an early sign of her genuine political leanings, had a great campaign idea. She said, "I will gather one hundred children from my school and give them flags, then we will come to the parliament to ask the MPs to vote for you." I gave her a big kiss of thanks. I was surprised how sophisticated her idea was for a child of six and extremely proud that she was already learning to think big.

Shaharzad is a gentle and thoughtful child who reminds me so much of her father. She took my hand and gave me a long, earnest look as she said, "Mother, one of the women should have a senior position in this parliament. And it is better it is you who has it, because I know you are the best. I know it means you will be away from us even more and working very hard, but that's okay with us." I almost cried. It is exactly what Hamid would have said. I decided to run.

The corridors in the parliament building resonated with talk of only one thing: Who was going to run for the positions? My candidacy seemed like a big joke to many MPs, especially the ones who had made plenty of money through war profiteering and involvement in criminal activities. This only strengthened my resolve to win the post of deputy speaker. The wealthier MPs started to court favor by throwing lavish evening parties at their homes and in some of Kabul's smartest restaurants and hotels, inviting those who might vote for them. I didn't have any spare cash for that kind of thing, and it had been noted that I was the only candidate who hadn't organized an event. The night before the voting, my sister helped organize a small dinner party for me at a very inexpensive, low-key restaurant. It was by no means a smart place, but it was all I could afford. Around twenty MPs turned up.

The night of the dinner was freezing, and the restaurant was so cold inside that you could see your breath when you exhaled. I asked the restaurant manager to try to sort out some heating. He brought out a very cheap, old oil heater called a *bukhari,* which leaked noxious fumes. The food was awful, cold and congealed. After a while, guests could barely even see each other because the *bukhari* was giving off so much smoke. I was extremely tense, but I tried my best to cover it up and be a good hostess. But when we got home, I shook my head and sighed, telling my sister that I'd blown it. After such a disastrous social function, no one was going to vote for me. Being able to entertain people and be a gracious host is an important part of our culture, and if you fail at it people judge you harshly.

The children were already asleep. I climbed into bed next to them, but I couldn't sleep. The voting was the next day, and all the candidates were supposed to give a short speech before it began. In the middle of the night, I got up to write mine. I sat there until the early hours staring at a blank piece of paper, not knowing where to start or what to say. Usually I love writing speeches and it comes straight from my heart, but with this one I was at a loss of what say. I started to write, promising this and that, only to tear it up because it just didn't sound right. All the candidates had been told to prepare only very short speeches. But I wanted to write something that defined me and my values, and it was almost impossible to express that in just a few sentences. Dawn started to creep across the clouds and into my bedroom. By now, I was on my third or fourth attempt; I looked at it again. It still didn't work. I tore up the piece of paper and resolved to just ad lib. I was sure that once I was standing there in front of my fellow MPs, I'd know what I needed to say.

The next morning, all the candidates and their supporters were running along the corridors of parliament making last-ditch attempts to win supporters. There were ten other candidates for the position of deputy speaker. All of them were well known except for me. Some of them were powerful people. Around 10 A.M., I had a visit from a staff member of one of my opponents, asking me to withdraw my candidacy and offering to pay me a substantial amount of money if I did so. I was horrified but sadly not shocked. How could these people try to win such an important vote by paying to win? And how dare they think I would be bribed?

The plenary voting session started. I sat quietly in a corner just gathering my thoughts and watching the situation unfold. If nothing else, it was certainly an exciting scene to witness and be a part of.

Then, I was called to give my introductory speech. I walked up to the podium, aware of some male MPs watching me with mocking or angry eyes. Out of the corner of my eye, I saw my good friend Sabrina give me a supportive smile, which helped control my nerves. This was the first time I had given any kind of speech in front of the other MPs, and I struggled to keep my body from shaking. Then suddenly I remembered that I had won over eight thousand votes. I had every right to be there.

As I looked around, my sense of confidence and self-esteem grew. I took a deep breath and started by introducing myself. Then I told them that I wanted to run for this position to demonstrate that women in Afghanistan are able to do big things and hold senior posts; that my mission would be to put my country's interests before my personal interests; that I saw an Afghanistan that had been severely damaged in every way and needed new voices and new energy to rebuild it. I told them that although I was only thirty, I was not a novice and already had a huge amount of professional experience. I went on to say how much I loved Afghanistan and our culture, and how my entire commitment was to change this country for the better. I was talking quickly, as I usually do when speaking from the heart, and I was so focused that at first I almost didn't hear the clapping. Then it became louder. By the time I finished, several MPs—men, women, traditionalists, the powerful—were clapping loudly.

Many MPs came up to me, congratulating me on the sincerity of the speech. An old friend of my father's, a Pashtun man from Kunduz province, came and kissed me gently on the forehead and whispered that I had done my father justice. The reaction was so positive that for the first time I started to think I might actually win. I could barely breathe when the counting started.

I won with a large majority.

It was the first time in Afghan history that a woman, a "poor girl," had been elected to such a senior political position. I couldn't take it all in. My face was as radiant as a blooming flower and for a moment I thought I was flying through the air.

Suddenly, I was surrounded by journalists firing questions at me. What were my priorities on women? How would I bring change? How would a woman cope with the scrutiny of such a senior parliamentary position? This was my first real press conference experience and it was fairly intimidating, but I tried to answer honestly and clearly. I am not an MP who dislikes journalists. I think in our country many journalists do a fantastic job of sharing information with the public and challenging those in power, so I have always tried to treat the media with the respect it deserves. Over the next few days, I was almost besieged by media attention. No one had expected a woman to achieve what I had, and I became a national novelty. But I was determined to make each interview show that I was more than just a point of curiosity; I was a serious politician who was more than capable of doing the job I held.

Karzai then announced his cabinet of ministers. The only female minister was Masooda Jalal, a former medical doctor. She had been the only woman to run against Hamid Karzai in the presidential race. She had lost, gaining only a small number of votes, but Karzai appointed her minister of women's affairs. To this day, a woman hasn't held any other mainstream ministerial post, something I find very disappointing. If a woman can be the women's minister, why can't she be the minister for business? Or communications? Or indeed any of the other senior posts, provided she has the relevant experience, of course. Karzai did make one other high-profile appointment. A highly-respected woman by the name of Habiba Sorabi was given the post of governor of central Bamiyan province in March 2005. She has since become a very well-known and popular figure in Afghan politics.

With all the roles in place, the parliament opened for business. This was another truly historic event, and it was broadcast on live TV both in Afghanistan and around the world. As the speaker was not present, I had to chair the first plenary session. I looked around and once again realized that here I was chairing a parliament in which former presidents, ministers, and mujahideen leaders were all sitting. But I wasn't nervous. Debating is one of the things I enjoy most in life, so to have the chance of chairing such an important debate was wonderful. I simply loved it.

That day went very well, and afterwards a number of male MPs commented on how surprised they had been that a woman had managed the task of keeping order so well. They too now recognized what an important symbol this was for Afghan women and for the nation.

But very soon the jealousy started. Some of the old MPs, the corrupt ones, are losing power and public support day by day. And they know it. These old-style politicians who use guns and intimidation as their means of communication could not stomach the fact that a young woman like me was growing in political popularity and influence. When I would walk past them in the corridors or step down from the podium, I would hear them muttering, "A woman is chairing our parliament and we must just sit here and watch? She cannot be allowed to continue."

I tried to ignore them and started focusing on providing the services that voters had wanted when they elected me. The Kabul-Faizabad road, for example, was still a dirt track with no asphalt. I started to lobby for funds to build a proper highway that would for the first time link Badakhshan with the capital city. On a political visit to the United States, I met President George W. Bush and his wife, Laura. I found Laura to be a very pleasant, warm woman and I liked her immensely. She seemed genuinely committed to civil issues—children's rights, education for women, school-building projects, human rights. I got the sense that as a mother herself she understood the plight of women and children in developing countries. She asked me many intelligent questions about the situation in my country and listened carefully as I outlined what I thought she and the United States could do to help. I felt encouraged by her support.

I also used my time in the United States to try to gain wider support for construction of the road. The US ambassador told me he couldn't make me any promises, but that my request had been noted. Four months later, I learned that the US Agency for International Development had approved the budget for the road. I was thrilled.

The road is now complete and it has improved the lot of Badakhshanis immeasurably. What was once a three-day journey to Kabul now takes less than a day. The road takes in some wonderful scenery, and I think it's the most beautiful in all Afghanistan. Some Badakhshanis have nicknamed it "Fawzia's road." The road on the other side of the Atanga Pass is still not complete, despite my best efforts. But I will not rest until this road is also built. I feel I owe it to my father to complete the dream that he so bravely started.

In recent years, I have met several other famous international politicians, including Tony Blair, Gordon Brown, and David Cameron, the previous and current prime ministers of the United Kingdom. I met Hillary Clinton twice. I find her an incredibly inspiring woman who has a definite grace and power about her. I also met Stephen Harper, the Canadian prime minister, and Peter MacKay, the Canadian defense minister.

I have yet to meet President Obama, but I hope I shall. Afghans followed his campaign and subsequent election very closely, and he became a very popular figure here. There was something very inspiring to us about his journey to become the first black president of the United States. Many Afghans also regarded him as someone who would favor negotiation over war and who had a very strong understanding of foreign policy and global issues.

As the years have passed, I have made some very good friends and allies at the international level, among the fraternity of diplomats and among aid workers and journalists. I believe we all have something to learn from each other and that cooperation between nations is essential. For too long, Afghanistan has allowed itself to be a pawn that is moved and shifted by the hands of more powerful players. I believe that Afghanistan can and will one day take its rightful role as a power player within the Asian region. As a nation, we need to learn to work more strategically with our allies and stand up to our enemies.

We don't have to be a nation that the world either fears as terrorists or pities as victims. We are a great people and we can be a great nation. Achieving this for my country is my life's ambition. I'm not certain what God's purpose is for me, only that he has one. It may be that he has chosen me to lead my country out of the abyss of corruption and poverty or simply that he wants me to be a hard-working MP and a good mother who will raise two shining stars as daughters.

Whatever the future holds for me and my nation, I know that God alone wills it.

Dear Father,

I was almost four years old when you were martyred. In that short time you only addressed me directly once, and that was to tell me to go away.

I don't know how you would react to seeing me in the position that I am in today. But I like to think that you'd be proud of what the youngest child of your favorite wife has achieved.

I barely knew you, my father, but I know I have inherited many of your qualities. When I hear people tell stories about you I am always proud of your honesty, frankness, and hard work. So many years after your death and you are still remembered for these qualities.

I think that if you are not honest with yourself then you cannot be honest with others. I know your frankness made you different from the other members of parliament. I know you always believed in what you did and would stand by your values and the decisions you took on behalf of your people. These characteristics made you a great man.

In my job as an MP, the very same job that you used to do before me, I often think of you and wonder how you would react to a difficult situation.

Remembering you gives me the courage to remain fearless and determined—over 30 years later and you still lead by example.

I inherited more than your values, Father. I inherited your political legacy. It is a legacy I will never betray. Even if I know that one day, just like you, I will probably be killed because of this work.

But I don't want that to happen, Father. And perhaps, God willing, it won't. If I stay alive then perhaps one day I might even get to be president. What do you think of that, Father? I hope that thought makes you smile in heaven.

With love,
Your daughter

TWENTY

A DREAM FOR A
WAR-TORN NATION

Let me share with you a memory.

Two years ago I went to one of the villages in Badakhshan in order to hear the problems of the people and to find out what I could do to help them. On the way the weather became dark and we had to spend the night in one of the houses in the village. The family that we spent the night with was one of the richest families of what was a very poor village. The house owner guided us toward his home, and the young people of the village had lined up on the both sides of the road to welcome us. After greeting them we went on toward our host's house.

A beautiful young woman, about 30 years old, wearing ragged clothes and a red scarf came out of the house to welcome us. I greeted the woman and she bent to kiss my hands. I was embarrassed. I did not expect the young and beautiful woman to respect me in that way. I hadn't done anything for this woman or for her village, so I didn't allow her to kiss my hands. The woman, who seemed unhappy and worried, invited us into the living room. The room was small and dark. It took a while for my eyes to adjust to the darkness. When they did I noticed she was heavily pregnant.

The woman brought us green tea, dried mulberries, and walnuts. I asked her how many children she had. She replied that she had five children and was now seven months pregnant.

I was worried about the woman because she did not look right. She left the room again and came back with a big plate of sweet Afghan rice pudding that she had made for us. She spread out a cloth and then put the big wooden bowl of rice on it.

Dinner was a good time for me to try and engage her in conversation in order to get more information. I started by talking about the weather. I said: "It's summer but your village is high in the mountains and the weather still feels cold; in winter it must be very cold here." The shy woman replied: "Yes, in winter we have a lot of snow, we can't even get out of the house it snows so heavily." I asked her: "How do you work then? Is someone helping you with the house work?"

She replied: "No one helps me. I wake up at four in the morning. I clear the snow until the doors of the stable are accessible, then I feed the cows and other animals. After that I prepare dough and bake bread in the tandoor oven. Then I clean the house."

"But you are heavily pregnant," I said. "Do you still do all this on your own even when pregnant?"

"Yes," she replied. She seemed surprised that I was surprised by her answer.

I told her I didn't think she looked well and that I was worried about her. She told me she felt very ill: "I work all day and at night I cannot move because I am in so much pain."

I asked her why she didn't see a doctor. She told me that it wasn't possible because the hospital was far away.

I told her that I would talk to her husband on her behalf and tell him he must take her.

She replied: "If my husband takes me to the hospital then we would have to sell a goat or a sheep in order to pay for my treatment. He would never agree to that. On top of that, how would we get there? The hospital is three days walking and we don't have a donkey or horse."

I told her that her life should be more important than a goat or a sheep. If she is healthy she can take care of the whole family, but if she is sick then she can't look after anyone.

She shook her head and smiled a slow, wistful smile of sadness: "If I die then my husband will marry somebody else, but the whole family is fed by the milk of the goats and the meat from the sheep. If we lose a goat or sheep then who will feed this family? From where will this family get food then?"

I HAVE NEVER FORGOTTEN this poor woman. And I doubt she is alive today. Her multiple pregnancies, her poor diet, her exhaustion, her lack of access to a doctor. Any one of these things could have killed her.

There are hundreds of thousands of women like her across Afghanistan.

Her attitude was typical of many. The typical Afghan woman does not fear death and wants to keep her family happy and satisfied at any cost.

Brave and kind, she is ready to sacrifice herself for the sake of others, but what does she get in return? Normally very little. And a husband who puts the cost of a goat or a sheep above his wife's life.

When I remember this woman, tears come to my eyes and I feel more compelled than ever to help all those others like her.

I have a dream that one day all the humans in Afghanistan will have equal rights. Afghan girls have talent, skill, and the capacity to be educated. They should be given every opportunity to be educated and literate, and to participate fully in the political and social future of the country.

I dream that the culture of ethnic division disappears in Afghanistan. I hope also that the Islamic values that have shaped our history and our culture are kept safe from false and wrong interpretations.

The Afghan people are the main victims of terrorism worldwide, but Afghanistan is also known to the world as the main producer of terrorists. I hope that with active diplomacy and good representation we will be able to change this understanding.

Afghanistan is traditionally a poor country but we have great resources. I hope our untapped mineral wealth can be used to combat poverty and give our country importance.

Afghanistan as a nation has witnessed great struggles. We have never accepted invasion nor been colonized or conquered. That is something we Afghans are proud of. We are warriors by nature. But this does not mean that the doors of globalization and global opportunities and cooperation should be closed for Afghanistan.

I dream that one day Afghanistan will be a nation free from the shackles of poverty. I dream it will no longer be labeled the worst place in the world for a woman or a child to be born.

Since 2001 and the fall of the Taliban billions of dollars of aid money have been spent in Afghanistan. I am grateful for every penny of it, but unfortunately much of it has been wasted or misdirected, or fell into the wrong hands, such as those of corrupt local politicians or American contracting companies who took great profits but built poor quality roads and new hospitals without proper plumbing.

Despite their good intentions some of the decisions taken by the United Nations and the international community have proved only mixed successes. At a meeting in Geneva in 2002 it was decided that the United States would train the newly formed Afghan National Army, Germany would be responsible for the police, Italy would look after the justice system, Britain would take counter narcotics, and Japan would focus on disarming illegal groups. This so-called Five Pillar approach had at its heart the issue of security, yet almost ten years after Operation Enduring Freedom began Afghanistan is still far from stable.

A large part of the problem is that for far too long Afghanistan's leaders have acted like the country is theirs to do with as they please. They forget that there's a whole nation of people living here—real people, good people, with families and businesses and children and dreams for their future. Instead Afghanistan has been run like the personal fiefdom of a few powerful men. Their agenda has generally been entirely selfish.

In the case of the Soviets, Afghanistan was as a stepping stone in their ambitions for empire, as they jealously eyed Pakistan's warm-water ports. Afghanistan lay in the way, and as such was largely an inconvenience to be subjugated as part of a greater game.

Then the mujahideen cloaked themselves in nationalism. They were the liberating heroes of our nation and while all Afghans are proud of their long and tenacious victory over the Soviets, the mujahideen's grasp for personal power turned into civil war and nearly destroyed my country. It was their infighting and the chaos that followed it that opened the door for the Taliban.

The Taliban strove for a kind of great backward leap, propelling Afghanistan into a medieval era of Islamic conservatism and hyperbole barely seen in the history of the world or in Islam.

Little, if any, thought was given to the ambitions, hopes, and welfare of ordinary Afghans. Ironically, it was perhaps the Soviets who got closest, building hospitals and learning institutions to improve people's lives. But that was about a hegemonic pacification as a means of achieving a larger strategic goal, not the enrichment and development for the greater good of a diverse people who call Afghanistan home.

Ordinary Afghans, be they Pashtu, Takjiks, Hazaras, Uzbeks, Aimak, Turkmen, or Baluch, have hopes for this country. Unfortunately for far too long they have had leaders who are only interested in serving themselves, and in many ways that is still true to this day.

The average Afghan politician has the attitude that once they come to power their office and authority is a personal plaything, whether it is giving influential jobs to friends and relatives who are completely unqualified for the position, or enriching themselves through bribes and outright theft. The last thing on their minds is the welfare and happiness of the people they are supposed to represent.

Nepotism is rampant in Afghanistan's political system. Family and friends are incredibly important in my country, just as they rightly are every-where. However, our politicians have yet to realize that public office is about public service, not giving your nearest and dearest key positions in the ad-ministration. It is wrong, even when such appointments are well intended, for example: "I need someone I can trust. Well, who better than my cousin/nephew/old family friend?" It is not the way to run an effective government and is a catalyst for worse corruption. The new staff does not bring the desire to serve their nation with them. Instead, their loyalty lies with the person who hired them. Decisions are taken on the basis of what's best for each other, not what's best for the people. Accountability and transparency break down, and the fundamentals of good government are cast aside.

Sadly, while most Afghans dislike the way our government runs, many are accepting of it. Expectations of political leaders are low, and all too often dissenting voices can be bought off with a job, a contract, or maybe just cash. And if they can't be bought off? Well, sadly my country is a dangerous place. People die here all the time, and very few of the murders are ever solved. Much is written in the world media about the kidnapping of foreign aid workers, a rare but very unfortunate occurrence. These people have come only to help us and my heart weeps every time one of them lays down their life for a country that isn't even theirs. But what the media do not report is how commonly Af-ghans are kidnapped. Every rich businessman in our country knows someone who has been kidnapped for ransom. Even small children are not safe from the kidnap gangs who want their parents' money. Therefore most of the Af-ghan business people who hold dual passports have fled the country, creating a massive brain drain.

And that won't change until the system changes, and by that I mean the people whose job it is to run the country must start to do things for the right reasons. A person should be involved in public service only if they truly want to serve the public. If all our politicians and government officials were to adopt this mindset, there's no limit to what could be achieved. The billions of dollars of aid and development money that has been poured into Afghanistan would go where it is actually needed. The contract to do the work would be performed by the contractor best able to perform the service, not the one who pays the biggest bribe. The police and army would be solely loyal to their uniform and to the nation it represents, not to a corrupt boss. Local governors would diligently and honestly collect taxes and duties and deliver them to the central treasury. The central government in turn would see that the money gets spent wisely and efficiently on the ministries and projects the politicians have designated. And the politicians are beholden to listen to, and act upon, the wishes of their constituents.

I don't wish to sound politically naive at this point. All governments have their problems. But the best governments have mechanisms for improvement. That requires parliamentary inquiries where the members are free and willing to investigate and present their findings in an honest way. It requires a judiciary that can act independent of influence, and has the teeth to fight off any corrupting pressure. It requires a police force disciplined and proud enough to refuse committing petty larceny, and bold enough to investigate any level of criminal activity, no matter who is implicated.

So where does one start in a country that has the dubious honor of being rated one of the top three most corrupt countries in the world according to Transparency International's World Corruption Index? I believe it has to begin with the opposition. Only when there is the political will to listen to the people and act on their behalf with honesty and integrity can things begin to improve in Afghanistan. This is my personal opinion, but it is one formed by talking to hundreds, maybe thousands of ordinary people. Many Afghans have given up hope, or maybe resigned themselves to never having an honest government. They have been fed a diet of rubbish politics for 30 years, so it's no wonder the political health of this nation has suffered. As a country we are politically malnourished, and our growth has been stunted as a consequence. This is beginning to change, though. There is a rare breed of politicians who are listening to the electorate and acting with honesty and integrity. And in doing so they are winning the respect and trust of the people.

So much of Afghanistan's success as a democracy hinges on two things. The first is education. All people, all children, both boys and girls, must receive a decent, affordable education. They need it for their personal future, but they also need it to make informed decisions about the future of their country. The second is security. There needs to be law and order so that ordinary Afghan families can build their lives safely and in peace. And when it comes time to elect a government they need to feel safe both during the act of voting and in the knowledge that their vote actually counts. Afghans generally want the opportunity to elect their leaders. They don't, however, yet know what it means to have free and fair elections.

If a genuinely democratic government can be established then I hope that given time, all aspects of government, including the security forces, will form the backbone of a stable, free, and just society. There is something of a chicken and egg argument here. Does security produce better government? Or does good governance produce security? The answer is probably both.

And what about the Taliban, who stand for both and neither at the same time?

As I write this book, the world's powers are talking about withdrawal from Afghanistan. In my view, they are planning to withdraw before the job is finished and while war and conflict still blight our land. This conflict could at any point explode on an international scale. The warning that the great Ahmed Shah Massoud gave the West that terrorism would come to its shores is more relevant than ever. Unless our international friends start to work on a wider regional approach to tackle the Taliban issue, then the dangers to the world remain.

Recently, there have been many talks about Taliban reconciliation and reintegration into the government. Much of this process has been led by the international community and its purpose is to serve the agenda of withdrawing their troops as quickly as possible. But that is a mistake. It is another short-term quick fix that will do nothing to solve the world's problems, only store them up and make them worse for another day.

The Taliban will argue that their form of conservative Islam is the only form of government Afghanistan needs, and that they alone can bring stability to the country. But they've proven through their interpretation of education and health care policy that at least half the population suffers greatly under their rule. And their views on security and justice bear no resemblance to what most people want or expect. Should they be given a political voice? I suppose under the type of democratic system I believe in everybody has a say in politics. But that is the point—politics is about talking, reasoning, and persuading. It is hard to see how the Taliban will ever sit in a parliament alongside female politicians like me. I have just won a second term in the parliament and received even more votes than I did the first time. Like my father before me I am proud to say I am known as an honest politician who is not afraid to speak out when needed. I believe the Afghan public now sees me as a politician first and a woman second. This is something I am extremely proud of.

Yet the Taliban will never accept this and they make regular attempts on my life and on the lives of many other intellectuals, opponents, and friends of the West. Are these people who will ever understand or respect what democracy means? I doubt it.

Will they sit in debates with us and try to reach a common ground? Will they support new legislation or ideas put forward by me or other women? The answer is no. And it is naive of the international community to think this is possible. So much has been done in recent years to support and enhance the overall progress of Afghan women; bringing the Taliban back into the government will undo all of that.

As I drive through Kabul, I always smile when I see the beautiful sight of little girls dressed in the school uniform of black *shalwar kameez* and white head scarves. Within the past decade, hundreds of thousands of little girls, including my own daughters, have gained the opportunity to be educated. This not only gives them the chance of a future but also improves the future economic and physical health of their families. This in turn helps our entire nation grow stronger and powerful. If the Taliban returns, these little girls will once again be forced back indoors and silenced underneath their burqas and a set of arcane laws that accord women fewer rights than dogs. Our nation will once again slide backwards into darkness. To allow this to happen would be a betrayal of the highest order.

In October 2010, I won a second term in the parliament. I had not let my people down and, despite widespread fraud and cheating on the part of some of my opponents, I got even more votes than I did the first time.

I was also thrilled that my elder sister Qandigul (known as Maryam to her family) was elected as an MP. She is the sister who was beaten by the mujahideen the night my mother refused to show them where my father's weapons were hidden. She was illiterate and did not attend school as a child (I was the only female member of my family allowed to do so). But after she married and had children, she watched as I gained my education and saw what I had achieved. She too wanted to serve our country and do something important with her life, so she decided to educate herself. She started by going to night school to take computer and literacy classes and a few years later she graduated with a university degree. Now she is an MP like me and the latest member of the Koofis to take her place in the family business of politics. I am immensely proud of her achievements and I know she will work hard in her new role.

During the latest elections, there were even more threats on my life: gunmen trailing my car, roadside bombs laid along my route, warnings that I would be kidnapped. On the day of voting, two people were arrested who admitted that they had planned to kidnap me, take me to a different district, and then kill me. It was reported that they had links to other local politicians, but the politicians denied any involvement. One of the men has since been released while the other remains in custody. I cannot explain why one of these men was released without charge after admitting his evil project. I can only say that due to my outspokenness, I cannot always rely on our national security forces as much as I would like. Often I don't know who my would-be assassins are, whether they wear civilian clothes or official uniforms. At times in Kabul, I have had my car pulled off the road and been intimidated by our national intelligence forces, always without reason or explanation. This has become such a daily part of my life now. I will not say I am used to it—no one can ever get used to such threats—but I have learned to live with it.

Like my father, I am not afraid to speak out on difficult issues when needed. I have proven that I can deliver services and direct funds to those in need. Of course, the people I represent are still among the world's poorest and much work still needs to be done.

But I know I have improved their lives by bringing them roads, schools, jobs, and mosques. Recently I championed the building of a series of women's mosques in some remote and very conservative villages.

The mosques are a place to pray, and no man would deny his wife the chance to leave home for an hour a day to worship God. Sometimes it is the only opportunity these women have to get out of their homes. The mosques will make other services accessible to women. In these centers of religion, women can now get advice on nutrition and hygiene or take literacy classes.

Just one building like this can transform the dynamics of a poor village almost overnight.

Today I am probably the best known of all the female politicians in Afghanistan and am extremely popular with the public, both men and women. My supporters have suggested I run for president. I will not lie and say that the role of leading my nation is not something I would love to do. Of course I would. Name me a serious politician anywhere in the world who wouldn't want the top job if offered it. And I know it is a job I am capable of doing well. But in truth, I do not think the time is right. I don't think my country is ready to accept a woman in this role. Of course, I hope this will change one day. Until recently, no one thought a black man could be president of the United States but it happened. Other Islamic countries have had female heads of state. Megawati Sukarnoputri was president of Indonesia from 2001 to 2004; Begum Khaleda Zia was the first female prime minister of Bangladesh; in neighboring Pakistan, Benazir Bhutto was also prime minister and was on the verge of being elected president when she was killed. I think about my early political heroines, Margaret Thatcher and Indira Gandhi. They are women who are remembered not for their gender but for their policies and their strength as leaders. And I know it could one day be possible in Afghanistan.

For far too long politics in my country has been conducted at the end of a gun. It has had more to do with who's got the most soldiers or the best tanks. It hasn't been about policy, plans, or reforms. But it must be in the future.

These changes will take time. But while these changes germinate, take root, and grow, so too will the economy. A stable Afghanistan will sprout opportunities for its people. Whether it is the farmer who can use better and safer roads to get to market, the budding entrepreneur building an import-export business, or the hundreds of thousands of Afghans living abroad, many of them highly educated, the building blocks for a better future will begin to present themselves.

I don't wish to understate the challenges that lay ahead for my country. There are so many problems we must overcome. Afghanistan is awash with corruption, flawed religious extremism, and a river of money from the sea of opium poppies grown on our farmland. But through the generations of suffering this land has endured, there is a strength and resolve in the people that has never been broken. I believe and pray that the time is approaching for all Afghans to put aside the past and look to the future. After so many years of war and oppression we are left with virtually nothing. The only choice we have is to rebuild, and I believe that's what the majority of my countrymen and women genuinely want. They just need the framework to do it.

And if we can achieve that, my darling daughters, then perhaps someday your children's children will grow up free in a proud, successful, Islamic republic that has taken its rightful place in the developed world.

This is what I live for. And what I know I will die for.

If this should happen, my darling daughters, then know that every word in this book was written for you.

I want and need you, and all the boys and girls of Afghanistan, to understand. My dreams for this nation will live on in you.

And if the Taliban does not succeed in killing me? Well Shuhra, maybe I will try and beat you to the post of first female president of Afghanistan. And maybe we will form a new dynasty of powerful Islamic female leaders.

I know as I write these final words my mother is most definitely smiling in heaven.

A HISTORICAL TIMELINE OF AFGHANISTAN

1919   Afghanistan regains independence after a third war against British forces who were trying to bring the country under their sphere of influence.

1933   Zahir Shah becomes king and Afghanistan remains a monarchy for the next four decades.

1973   Mohammed Dawoud seizes power in a coup and declares a republic.

1978   General Dawoud is overthrown and killed in a coup by the leftist People's Democratic Party.

1979   A power struggle between leftist leaders Hafizullah Amin and Nur Muhammad Taraki in Kabul is won by Amin. Revolts in the countryside continue and the Afghan army faces collapse. The Soviet Union finally sends in troops to help remove Amin, who is executed.

1980   Babrak Karmal, leader of the People's Democratic Party Parcham faction, is installed as ruler, backed by Soviet troops. But anti-regime resistance intensifies with various mujahideen groups fighting Soviet forces. The United States, Pakistan, China, Iran, and Saudi Arabia supply money and arms.

1985   Mujahideen come together in Pakistan to form an alliance against Soviet forces. Half the Afghan population is now estimated to be displaced by war, with many fleeing to neighboring Iran or Pakistan.

1986   The United States begins supplying the mujahideen with Stinger missiles, enabling them to shoot down Soviet helicopter gunships. Babrak Karmal is replaced by Mohammad Najibullah as head of the Soviet-backed regime.

1988	Afghanistan, the Soviet Union, the United States and Pakistan sign peace accords and the Soviet Union begins pulling out troops.
1989	The last Soviet troops leave, but civil war continues as the mujahideen push to overthrow Najibullah.
1991	The United States and the Soviet Union agree to end military aid to both sides.
1992	Resistance closes in on Kabul and Najibullah falls from power. Rival militias vie for influence.
1993	Mujahideen factions form a government with an ethnic Takjik, Burhanuddin Rabbani, who is proclaimed president.
1996	The Taliban seize control of Kabul and introduce a hard-line version of Islam. Rabbani flees to join the anti-Taliban Northern Alliance.
1997	The Taliban are recognized as the legitimate rulers by Pakistan and Saudi Arabia. Most other countries continue to regard Rabbani as head of state. The Taliban now control about two-thirds of the country.
2001	Ahmed Shah Massoud, a legendary guerrilla and leader of the main opposition to the Taliban, is killed, apparently by assassins posing as journalists.
2001 October	The United States and Britain launch air strikes against Afghanistan after the Taliban refuse to hand over Osama Bin Laden, held responsible for the September 11 attacks on the United States.
2001 December 5	Afghan groups agree to a deal in Bonn forming an interim government.
2001 December 7	The Taliban finally give up the last stronghold of Kandahar, but Mullah Omar remains at large.
2001 December 22	Pashtun royalist Hamid Karzai is sworn in as the head of a thirty-member interim power-sharing government.
2002 April	Former king Zahir Shah returns, but says he makes no claim to the throne.
2002 May	The UN Security Council extends the mandate of the International Security Assistance Force until December 2002. Allied forces continue their military campaign to find remnants of al-Qaida and Taliban forces in the southeast.
2002 June	The *loya jirga*, or grand council, elects Hamid Karzai as interim head of state. Karzai picks members of his administration, which is to serve until 2004.
2003 August	NATO takes control of security in Kabul, its first-ever operational commitment outside Europe.

2004 January	The *loya jirga* adopts a new constitution that provides for a strong presidency.
2004 October–November	Presidential elections: Hamid Karzai is declared the winner, with 55 percent of the vote. He is sworn in, amid tight security, in December.
2005 September	The first parliamentary and provincial elections in more than thirty years are held.
2005 December	The new parliament holds its inaugural session.
2006 October	NATO assumes responsibility for security across the whole of Afghanistan, taking command in the east from a US-led coalition force.
2008 November	Taliban militants reject an offer of peace talks from President Karzai, saying there can be no negotiations until foreign troops leave Afghanistan.
2009 October	Hamid Karzai is declared winner of the August presidential election, after second-place opponent Abdullah Abdullah pulls out before the second round. Preliminary results had given Karzai 55 percent of the vote, but so many ballots are found to be fraudulent that a run-off was called.
2009 November	Hamid Karzai is sworn in for a second term as president.
2010 July	A major international conference endorses President Karzai's timetable for control of security to be transferred from foreign to Afghan forces by 2014.

"A Historical Timeline of Afghanistan" adapted with permission of BBC Online.

ACKNOWLEDGMENTS

I would like to thank the following people:

My daughters, for their patience and the time they gave me during the writing.

Nadene, who has been extremely helpful in co-writing and narrating the book.

Elsa, who has been a great support in shaping the stories, managing the team and editing the book so many times and with patience.

My brother Ennayat, who spent his one week off traveling with Nadene and I to the remote mountainous area of Badakhshan to remind ourselves of childhood stories.

The security people in my district for providing required security to all of the team during the trip to our village.

Kaka Yatim, the brave driver who drove us on some of the most difficult roads in Afghanistan non-stop for two days and nights.

Fawzia Koofi is a supporter of BEH Z Creations, which funds literacy projects in remote areas of Afghanistan. You can read more on www.fawziakoofi.org.

INDEX